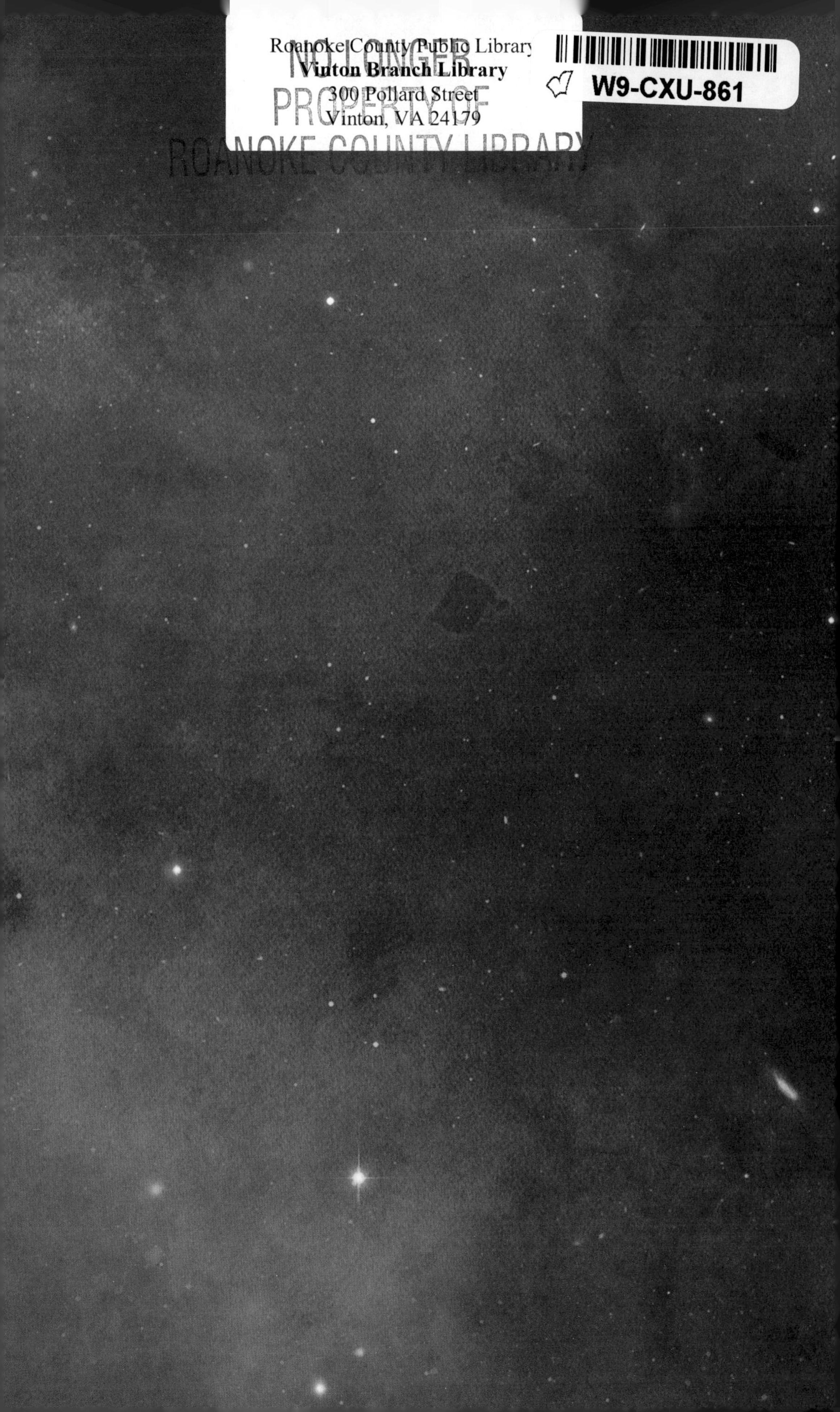

CREATED BY
JOSS WHEDON

firefly™

WATCH HOW I SOAR

JEFF **JENSEN** · ETHAN **YOUNG** · JORGE **CORONA**
JARED **CULLUM** · GIANNIS **MILONOGIANNIS**
JORGE **MONLONGO** · JORDI **PÉREZ**

Published by

Designer
Marie Krupina

Assistant Editor
Gavin Gronenthal

Editor
Sierra Hahn

Executive Editor
Jeanine Schaefer

Special Thanks to **Becca J. Sadowsky**,
Nicole Spiegel, and **Carol Roeder**.

Ross Richie CEO & Founder
Joy Huffman CFO
Matt Gagnon Editor-in-Chief
Filip Sablik President, Publishing & Marketing
Stephen Christy President, Development
Lance Kreiter Vice President, Licensing & Merchandising
Arune Singh Vice President, Marketing
Bryce Carlson Vice President, Editorial & Creative Strategy
Kate Henning Director, Operations
Spencer Simpson Director, Sales
Scott Newman Manager, Production Design
Elyse Strandberg Manager, Finance
Sierra Hahn Executive Editor
Jeanine Schaefer Executive Editor
Dafna Pleban Senior Editor
Shannon Watters Senior Editor
Eric Harburn Senior Editor
Sophie Philips-Roberts Associate Editor
Amanda LaFranco Associate Editor
Jonathan Manning Associate Editor
Gavin Gronenthal Assistant Editor
Gwen Waller Assistant Editor
Allyson Gronowitz Assistant Editor
Ramiro Portnoy Assistant Editor
Kenzie Rzonca Assistant Editor
Shelby Netschke Editorial Assistant
Michelle Ankley Design Coordinator
Marie Krupina Production Designer
Grace Park Production Designer
Chelsea Roberts Production Designer
Samantha Knapp Production Design Assistant
José Meza Live Events Lead
Stephanie Hocutt Digital Marketing Lead
Esther Kim Marketing Coordinator
Breanna Sarpy Live Events Coordinator
Amanda Lawson Marketing Assistant
Holly Aitchison Digital Sales Coordinator
Morgan Perry Retail Sales Coordinator
Megan Christopher Operations Coordinator
Rodrigo Hernandez Operations Coordinator
Zipporah Smith Operations Assistant
Jason Lee Senior Accountant
Sabrina Lesin Accounting Assistant

FIREFLY: WATCH HOW I SOAR, November 2020.
Published by BOOM! Studios, a division of Boom
Entertainment, Inc. © 2020 20th Century Studios. BOOM!
Studios™ and the BOOM! Studios logo are trademarks
of Boom Entertainment, Inc., registered in various
countries and categories. All characters, events, and
institutions depicted herein are fictional. Any similarity
between any of the names, characters, persons, events,
and/or institutions in this publication to actual names,
characters, and persons, whether living or dead,
events, and/or institutions is unintended and purely
coincidental. BOOM! Studios does not read or accept
unsolicited submissions of ideas, stories, or artwork.

BOOM! Studios, 5670 Wilshire Boulevard, Suite 400, Los
Angeles, CA 90036-5679. Printed in Canada. First Printing.

ISBN: 978-1-68415-655-9, eISBN: 978-1-64668-204-1

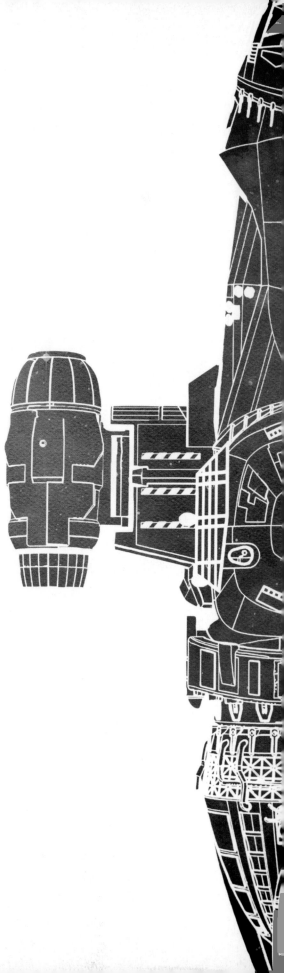

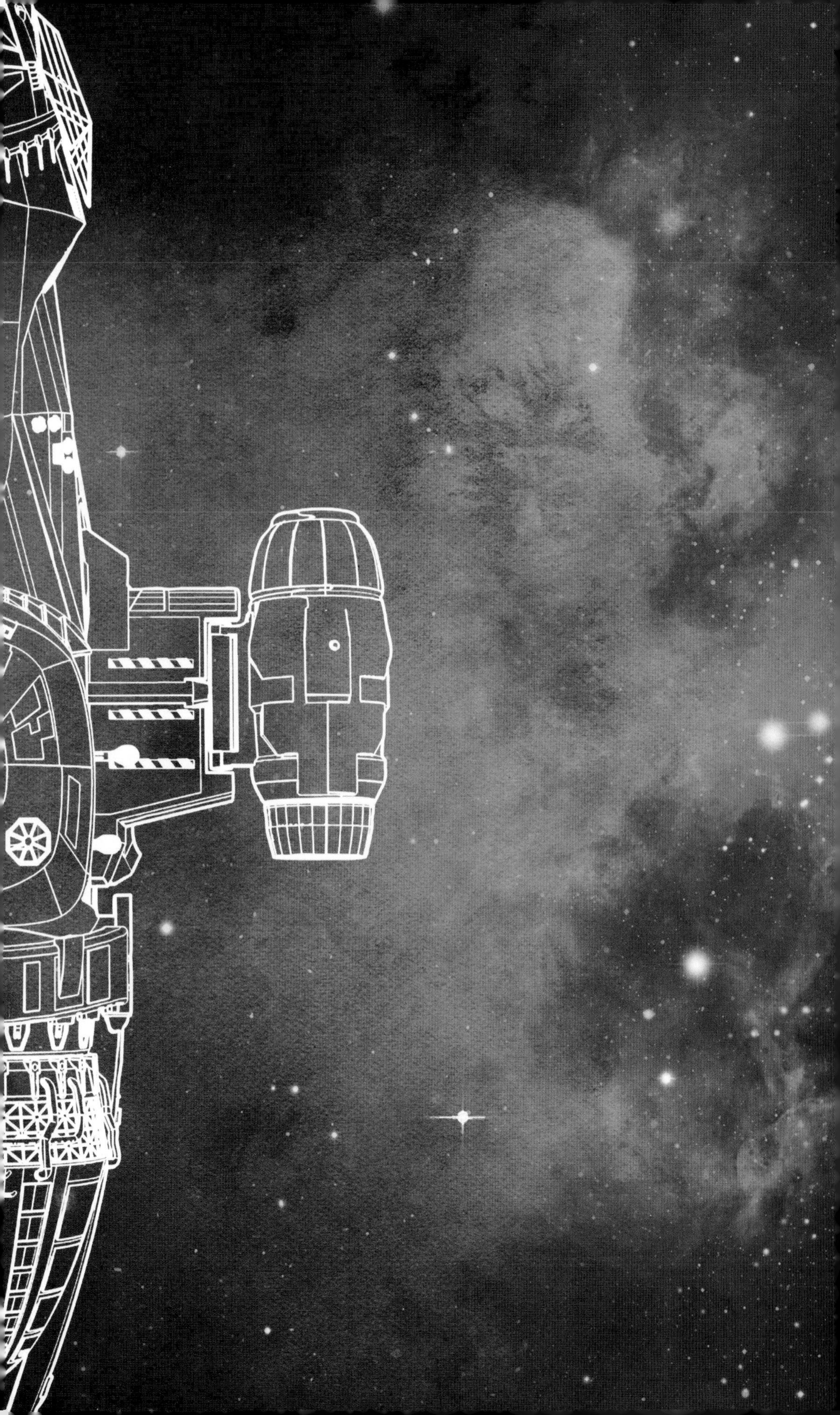

firefly™

WATCH HOW I SOAR

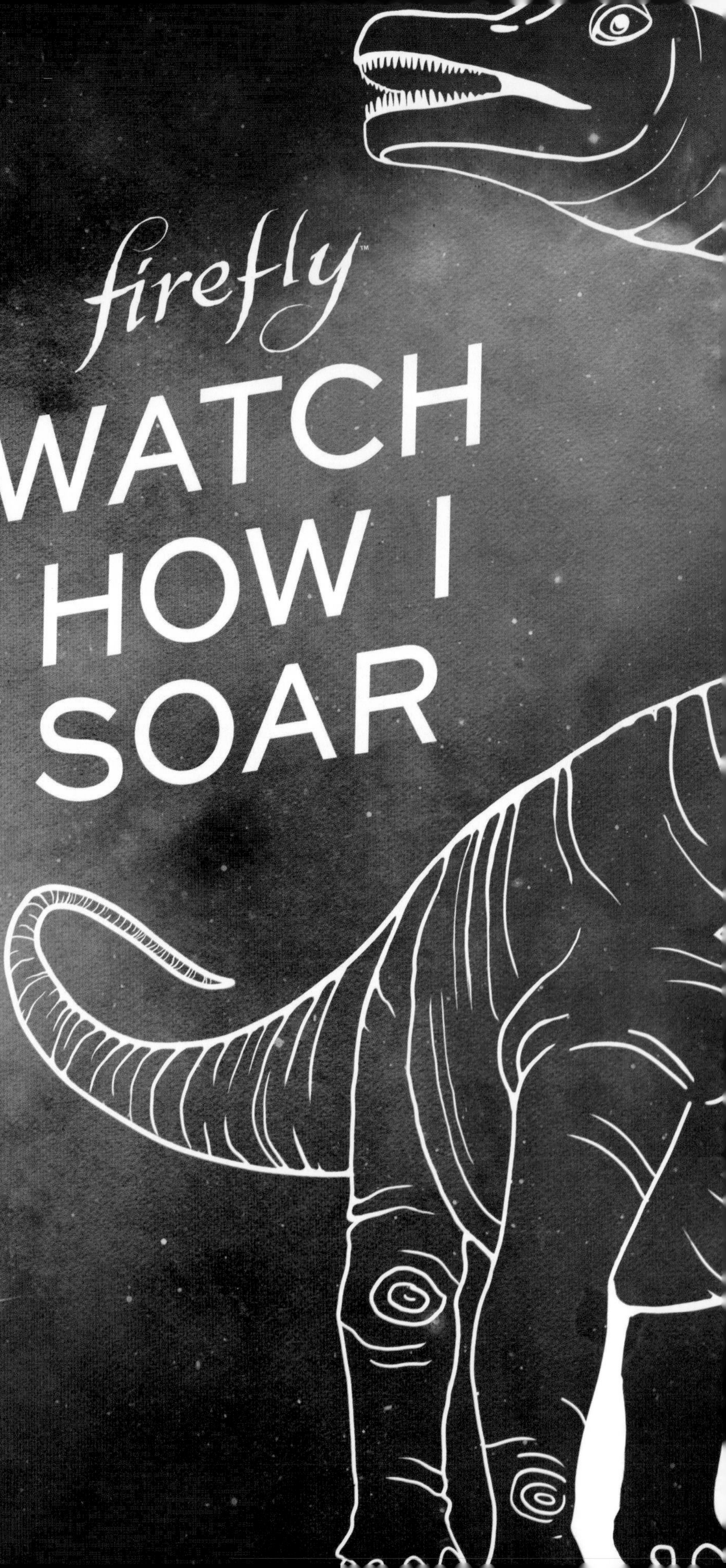

Created by
Joss Whedon

Lettered by
Fábio Amelia

Cover by
Miguel Mercado

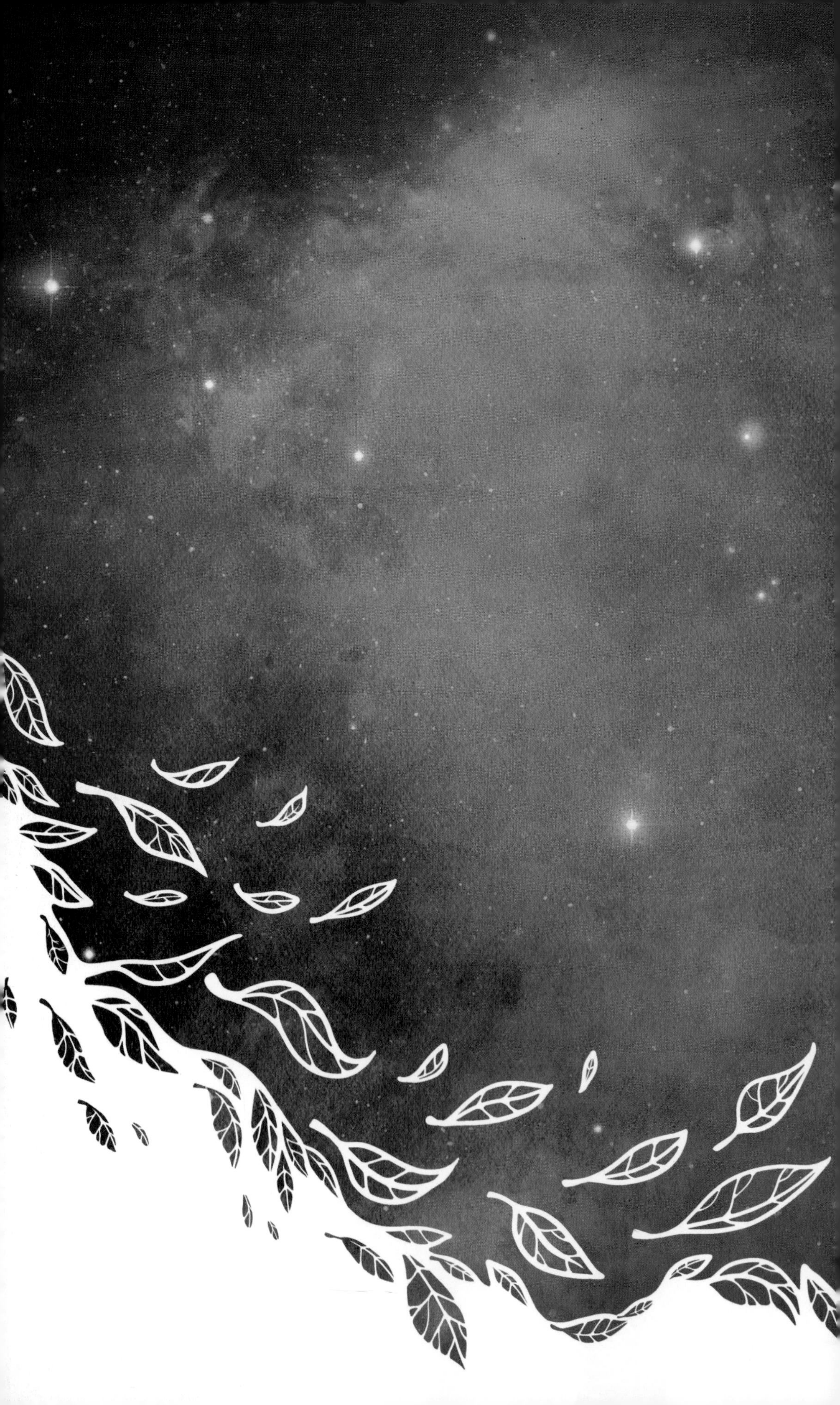

"WE GOTTA GO TO THE CRAPPY TOWN WHERE I'M A HERO."

—HOBAN WASHBURNE

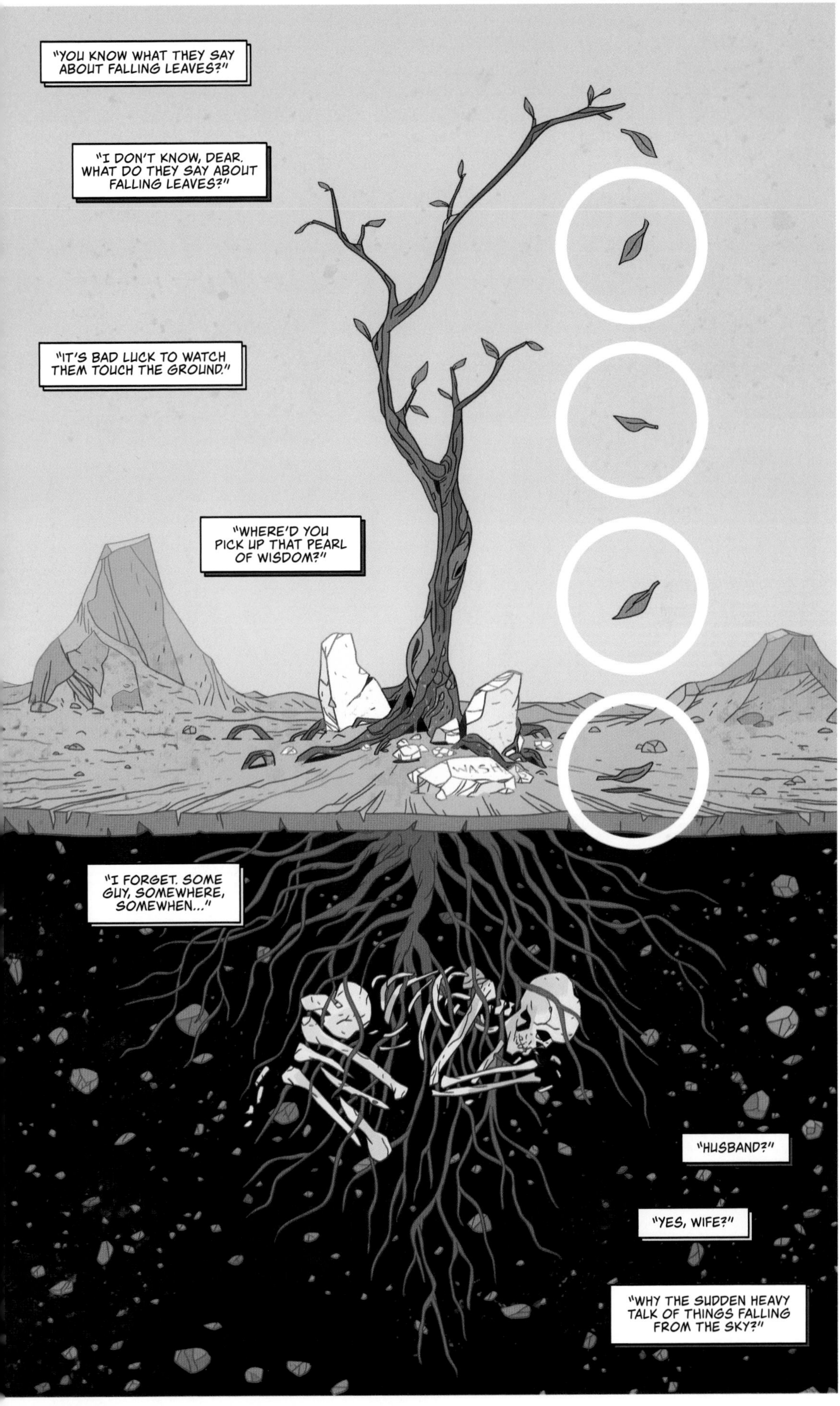
"YOU KNOW WHAT THEY SAY ABOUT FALLING LEAVES?"
"I DON'T KNOW, DEAR. WHAT DO THEY SAY ABOUT FALLING LEAVES?"
"IT'S BAD LUCK TO WATCH THEM TOUCH THE GROUND."
"WHERE'D YOU PICK UP THAT PEARL OF WISDOM?"
"I FORGET. SOME GUY, SOMEWHERE, SOMEWHEN..."
"HUSBAND?"
"YES, WIFE?"
"WHY THE SUDDEN HEAVY TALK OF THINGS FALLING FROM THE SKY?"

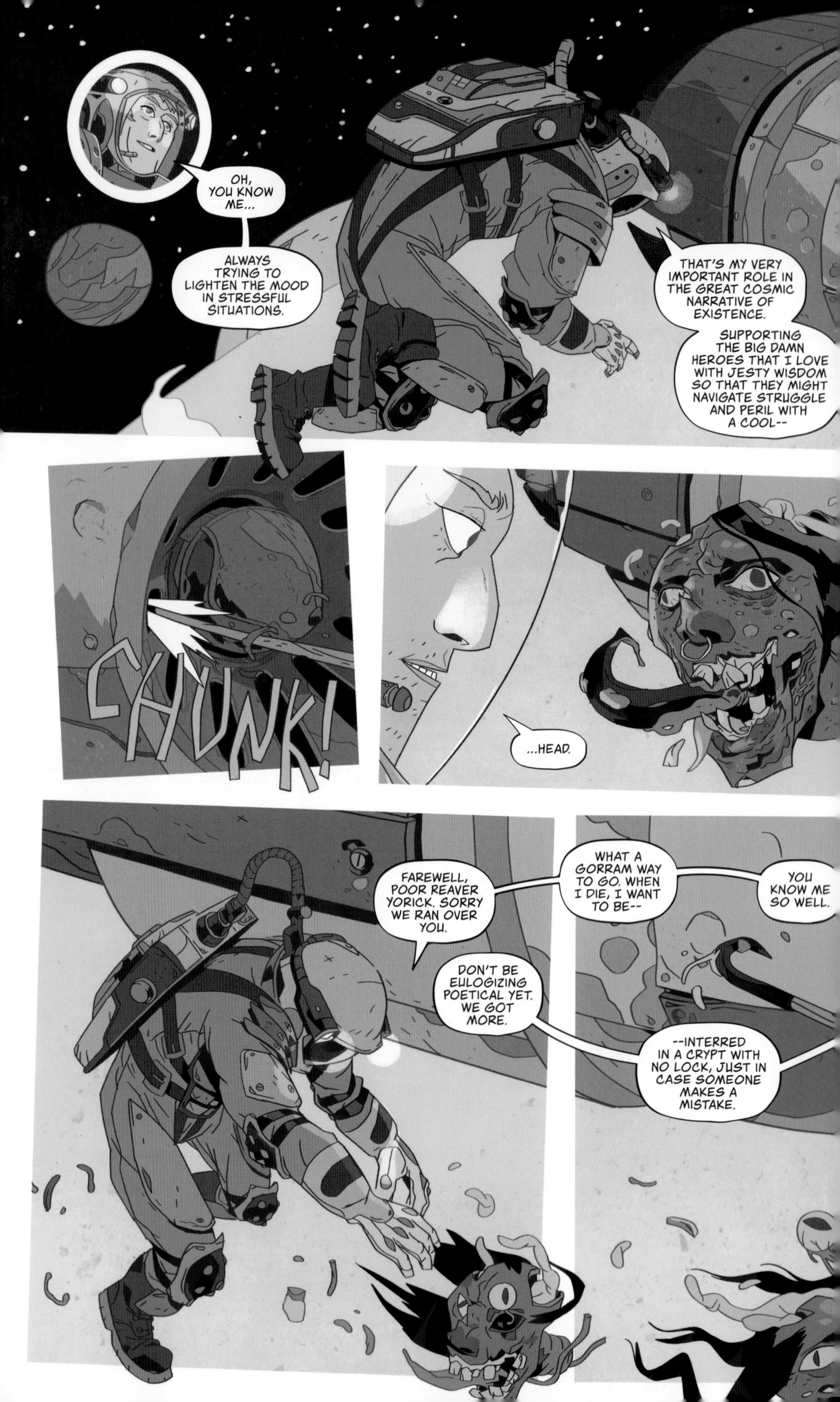
OH, YOU KNOW ME...
ALWAYS TRYING TO LIGHTEN THE MOOD IN STRESSFUL SITUATIONS.
THAT'S MY VERY IMPORTANT ROLE IN THE GREAT COSMIC NARRATIVE OF EXISTENCE.
SUPPORTING THE BIG DAMN HEROES THAT I LOVE WITH JESTY WISDOM SO THAT THEY MIGHT NAVIGATE STRUGGLE AND PERIL WITH A COOL--
CHUNK!
...HEAD.
FAREWELL, POOR REAVER YORICK. SORRY WE RAN OVER YOU.
DON'T BE EULOGIZING POETICAL YET. WE GOT MORE.
WHAT A GORRAM WAY TO GO. WHEN I DIE, I WANT TO BE--
--INTERRED IN A CRYPT WITH NO LOCK, JUST IN CASE SOMEONE MAKES A MISTAKE.
YOU KNOW ME SO WELL.

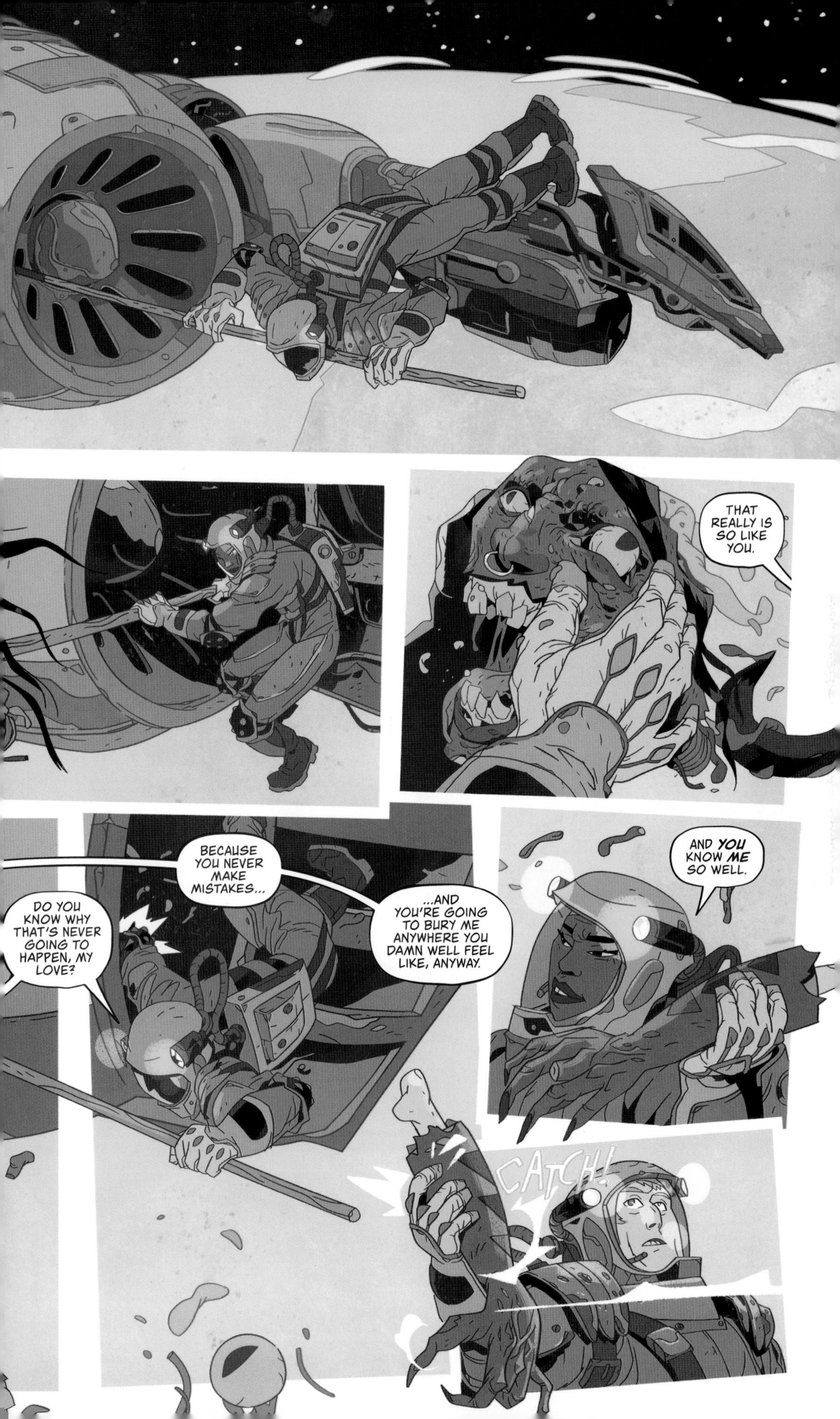
THAT REALLY IS SO LIKE YOU.
DO YOU KNOW WHY THAT'S NEVER GOING TO HAPPEN, MY LOVE?
BECAUSE YOU NEVER MAKE MISTAKES...
...AND YOU'RE GOING TO BURY ME ANYWHERE YOU DAMN WELL FEEL LIKE, ANYWAY.
AND YOU KNOW ME SO WELL.
CATCH!

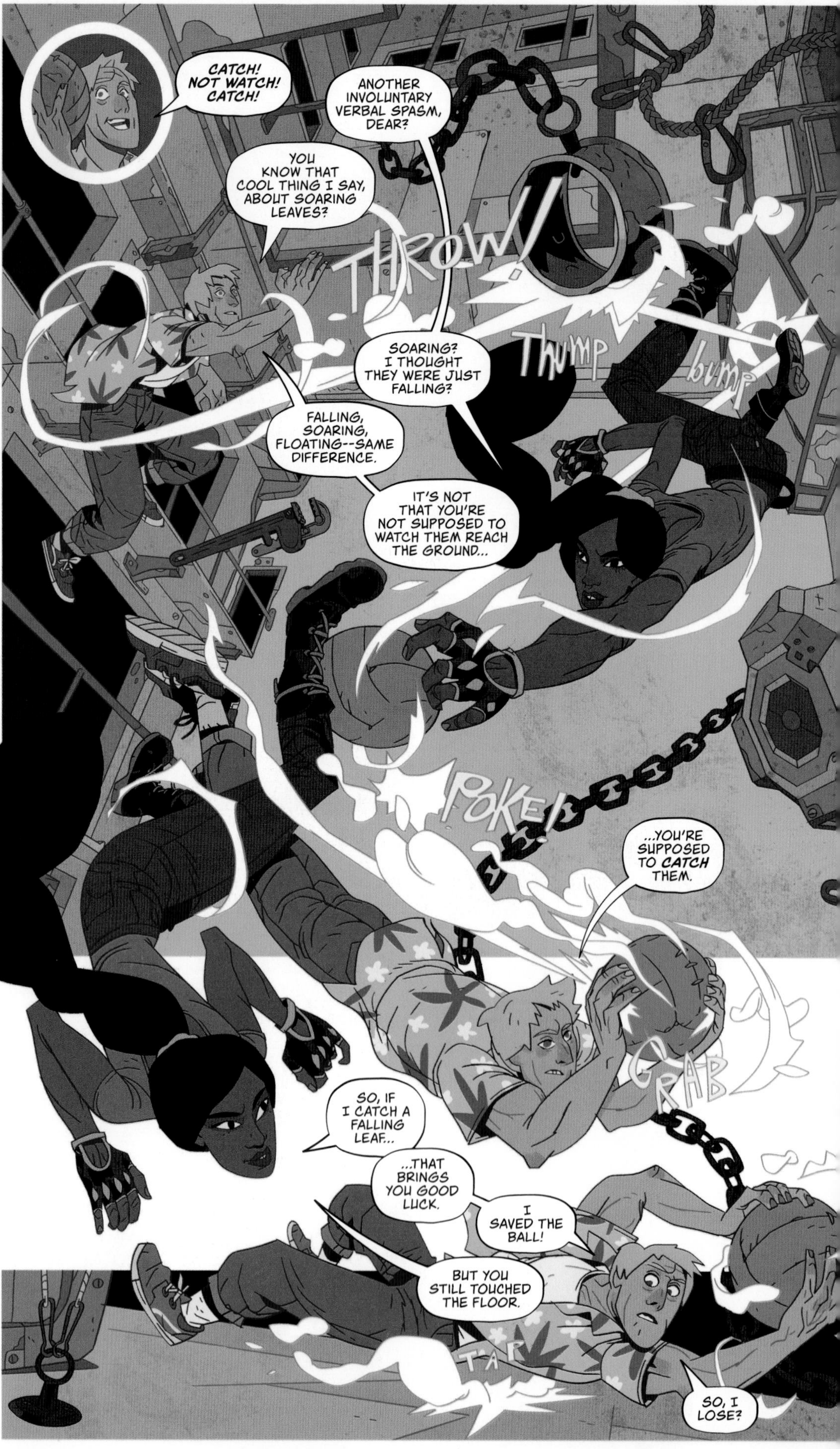
CATCH! NOT WATCH! CATCH!
ANOTHER INVOLUNTARY VERBAL SPASM, DEAR?
YOU KNOW THAT COOL THING I SAY, ABOUT SOARING LEAVES?
THROW!
SOARING? I THOUGHT THEY WERE JUST FALLING?
Thump
bump
FALLING, SOARING, FLOATING--SAME DIFFERENCE.
IT'S NOT THAT YOU'RE NOT SUPPOSED TO WATCH THEM REACH THE GROUND...
POKE!
...YOU'RE SUPPOSED TO CATCH THEM.
GRAB
SO, IF I CATCH A FALLING LEAF...
...THAT BRINGS YOU GOOD LUCK.
I SAVED THE BALL!
BUT YOU STILL TOUCHED THE FLOOR.
TAP
SO, I LOSE?

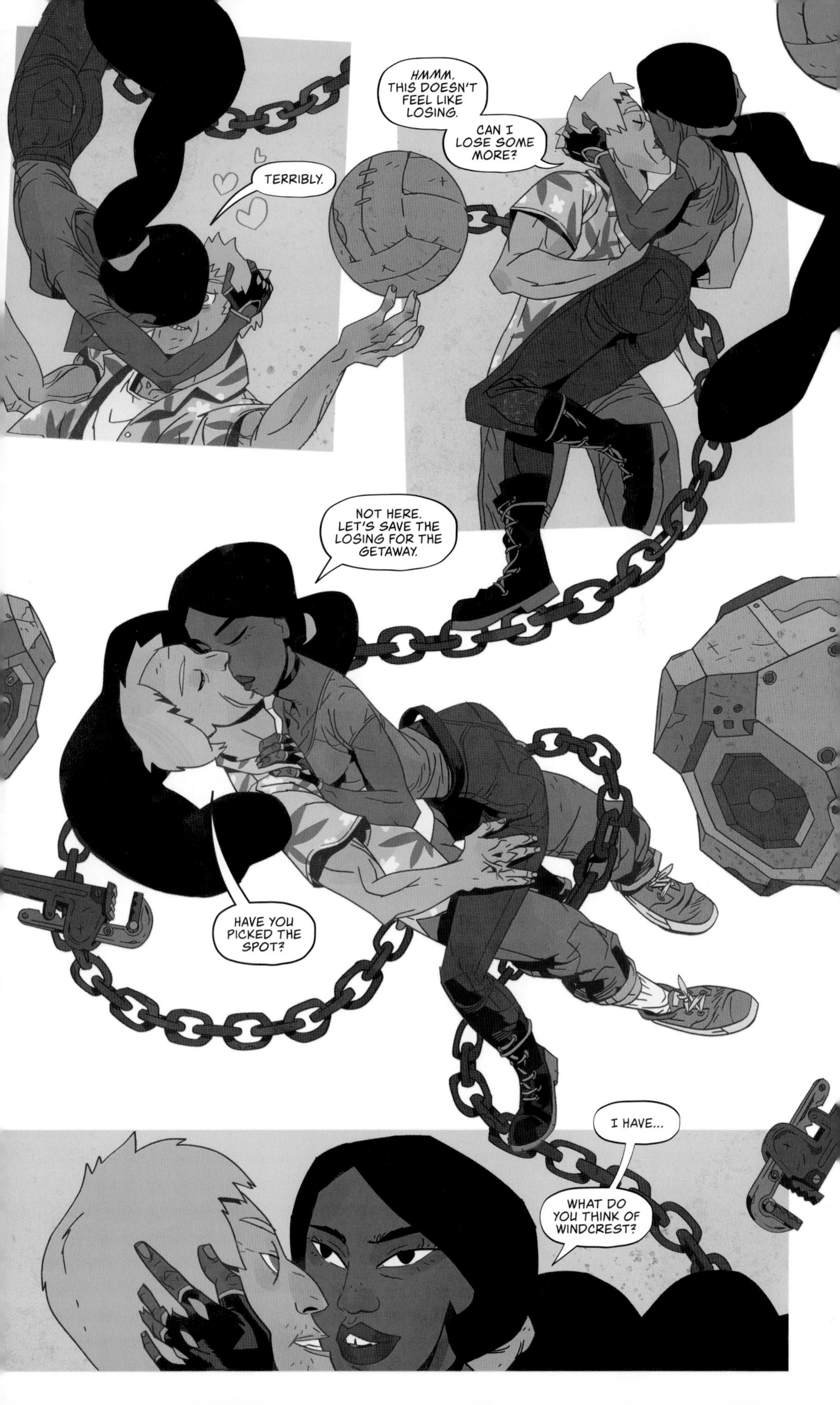
TERRIBLY.
HMMM. THIS DOESN'T FEEL LIKE LOSING.
CAN I LOSE SOME MORE?
NOT HERE. LET'S SAVE THE LOSING FOR THE GETAWAY.
HAVE YOU PICKED THE SPOT?
I HAVE...
WHAT DO YOU THINK OF WINDCREST?

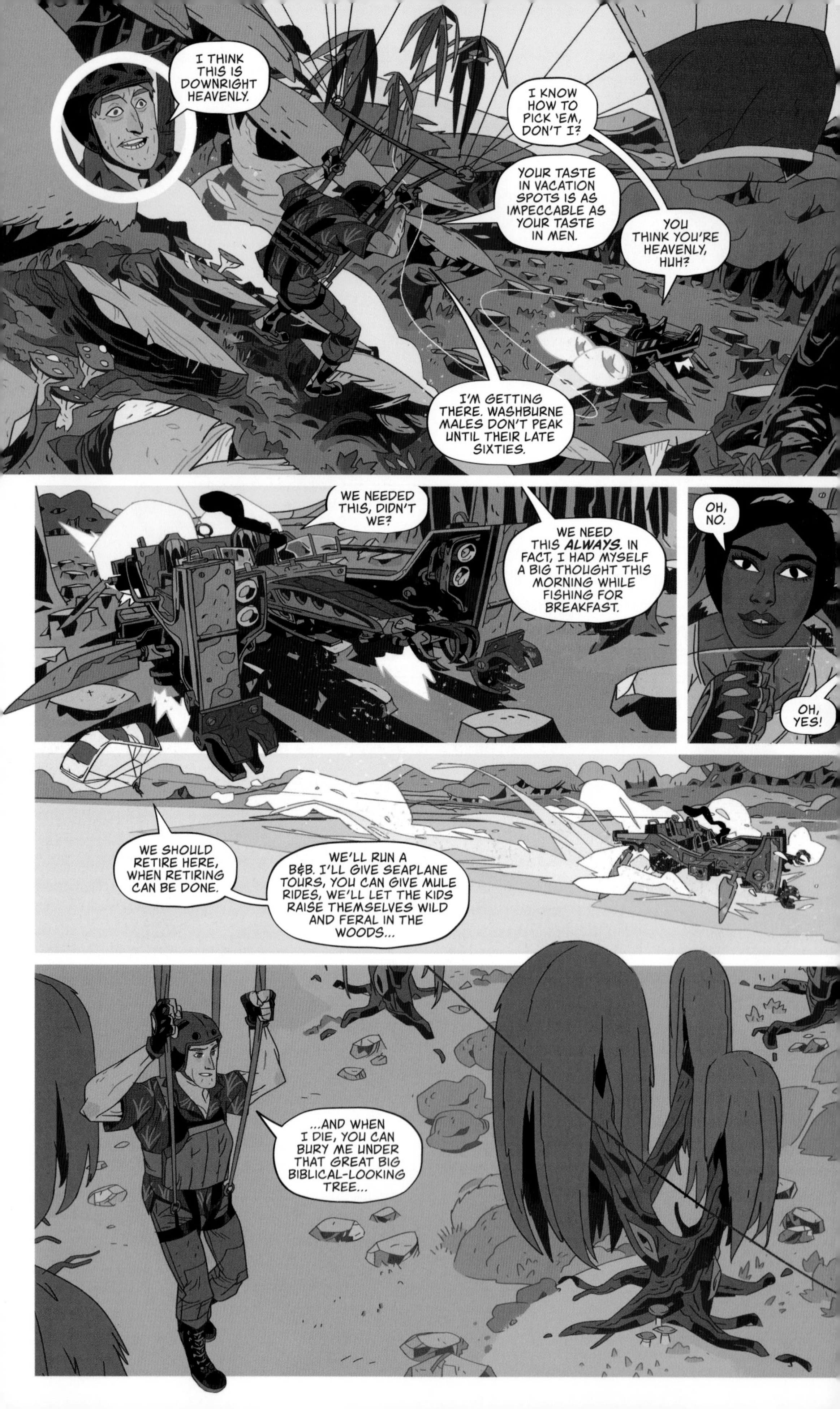
I THINK THIS IS DOWNRIGHT HEAVENLY.
I KNOW HOW TO PICK 'EM, DON'T I?
YOUR TASTE IN VACATION SPOTS IS AS IMPECCABLE AS YOUR TASTE IN MEN.
YOU THINK YOU'RE HEAVENLY, HUH?
I'M GETTING THERE. WASHBURNE MALES DON'T PEAK UNTIL THEIR LATE SIXTIES.
WE NEEDED THIS, DIDN'T WE?
WE NEED THIS ***ALWAYS.*** IN FACT, I HAD MYSELF A BIG THOUGHT THIS MORNING WHILE FISHING FOR BREAKFAST.
OH, NO.
OH, YES!
WE SHOULD RETIRE HERE, WHEN RETIRING CAN BE DONE.
WE'LL RUN A B&B. I'LL GIVE SEAPLANE TOURS, YOU CAN GIVE MULE RIDES, WE'LL LET THE KIDS RAISE THEMSELVES WILD AND FERAL IN THE WOODS...
...AND WHEN I DIE, YOU CAN BURY ME UNDER THAT GREAT BIG BIBLICAL-LOOKING TREE...

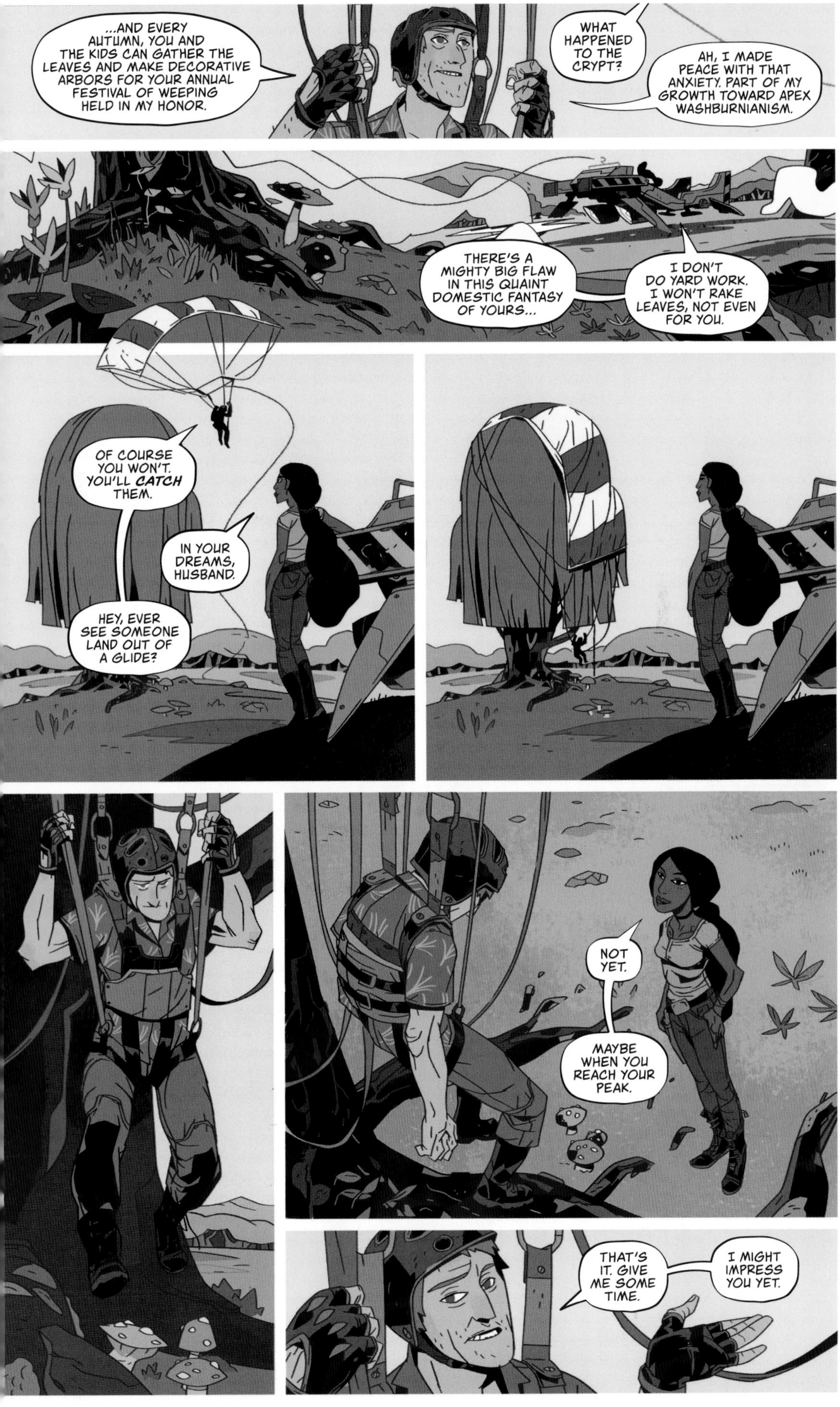
...AND EVERY AUTUMN, YOU AND THE KIDS CAN GATHER THE LEAVES AND MAKE DECORATIVE ARBORS FOR YOUR ANNUAL FESTIVAL OF WEEPING HELD IN MY HONOR.
WHAT HAPPENED TO THE CRYPT?
AH, I MADE PEACE WITH THAT ANXIETY. PART OF MY GROWTH TOWARD APEX WASHBURNIANISM.
THERE'S A MIGHTY BIG FLAW IN THIS QUAINT DOMESTIC FANTASY OF YOURS...
I DON'T DO YARD WORK. I WON'T RAKE LEAVES, NOT EVEN FOR YOU.
OF COURSE YOU WON'T. YOU'LL CATCH THEM.
IN YOUR DREAMS, HUSBAND.
HEY, EVER SEE SOMEONE LAND OUT OF A GLIDE?
NOT YET.
MAYBE WHEN YOU REACH YOUR PEAK.
THAT'S IT. GIVE ME SOME TIME.
I MIGHT IMPRESS YOU YET.

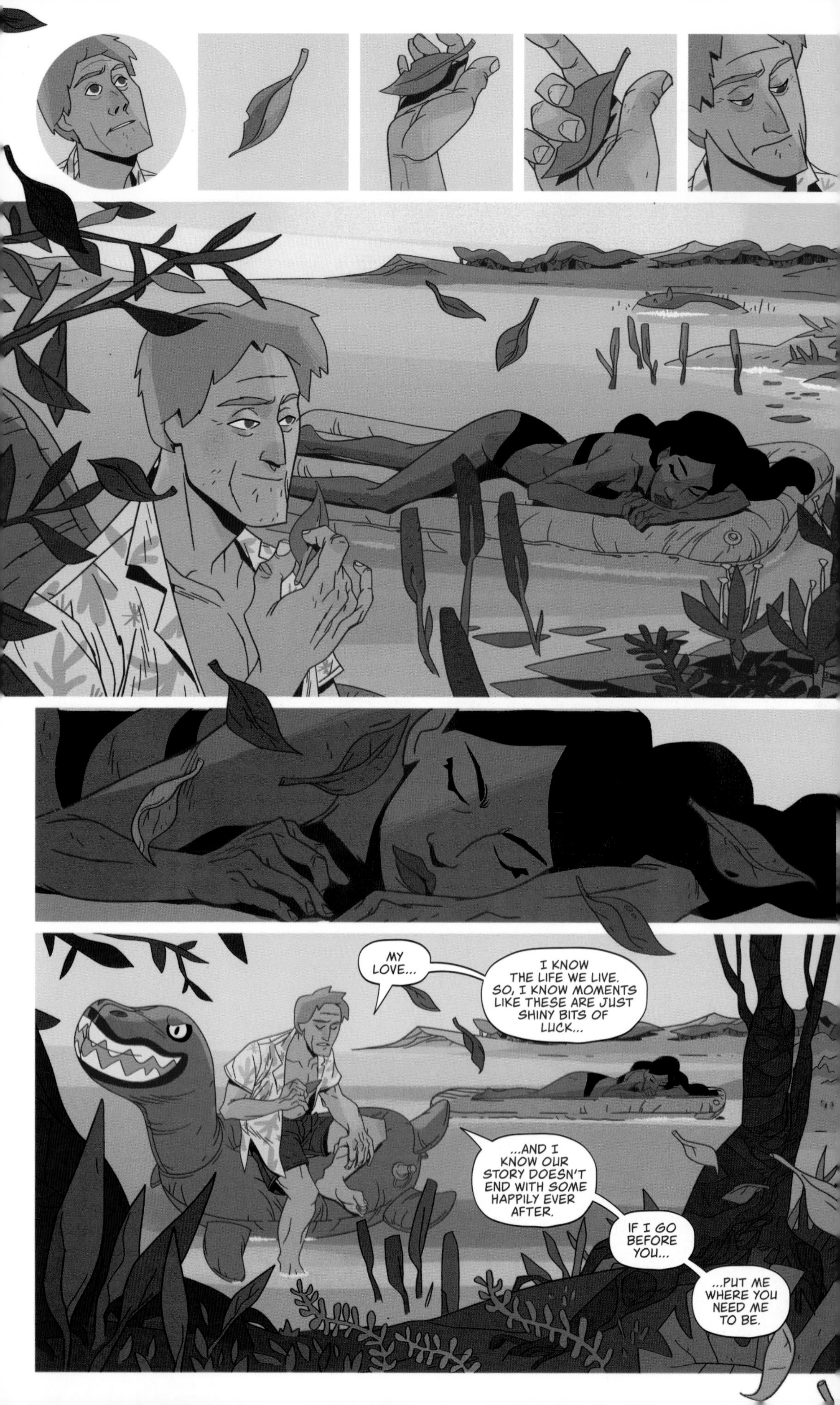
MY LOVE...
I KNOW THE LIFE WE LIVE. SO, I KNOW MOMENTS LIKE THESE ARE JUST SHINY BITS OF LUCK...
...AND I KNOW OUR STORY DOESN'T END WITH SOME HAPPILY EVER AFTER.
IF I GO BEFORE YOU...
...PUT ME WHERE YOU NEED ME TO BE.

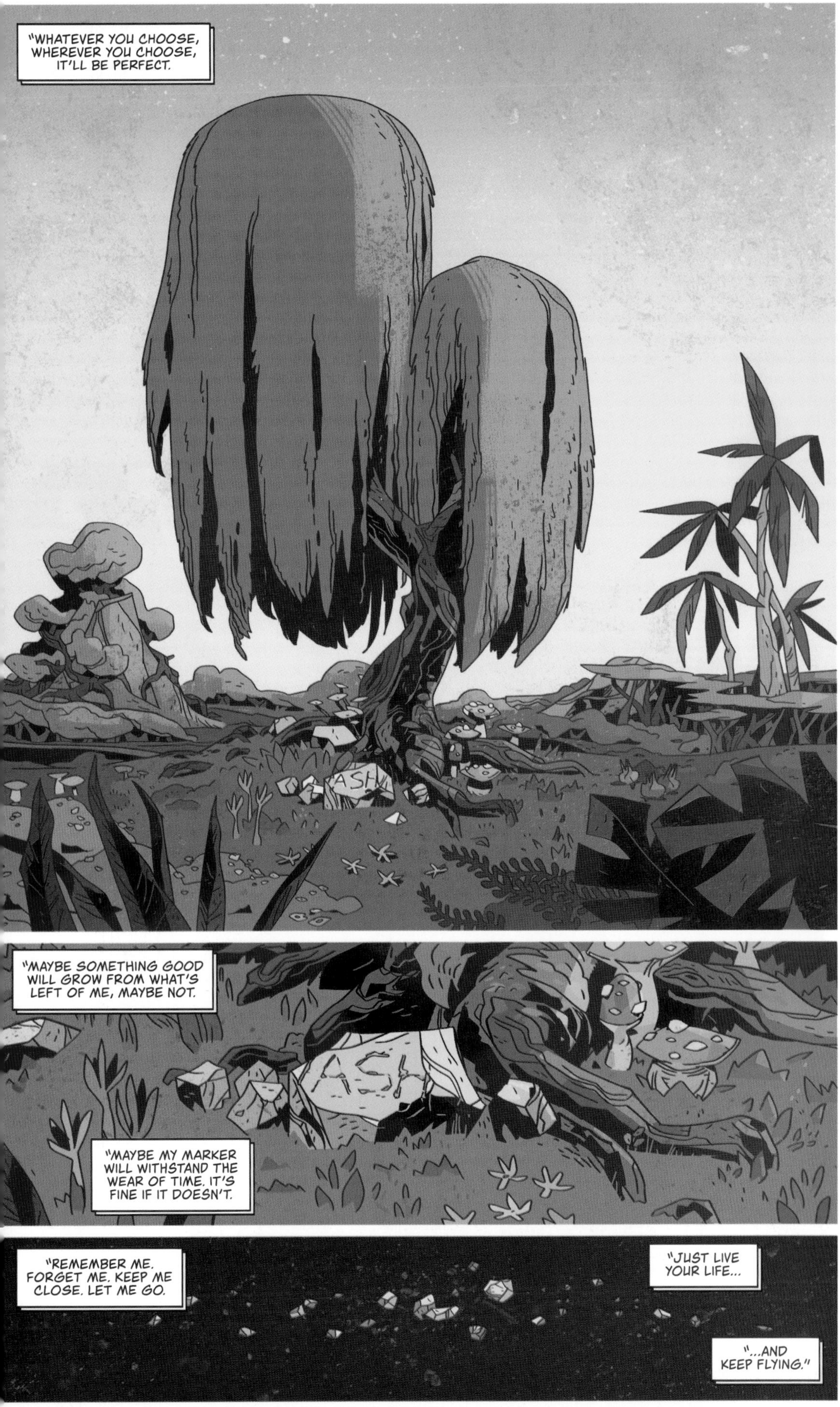
"WHATEVER YOU CHOOSE, WHEREVER YOU CHOOSE, IT'LL BE PERFECT.
ASH
"MAYBE SOMETHING GOOD WILL GROW FROM WHAT'S LEFT OF ME, MAYBE NOT.
"MAYBE MY MARKER WILL WITHSTAND THE WEAR OF TIME. IT'S FINE IF IT DOESN'T.
"REMEMBER ME. FORGET ME. KEEP ME CLOSE. LET ME GO.
"JUST LIVE YOUR LIFE...
"...AND KEEP FLYING."

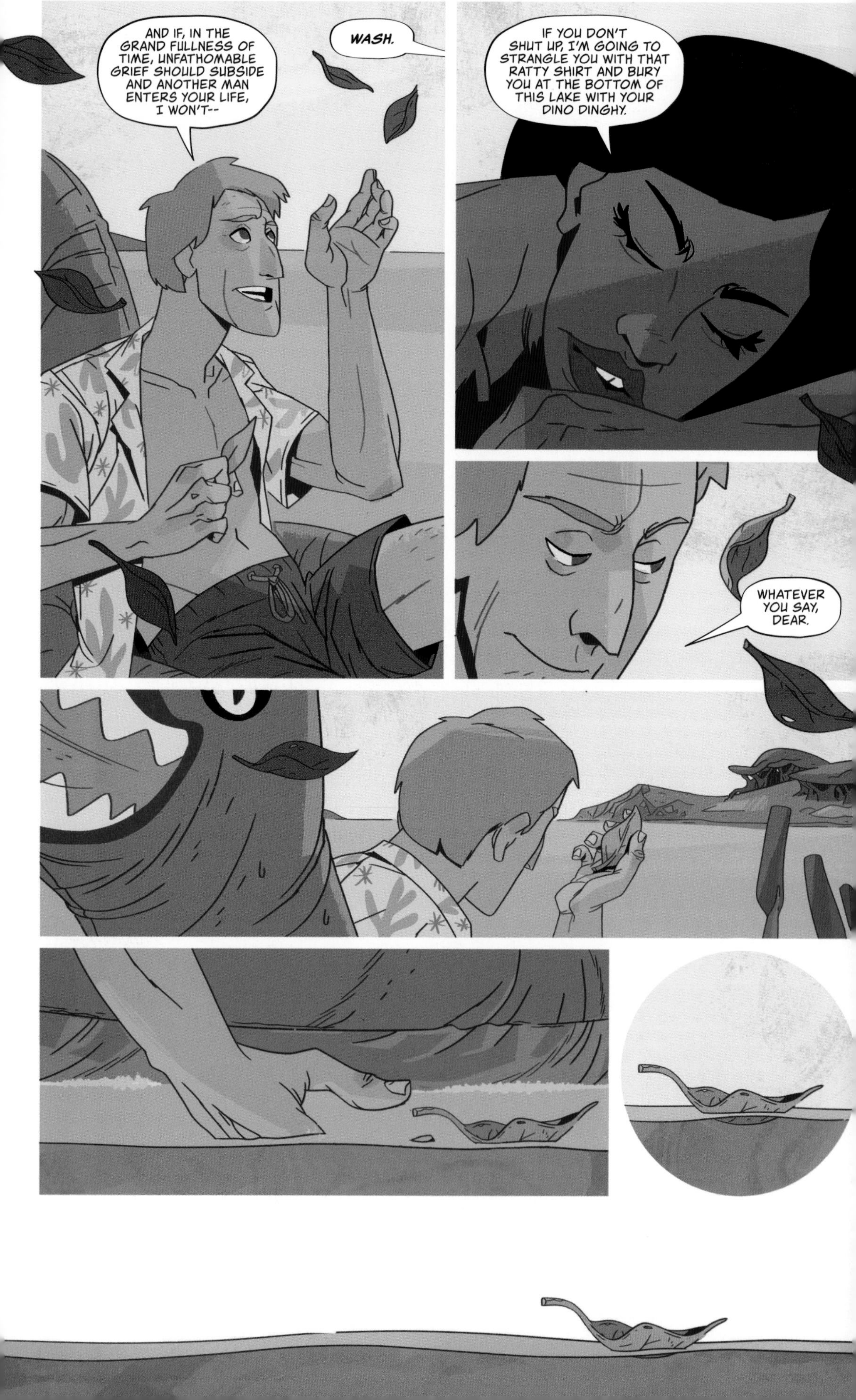
AND IF, IN THE GRAND FULLNESS OF TIME, UNFATHOMABLE GRIEF SHOULD SUBSIDE AND ANOTHER MAN ENTERS YOUR LIFE, I WON'T--
WASH.
IF YOU DON'T SHUT UP, I'M GOING TO STRANGLE YOU WITH THAT RATTY SHIRT AND BURY YOU AT THE BOTTOM OF THIS LAKE WITH YOUR DINO DINGHY.
WHATEVER YOU SAY, DEAR.

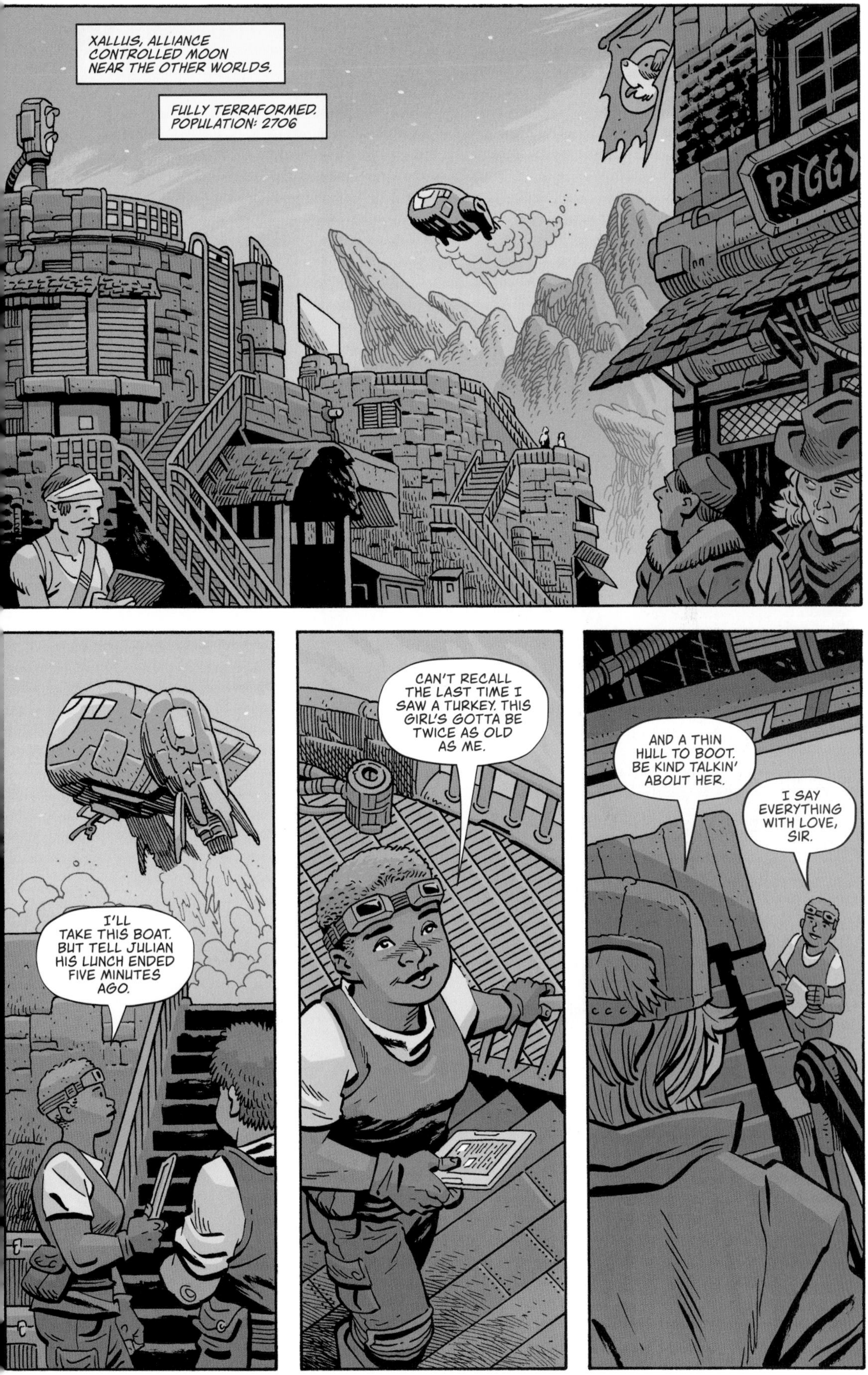
XALLUS, ALLIANCE CONTROLLED MOON NEAR THE OTHER WORLDS.
FULLY TERRAFORMED. POPULATION: 2706
I'LL TAKE THIS BOAT. BUT TELL JULIAN HIS LUNCH ENDED FIVE MINUTES AGO.
CAN'T RECALL THE LAST TIME I SAW A TURKEY. THIS GIRL'S GOTTA BE TWICE AS OLD AS ME.
AND A THIN HULL TO BOOT. BE KIND TALKIN' ABOUT HER.
I SAY EVERYTHING WITH LOVE, SIR.

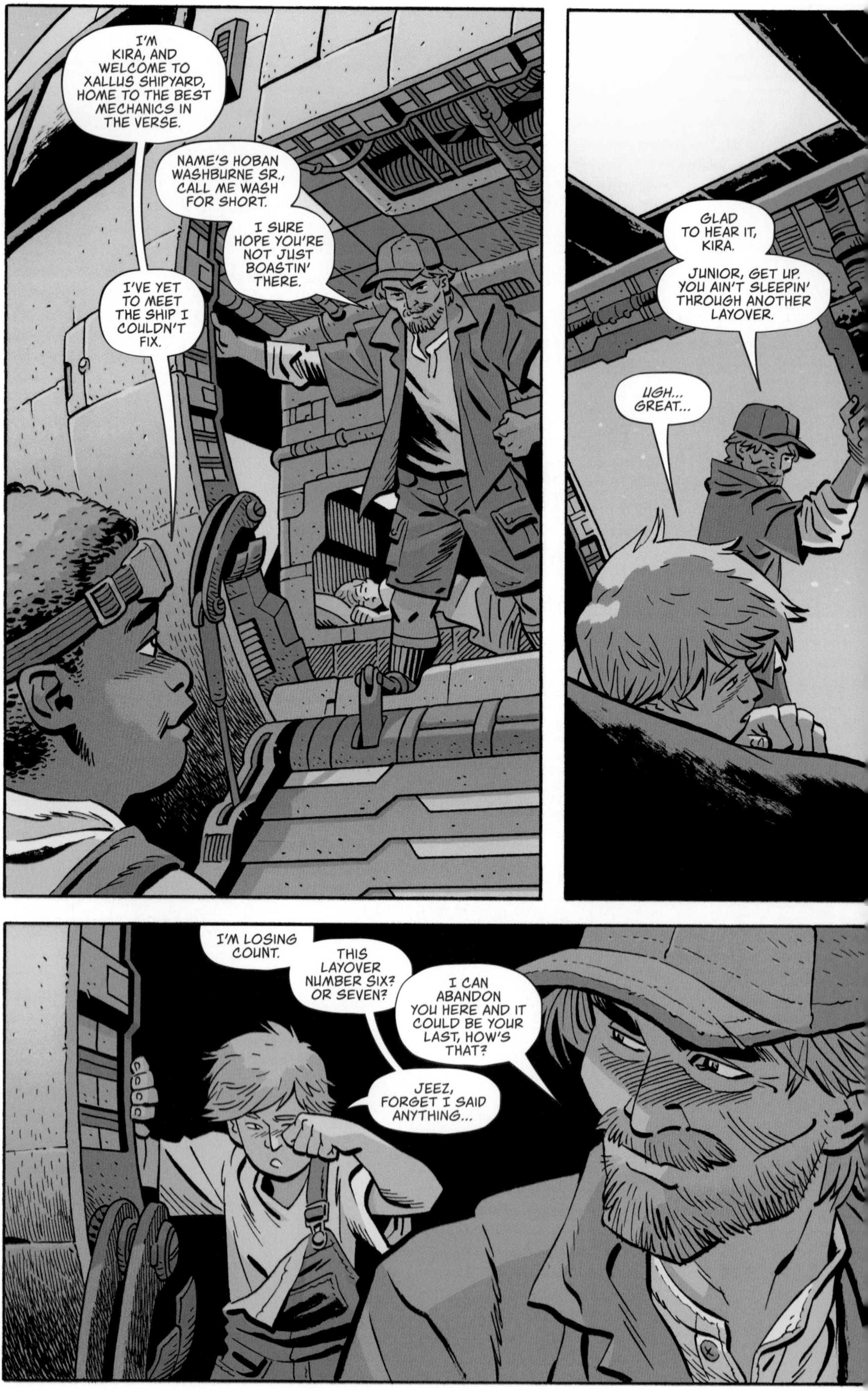
I'M KIRA, AND WELCOME TO XALLUS SHIPYARD, HOME TO THE BEST MECHANICS IN THE VERSE.
NAME'S HOBAN WASHBURNE SR., CALL ME WASH FOR SHORT.
I SURE HOPE YOU'RE NOT JUST BOASTIN' THERE.
I'VE YET TO MEET THE SHIP I COULDN'T FIX.
GLAD TO HEAR IT, KIRA.
JUNIOR, GET UP. YOU AIN'T SLEEPIN' THROUGH ANOTHER LAYOVER.
UGH... GREAT...
I'M LOSING COUNT.
THIS LAYOVER NUMBER SIX? OR SEVEN?
I CAN ABANDON YOU HERE AND IT COULD BE YOUR LAST, HOW'S THAT?
JEEZ, FORGET I SAID ANYTHING...

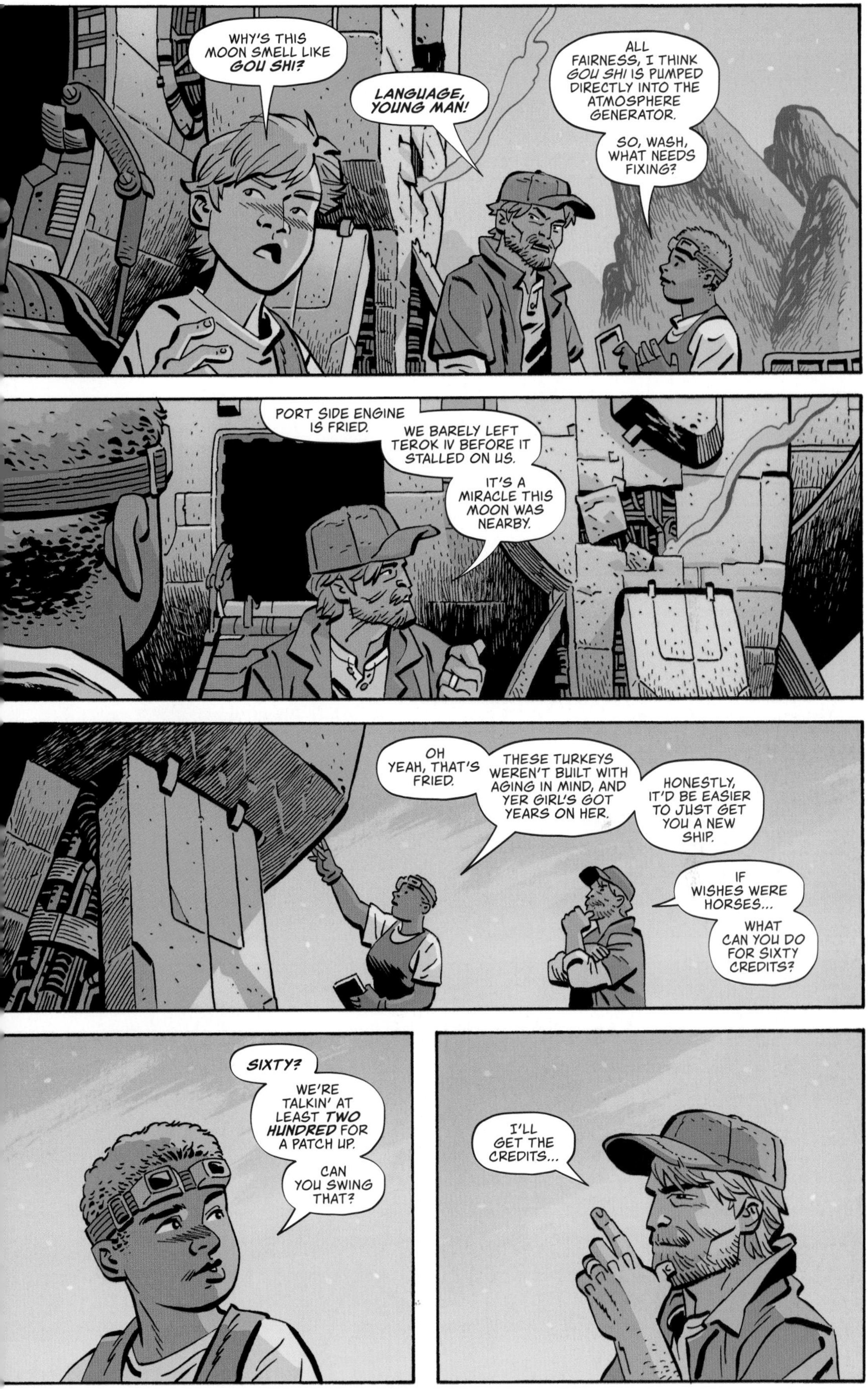
WHY'S THIS MOON SMELL LIKE GOU SHI?
LANGUAGE, YOUNG MAN!
ALL FAIRNESS, I THINK GOU SHI IS PUMPED DIRECTLY INTO THE ATMOSPHERE GENERATOR.
SO, WASH, WHAT NEEDS FIXING?
PORT SIDE ENGINE IS FRIED.
WE BARELY LEFT TEROK IV BEFORE IT STALLED ON US.
IT'S A MIRACLE THIS MOON WAS NEARBY.
OH YEAH, THAT'S FRIED.
THESE TURKEYS WEREN'T BUILT WITH AGING IN MIND, AND YER GIRL'S GOT YEARS ON HER.
HONESTLY, IT'D BE EASIER TO JUST GET YOU A NEW SHIP.
IF WISHES WERE HORSES...
WHAT CAN YOU DO FOR SIXTY CREDITS?
SIXTY?
WE'RE TALKIN' AT LEAST TWO HUNDRED FOR A PATCH UP.
CAN YOU SWING THAT?
I'LL GET THE CREDITS...

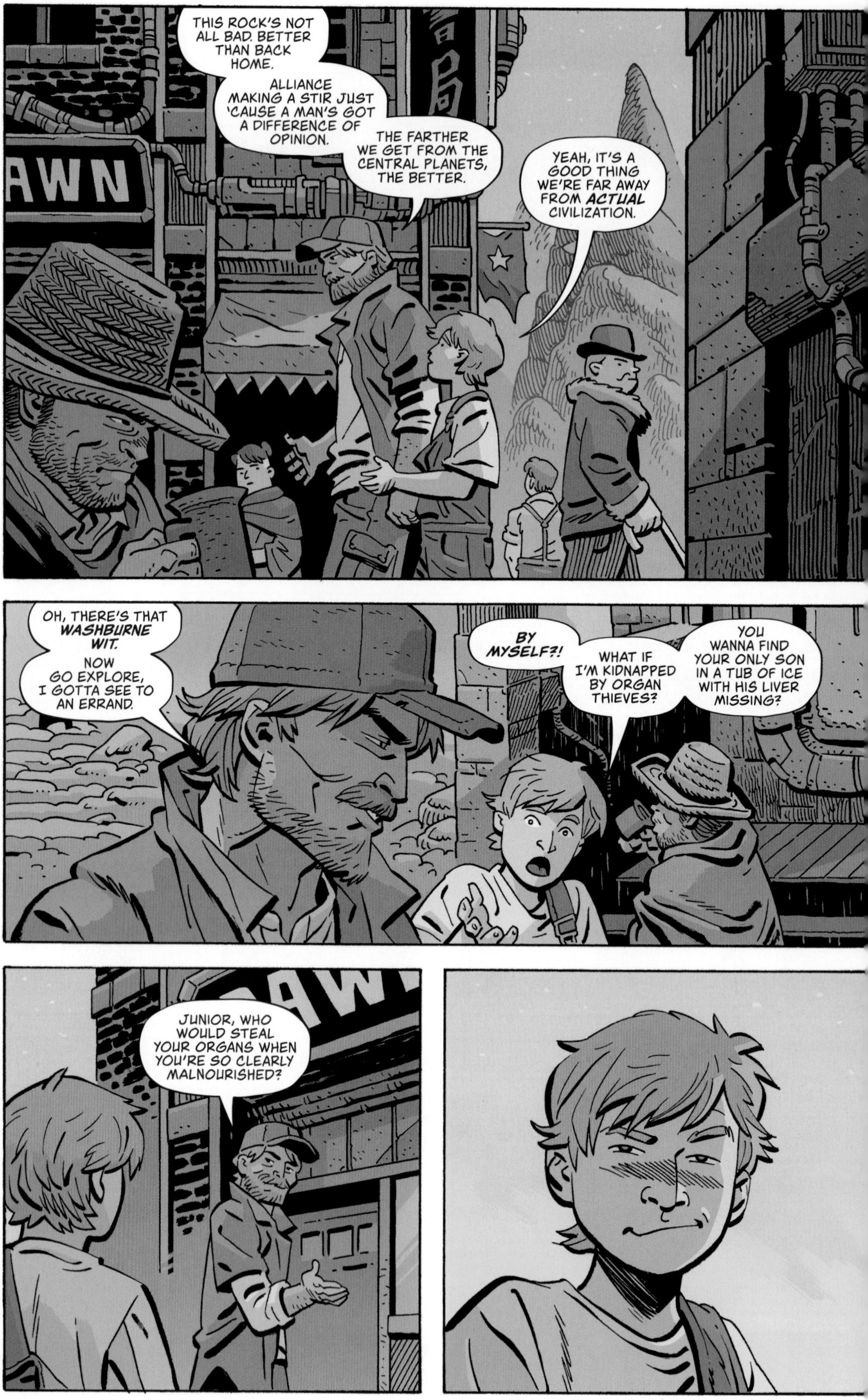
AWN
THIS ROCK'S NOT ALL BAD. BETTER THAN BACK HOME.
ALLIANCE MAKING A STIR JUST 'CAUSE A MAN'S GOT A DIFFERENCE OF OPINION.
THE FARTHER WE GET FROM THE CENTRAL PLANETS, THE BETTER.
YEAH, IT'S A GOOD THING WE'RE FAR AWAY FROM ACTUAL CIVILIZATION.
OH, THERE'S THAT WASHBURNE WIT.
NOW GO EXPLORE, I GOTTA SEE TO AN ERRAND.
BY MYSELF?!
WHAT IF I'M KIDNAPPED BY ORGAN THIEVES?
YOU WANNA FIND YOUR ONLY SON IN A TUB OF ICE WITH HIS LIVER MISSING?
JUNIOR, WHO WOULD STEAL YOUR ORGANS WHEN YOU'RE SO CLEARLY MALNOURISHED?

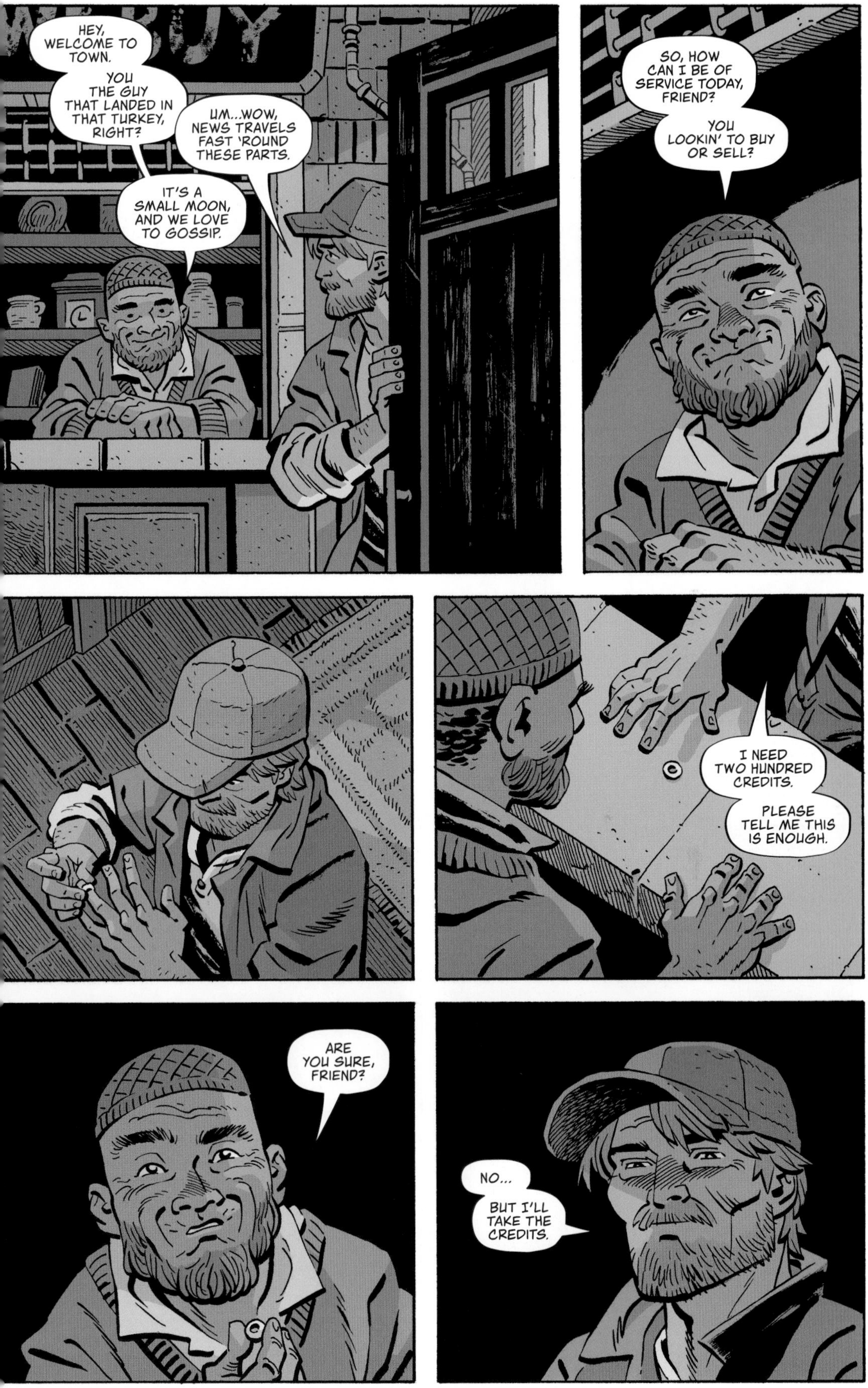

HEY, WELCOME TO TOWN.
YOU THE GUY THAT LANDED IN THAT TURKEY, RIGHT?
UM...WOW, NEWS TRAVELS FAST 'ROUND THESE PARTS.
IT'S A SMALL MOON, AND WE LOVE TO GOSSIP.
SO, HOW CAN I BE OF SERVICE TODAY, FRIEND?
YOU LOOKIN' TO BUY OR SELL?
I NEED TWO HUNDRED CREDITS.
PLEASE TELL ME THIS IS ENOUGH.
ARE YOU SURE, FRIEND?
NO...
BUT I'LL TAKE THE CREDITS.

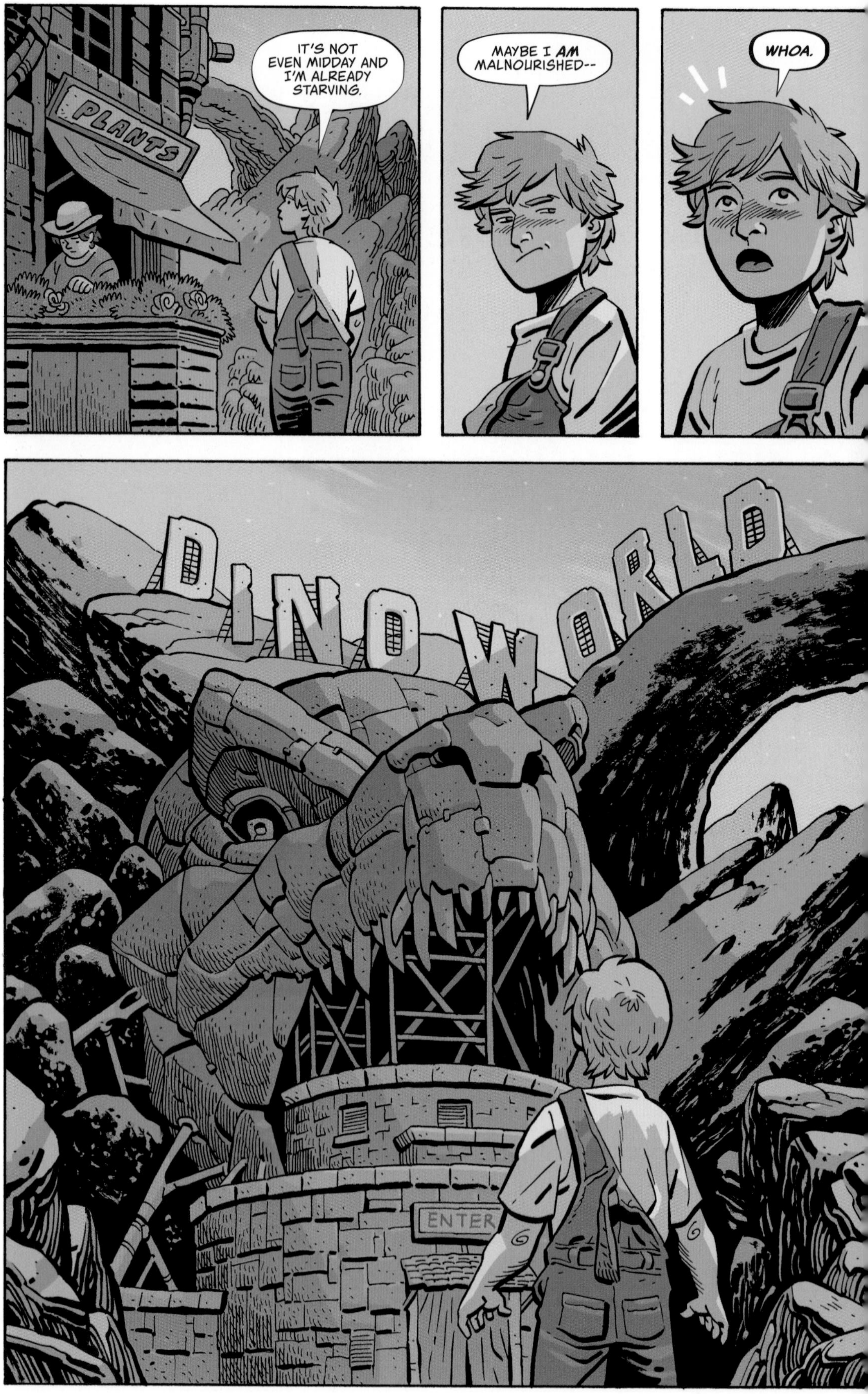
PLANTS
IT'S NOT EVEN MIDDAY AND I'M ALREADY STARVING.
MAYBE I AM MALNOURISHED--
WHOA.
DINO WORLD
ENTER

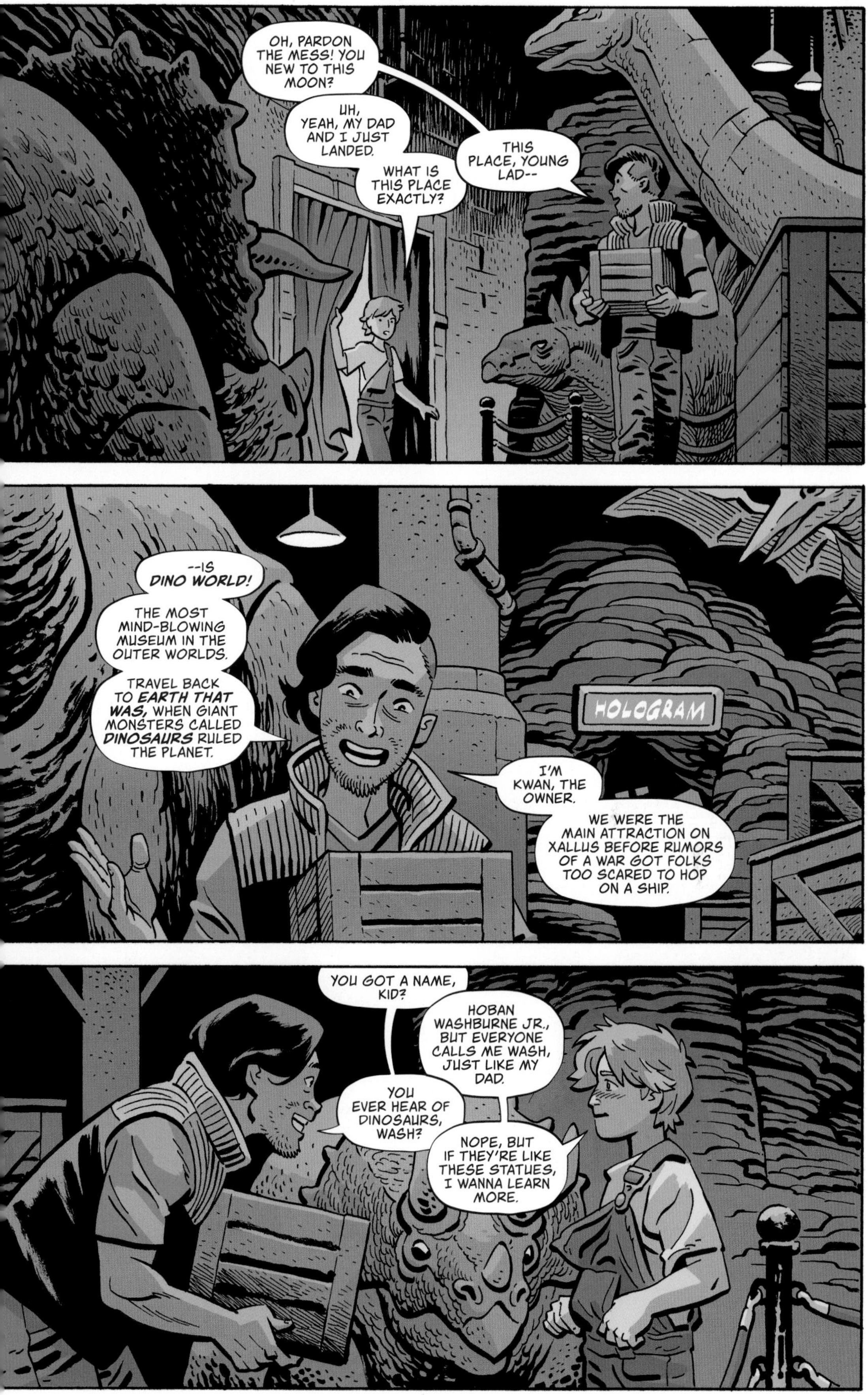
OH, PARDON THE MESS! YOU NEW TO THIS MOON?
UH, YEAH, MY DAD AND I JUST LANDED.
WHAT IS THIS PLACE EXACTLY?
THIS PLACE, YOUNG LAD--
--IS DINO WORLD!
THE MOST MIND-BLOWING MUSEUM IN THE OUTER WORLDS.
TRAVEL BACK TO EARTH THAT WAS, WHEN GIANT MONSTERS CALLED DINOSAURS RULED THE PLANET.
HOLOGRAM
I'M KWAN, THE OWNER.
WE WERE THE MAIN ATTRACTION ON XALLUS BEFORE RUMORS OF A WAR GOT FOLKS TOO SCARED TO HOP ON A SHIP.
YOU GOT A NAME, KID?
HOBAN WASHBURNE JR., BUT EVERYONE CALLS ME WASH, JUST LIKE MY DAD.
YOU EVER HEAR OF DINOSAURS, WASH?
NOPE, BUT IF THEY'RE LIKE THESE STATUES, I WANNA LEARN MORE.

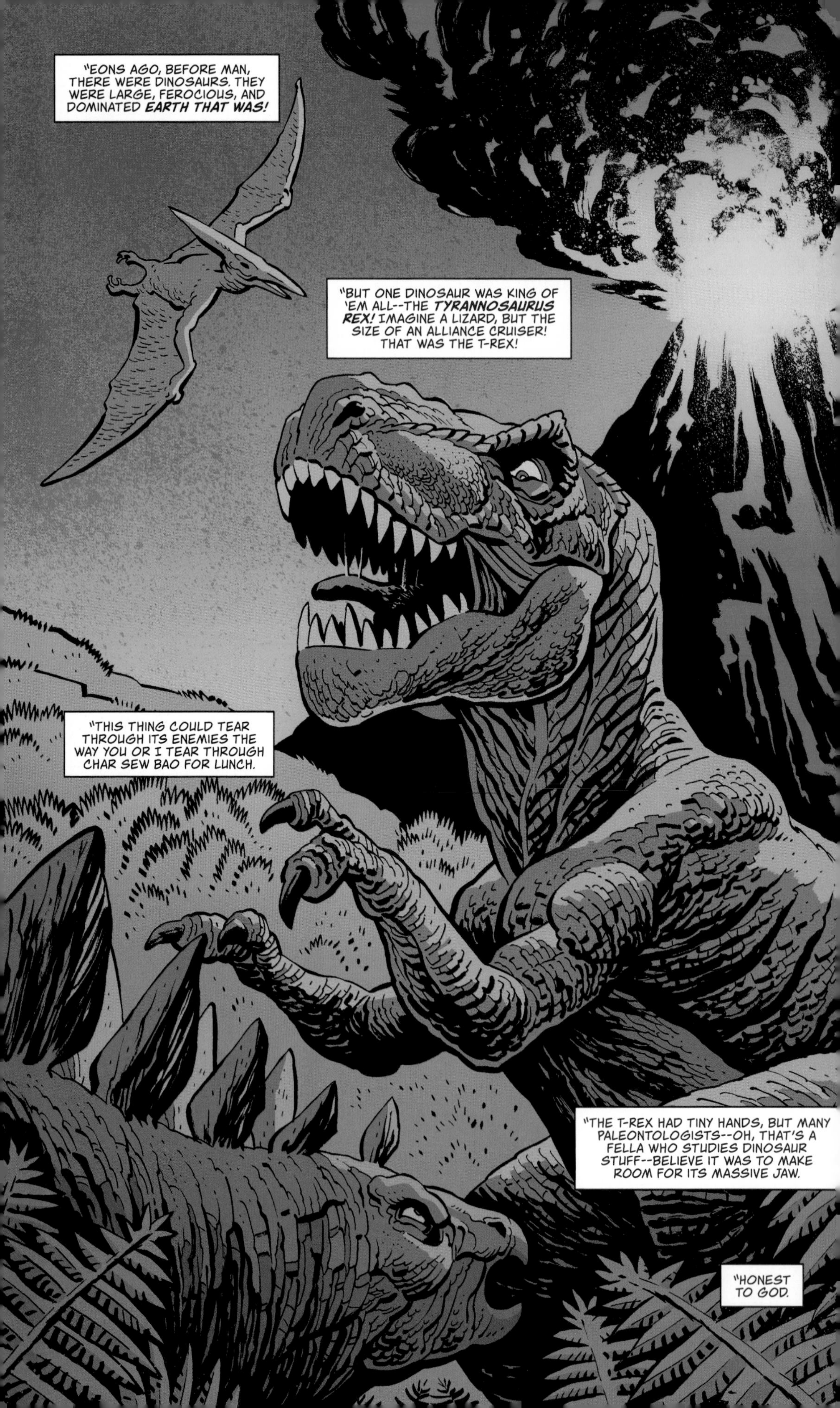
"EONS AGO, BEFORE MAN, THERE WERE DINOSAURS. THEY WERE LARGE, FEROCIOUS, AND DOMINATED **EARTH THAT WAS!**
"BUT ONE DINOSAUR WAS KING OF 'EM ALL--THE ***TYRANNOSAURUS REX!*** IMAGINE A LIZARD, BUT THE SIZE OF AN ALLIANCE CRUISER! THAT WAS THE T-REX!
"THIS THING COULD TEAR THROUGH ITS ENEMIES THE WAY YOU OR I TEAR THROUGH CHAR SEW BAO FOR LUNCH.
"THE T-REX HAD TINY HANDS, BUT MANY PALEONTOLOGISTS--OH, THAT'S A FELLA WHO STUDIES DINOSAUR STUFF--BELIEVE IT WAS TO MAKE ROOM FOR ITS MASSIVE JAW.
"HONEST TO GOD.

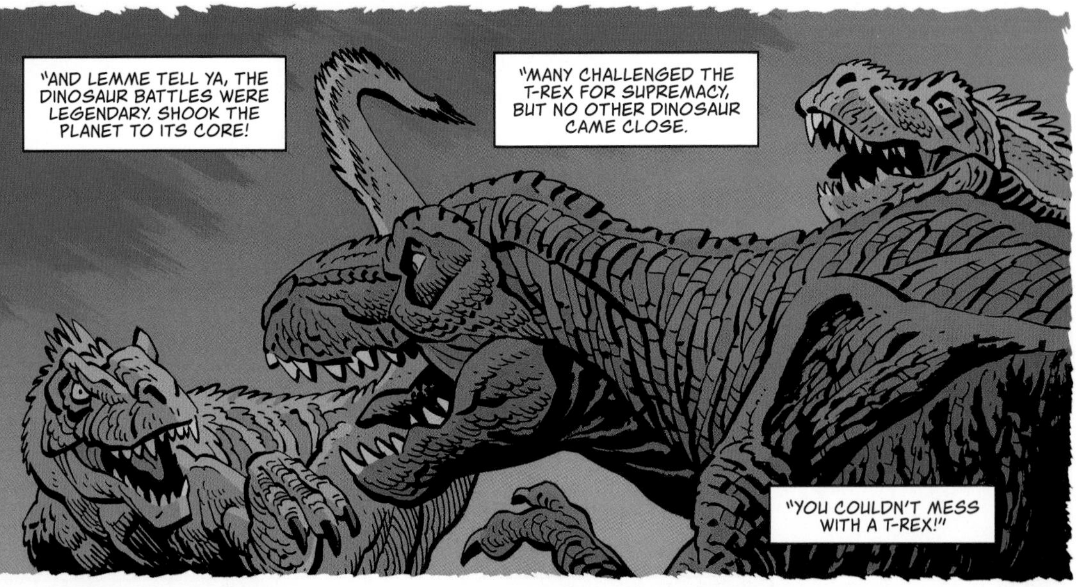
"AND LEMME TELL YA, THE DINOSAUR BATTLES WERE LEGENDARY. SHOOK THE PLANET TO ITS CORE!
"MANY CHALLENGED THE T-REX FOR SUPREMACY, BUT NO OTHER DINOSAUR CAME CLOSE.
"YOU COULDN'T MESS WITH A T-REX!"

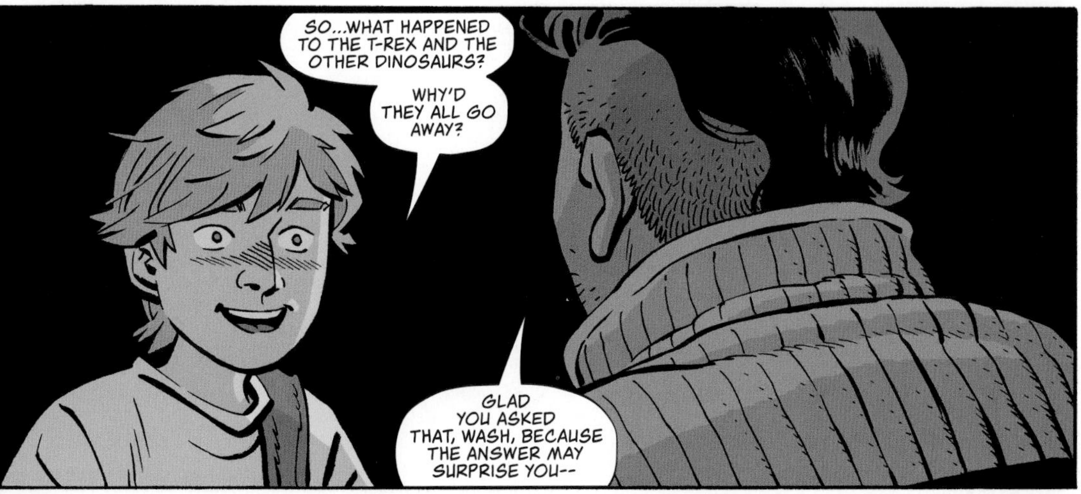
SO...WHAT HAPPENED TO THE T-REX AND THE OTHER DINOSAURS?
WHY'D THEY ALL GO AWAY?
GLAD YOU ASKED THAT, WASH, BECAUSE THE ANSWER MAY SURPRISE YOU--

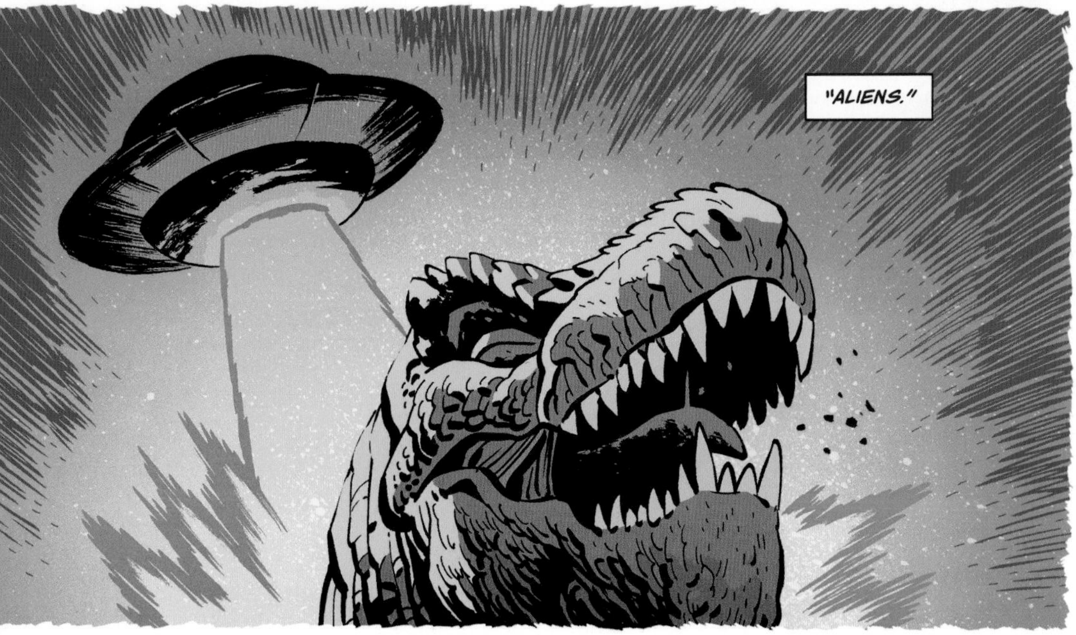
"ALIENS."

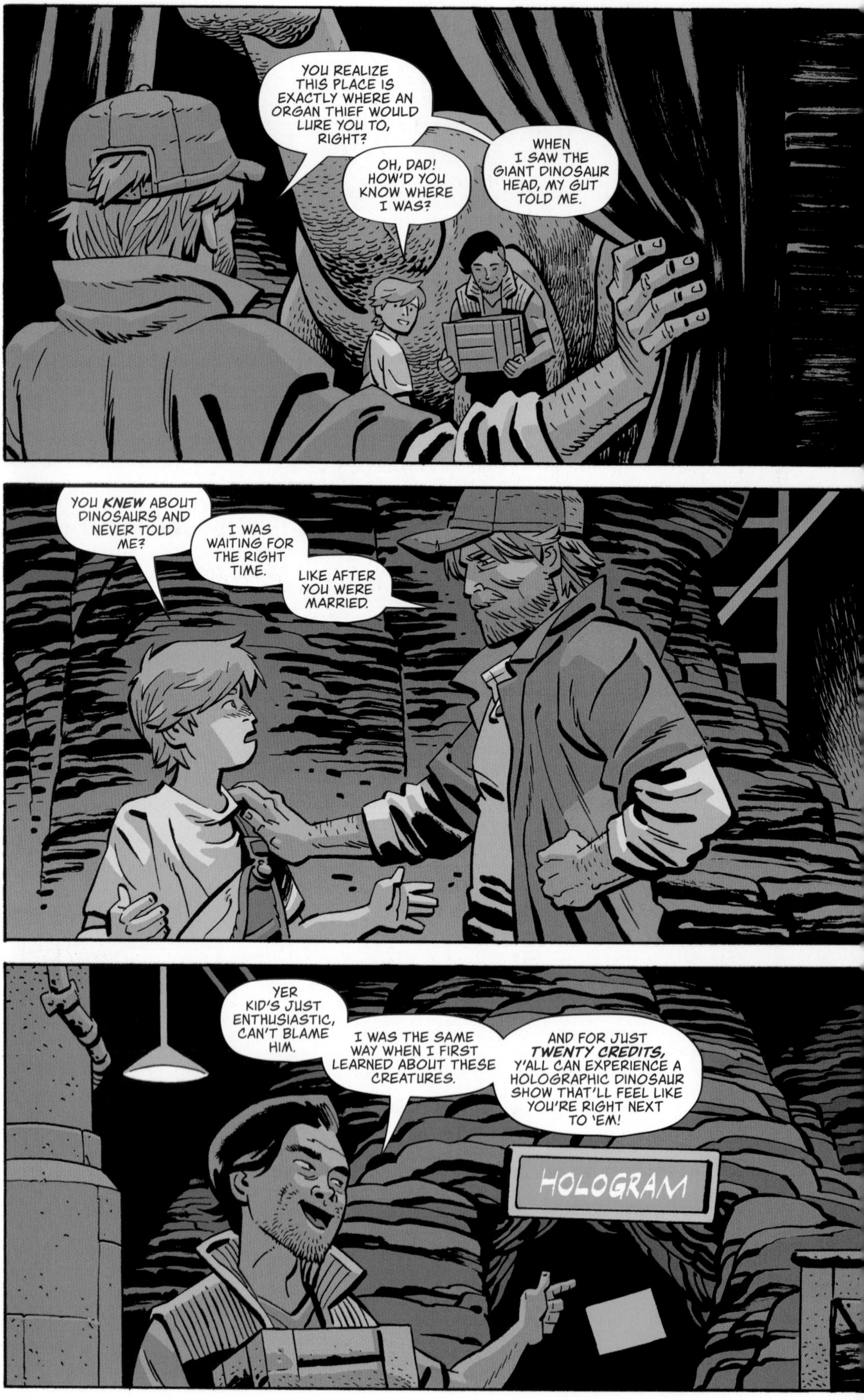
YOU REALIZE THIS PLACE IS EXACTLY WHERE AN ORGAN THIEF WOULD LURE YOU TO, RIGHT?
OH, DAD! HOW'D YOU KNOW WHERE I WAS?
WHEN I SAW THE GIANT DINOSAUR HEAD, MY GUT TOLD ME.
YOU **KNEW** ABOUT DINOSAURS AND NEVER TOLD ME?
I WAS WAITING FOR THE RIGHT TIME.
LIKE AFTER YOU WERE MARRIED.
YER KID'S JUST ENTHUSIASTIC, CAN'T BLAME HIM.
I WAS THE SAME WAY WHEN I FIRST LEARNED ABOUT THESE CREATURES.
AND FOR JUST ***TWENTY CREDITS,*** Y'ALL CAN EXPERIENCE A HOLOGRAPHIC DINOSAUR SHOW THAT'LL FEEL LIKE YOU'RE RIGHT NEXT TO 'EM!
HOLOGRAM

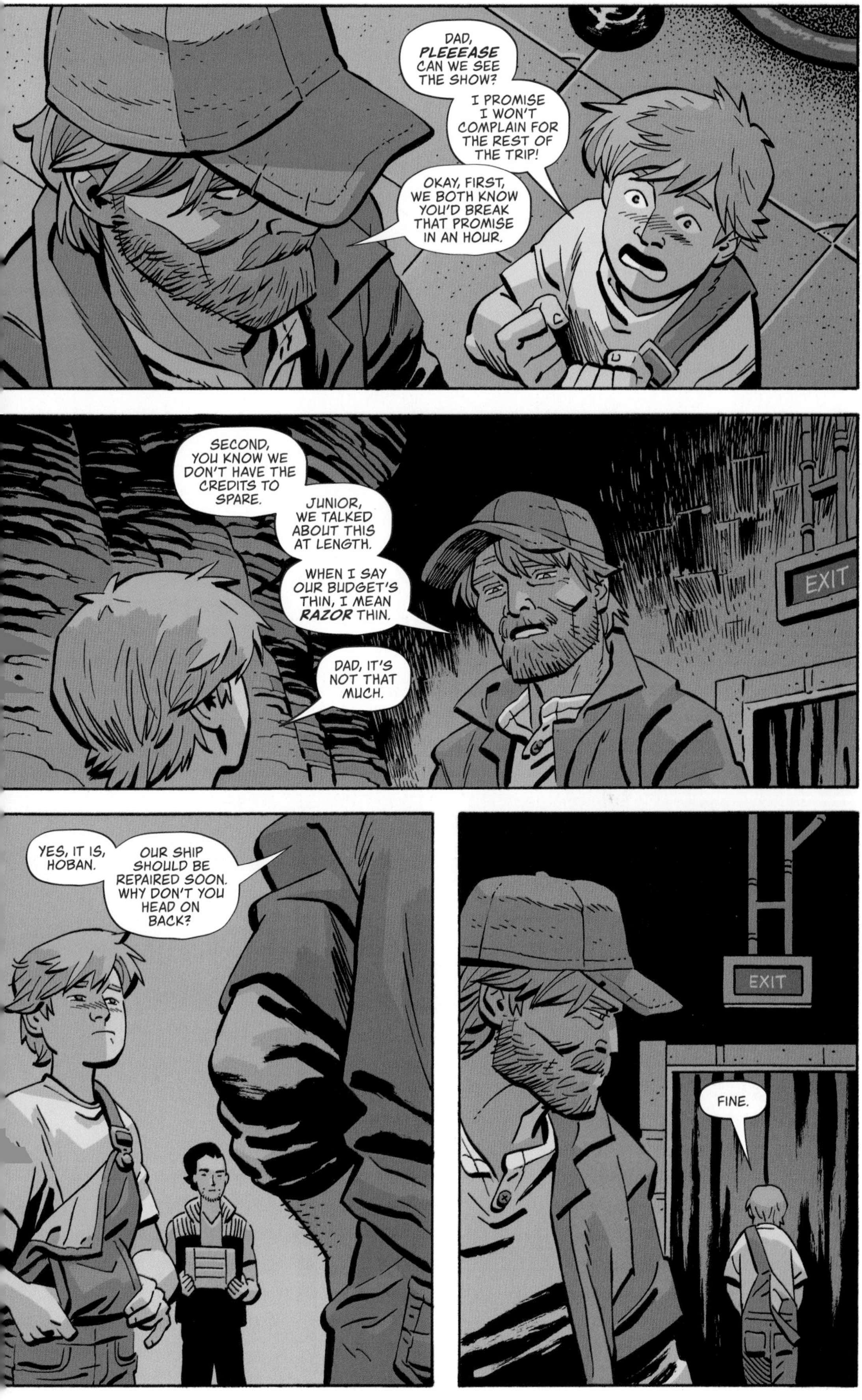
DAD, *PLEEEASE* CAN WE SEE THE SHOW?
I PROMISE I WON'T COMPLAIN FOR THE REST OF THE TRIP!
OKAY, FIRST, WE BOTH KNOW YOU'D BREAK THAT PROMISE IN AN HOUR.
SECOND, YOU KNOW WE DON'T HAVE THE CREDITS TO SPARE.
JUNIOR, WE TALKED ABOUT THIS AT LENGTH.
WHEN I SAY OUR BUDGET'S THIN, I MEAN *RAZOR* THIN.
EXIT
DAD, IT'S NOT THAT MUCH.
YES, IT IS, HOBAN.
OUR SHIP SHOULD BE REPAIRED SOON. WHY DON'T YOU HEAD ON BACK?
EXIT
FINE.

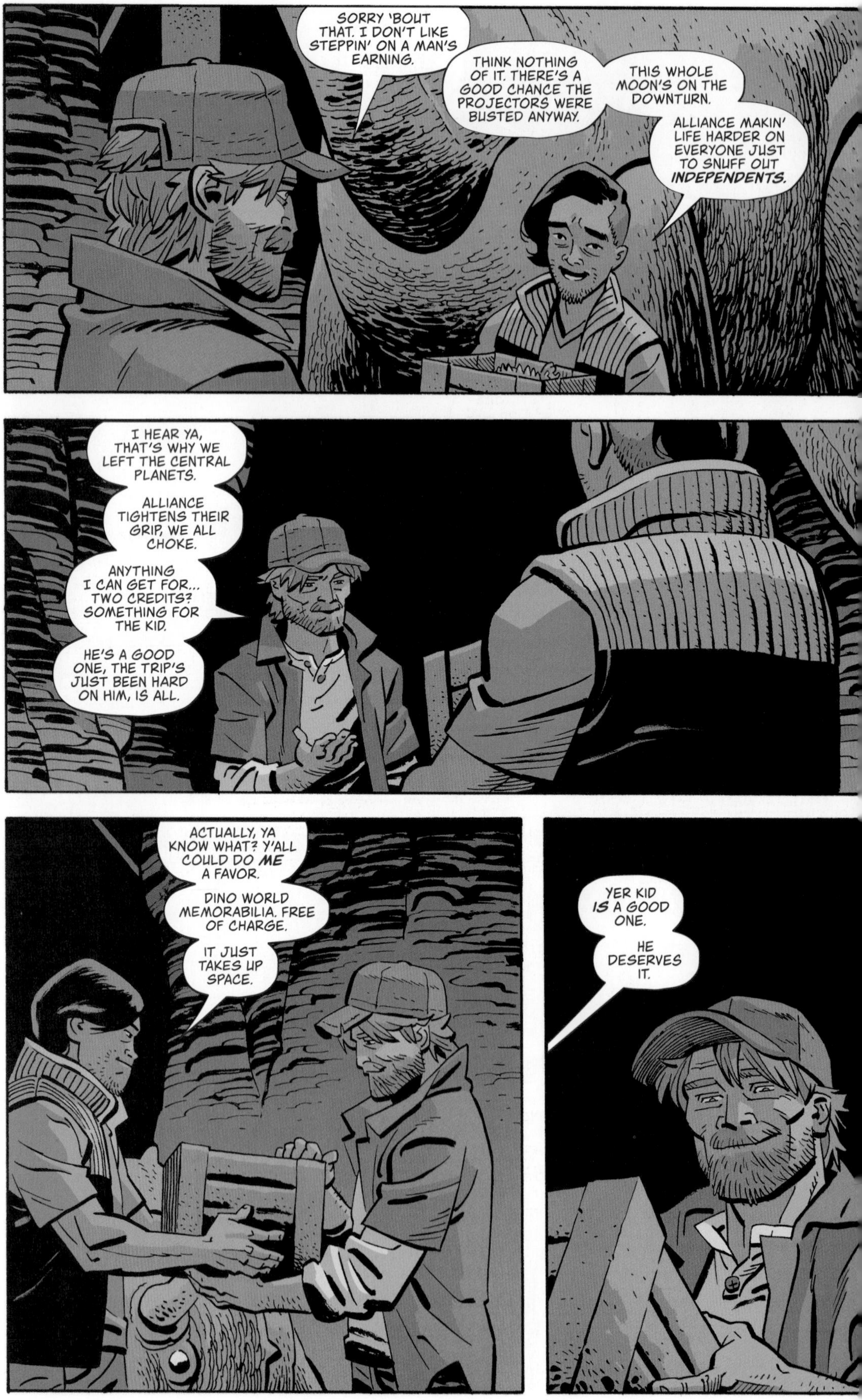
SORRY 'BOUT THAT. I DON'T LIKE STEPPIN' ON A MAN'S EARNING.
THINK NOTHING OF IT. THERE'S A GOOD CHANCE THE PROJECTORS WERE BUSTED ANYWAY.
THIS WHOLE MOON'S ON THE DOWNTURN.
ALLIANCE MAKIN' LIFE HARDER ON EVERYONE JUST TO SNUFF OUT ***INDEPENDENTS.***
I HEAR YA, THAT'S WHY WE LEFT THE CENTRAL PLANETS.
ALLIANCE TIGHTENS THEIR GRIP, WE ALL CHOKE.
ANYTHING I CAN GET FOR... TWO CREDITS? SOMETHING FOR THE KID.
HE'S A GOOD ONE, THE TRIP'S JUST BEEN HARD ON HIM, IS ALL.
ACTUALLY, YA KNOW WHAT? Y'ALL COULD DO ***ME*** A FAVOR.
DINO WORLD MEMORABILIA. FREE OF CHARGE.
IT JUST TAKES UP SPACE.
YER KID ***IS*** A GOOD ONE.
HE DESERVES IT.

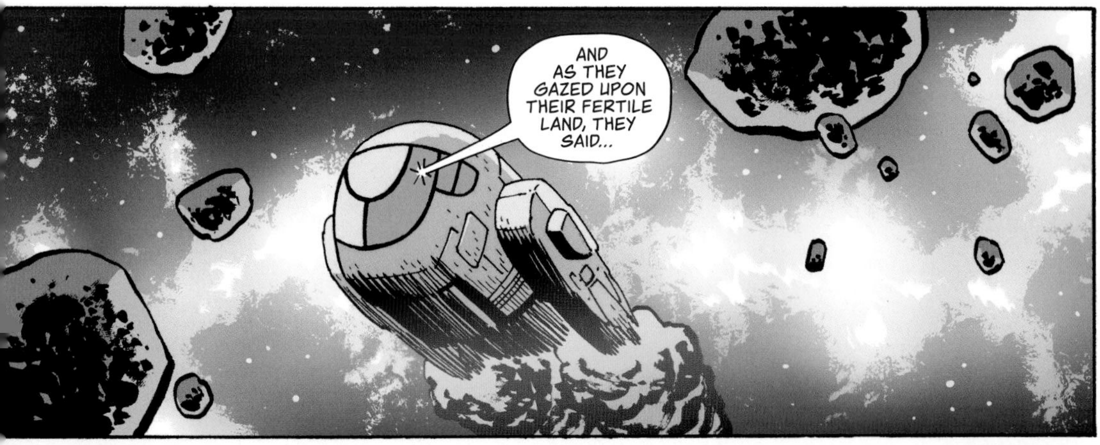
AND AS THEY GAZED UPON THEIR FERTILE LAND, THEY SAID...

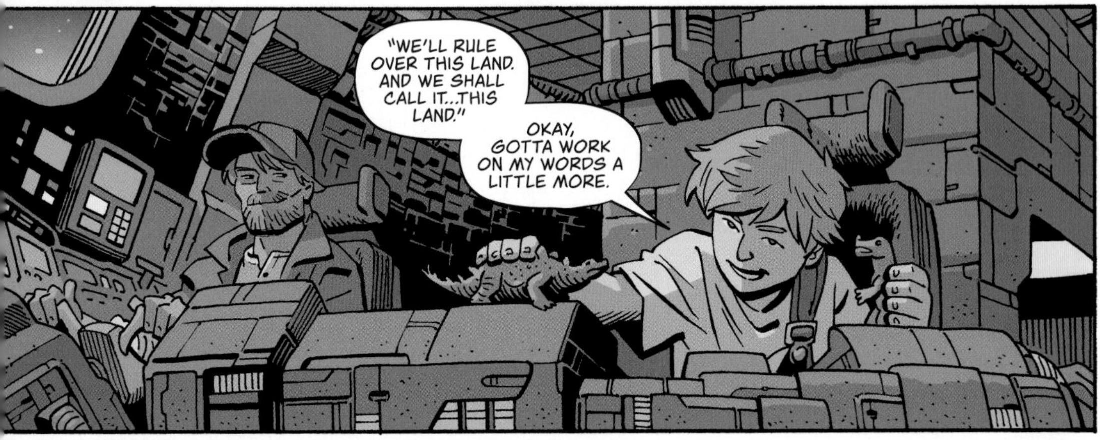
"WE'LL RULE OVER THIS LAND. AND WE SHALL CALL IT...THIS LAND."
OKAY, GOTTA WORK ON MY WORDS A LITTLE MORE.

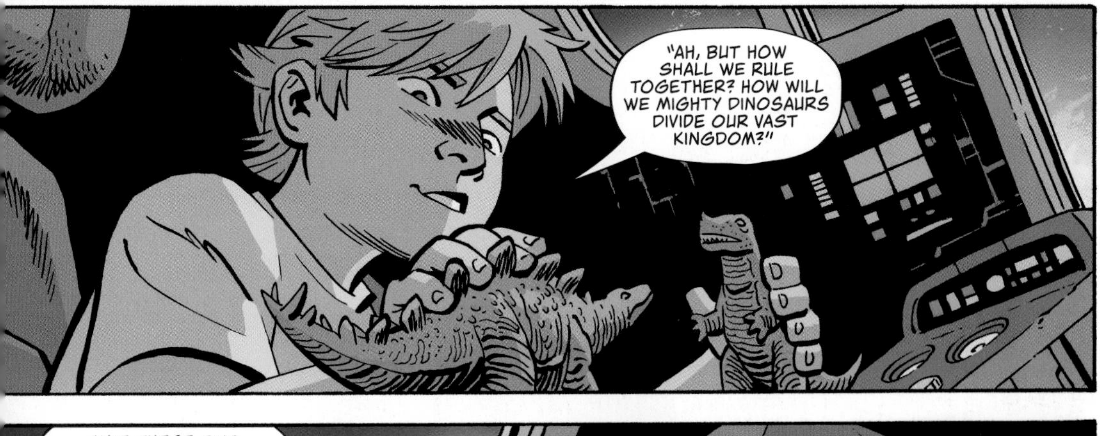
"AH, BUT HOW SHALL WE RULE TOGETHER? HOW WILL WE MIGHTY DINOSAURS DIVIDE OUR VAST KINGDOM?"

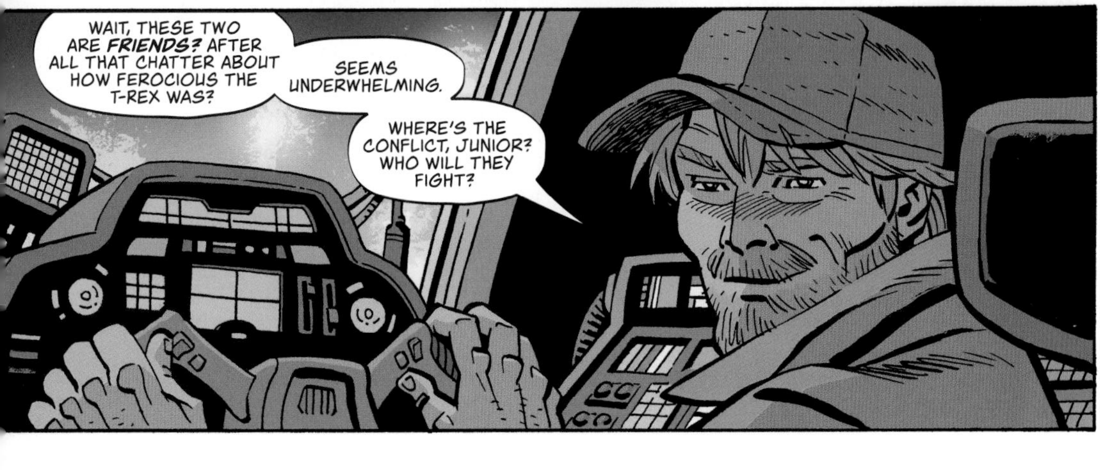
WAIT, THESE TWO ARE ***FRIENDS?*** AFTER ALL THAT CHATTER ABOUT HOW FEROCIOUS THE T-REX WAS?
SEEMS UNDERWHELMING.
WHERE'S THE CONFLICT, JUNIOR? WHO WILL THEY FIGHT?

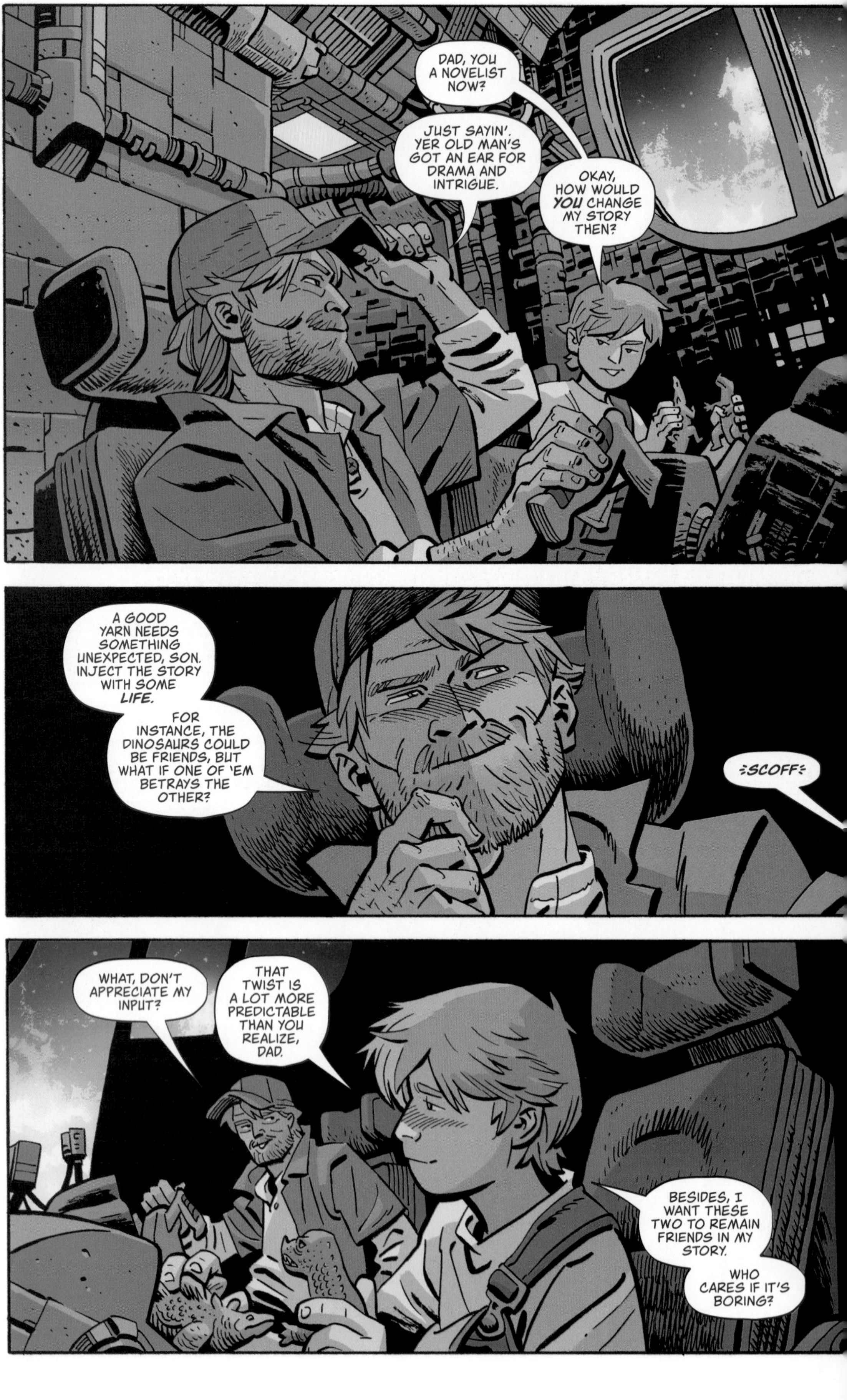
DAD, YOU A NOVELIST NOW?
JUST SAYIN'. YER OLD MAN'S GOT AN EAR FOR DRAMA AND INTRIGUE.
OKAY, HOW WOULD YOU CHANGE MY STORY THEN?
A GOOD YARN NEEDS SOMETHING UNEXPECTED, SON. INJECT THE STORY WITH SOME LIFE.
FOR INSTANCE, THE DINOSAURS COULD BE FRIENDS, BUT WHAT IF ONE OF 'EM BETRAYS THE OTHER?
SCOFF
WHAT, DON'T APPRECIATE MY INPUT?
THAT TWIST IS A LOT MORE PREDICTABLE THAN YOU REALIZE, DAD.
BESIDES, I WANT THESE TWO TO REMAIN FRIENDS IN MY STORY.
WHO CARES IF IT'S BORING?

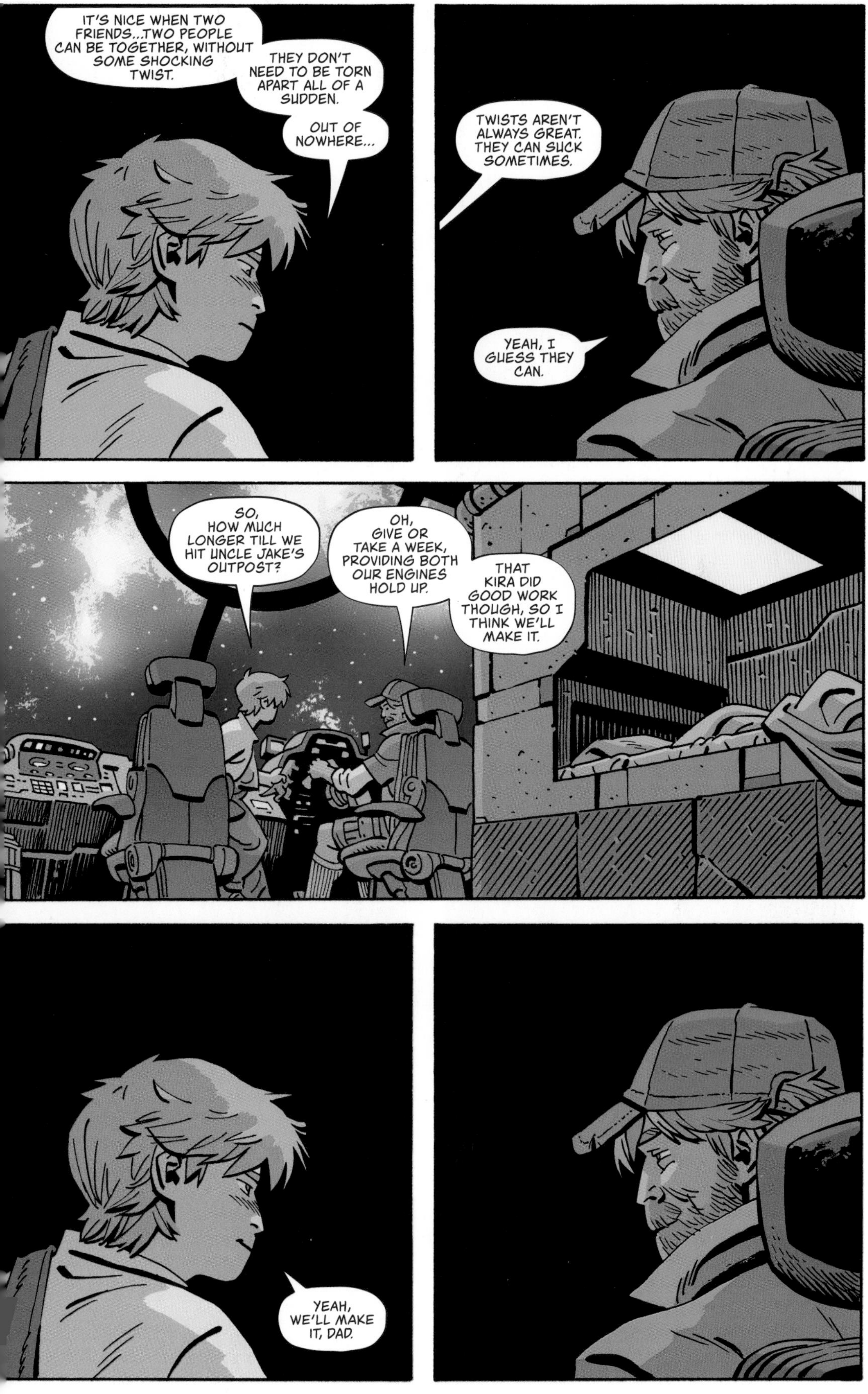
IT'S NICE WHEN TWO FRIENDS...TWO PEOPLE CAN BE TOGETHER, WITHOUT SOME SHOCKING TWIST.
THEY DON'T NEED TO BE TORN APART ALL OF A SUDDEN.
OUT OF NOWHERE...
TWISTS AREN'T ALWAYS GREAT. THEY CAN SUCK SOMETIMES.
YEAH, I GUESS THEY CAN.
SO, HOW MUCH LONGER TILL WE HIT UNCLE JAKE'S OUTPOST?
OH, GIVE OR TAKE A WEEK, PROVIDING BOTH OUR ENGINES HOLD UP.
THAT KIRA DID GOOD WORK THOUGH, SO I THINK WE'LL MAKE IT.
YEAH, WE'LL MAKE IT, DAD.

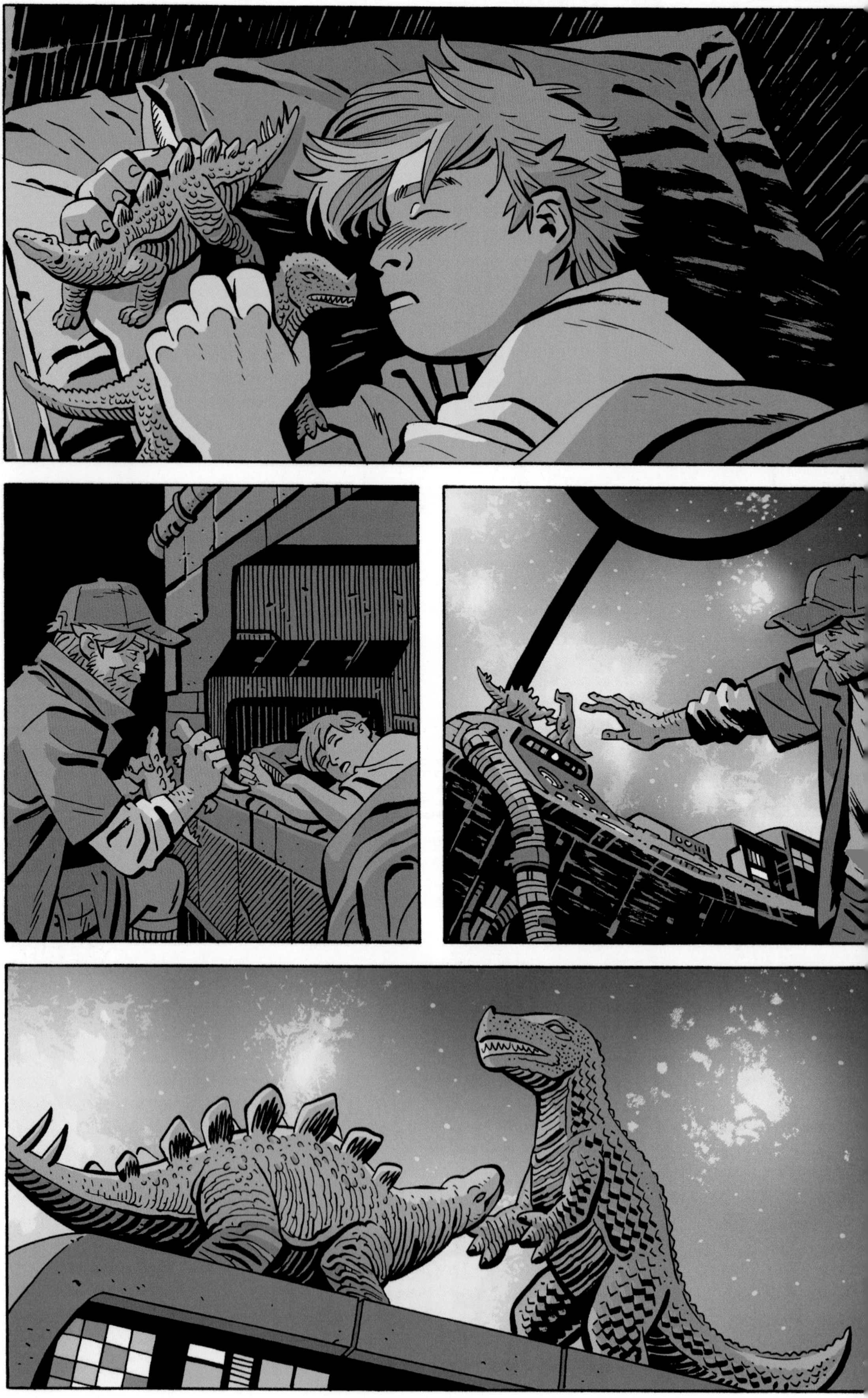

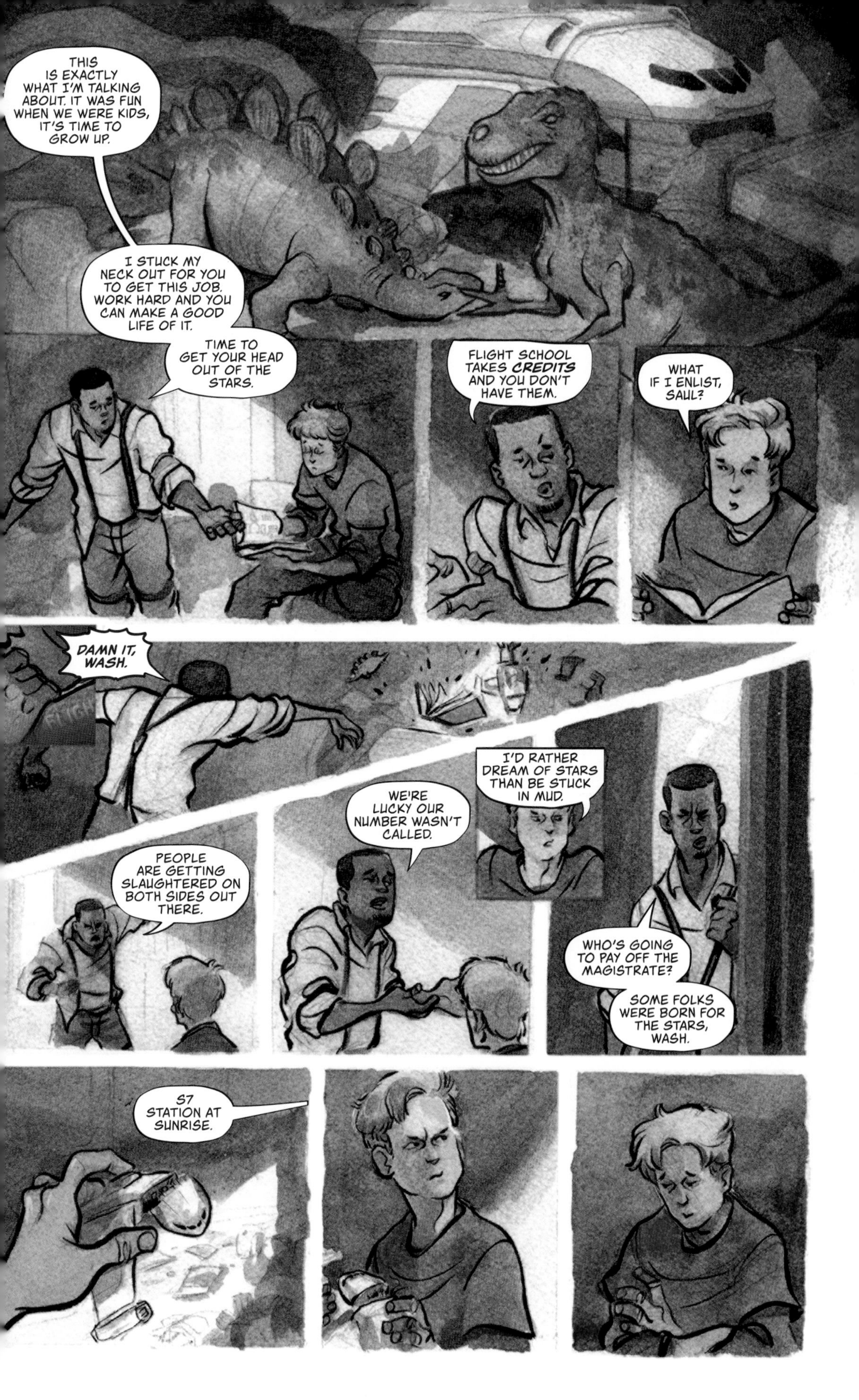
THIS IS EXACTLY WHAT I'M TALKING ABOUT. IT WAS FUN WHEN WE WERE KIDS, IT'S TIME TO GROW UP.
I STUCK MY NECK OUT FOR YOU TO GET THIS JOB. WORK HARD AND YOU CAN MAKE A GOOD LIFE OF IT.
TIME TO GET YOUR HEAD OUT OF THE STARS.
FLIGHT SCHOOL TAKES CREDITS AND YOU DON'T HAVE THEM.
WHAT IF I ENLIST, SAUL?
DAMN IT, WASH.
PEOPLE ARE GETTING SLAUGHTERED ON BOTH SIDES OUT THERE.
WE'RE LUCKY OUR NUMBER WASN'T CALLED.
I'D RATHER DREAM OF STARS THAN BE STUCK IN MUD.
WHO'S GOING TO PAY OFF THE MAGISTRATE?
SOME FOLKS WERE BORN FOR THE STARS, WASH.
S7 STATION AT SUNRISE.

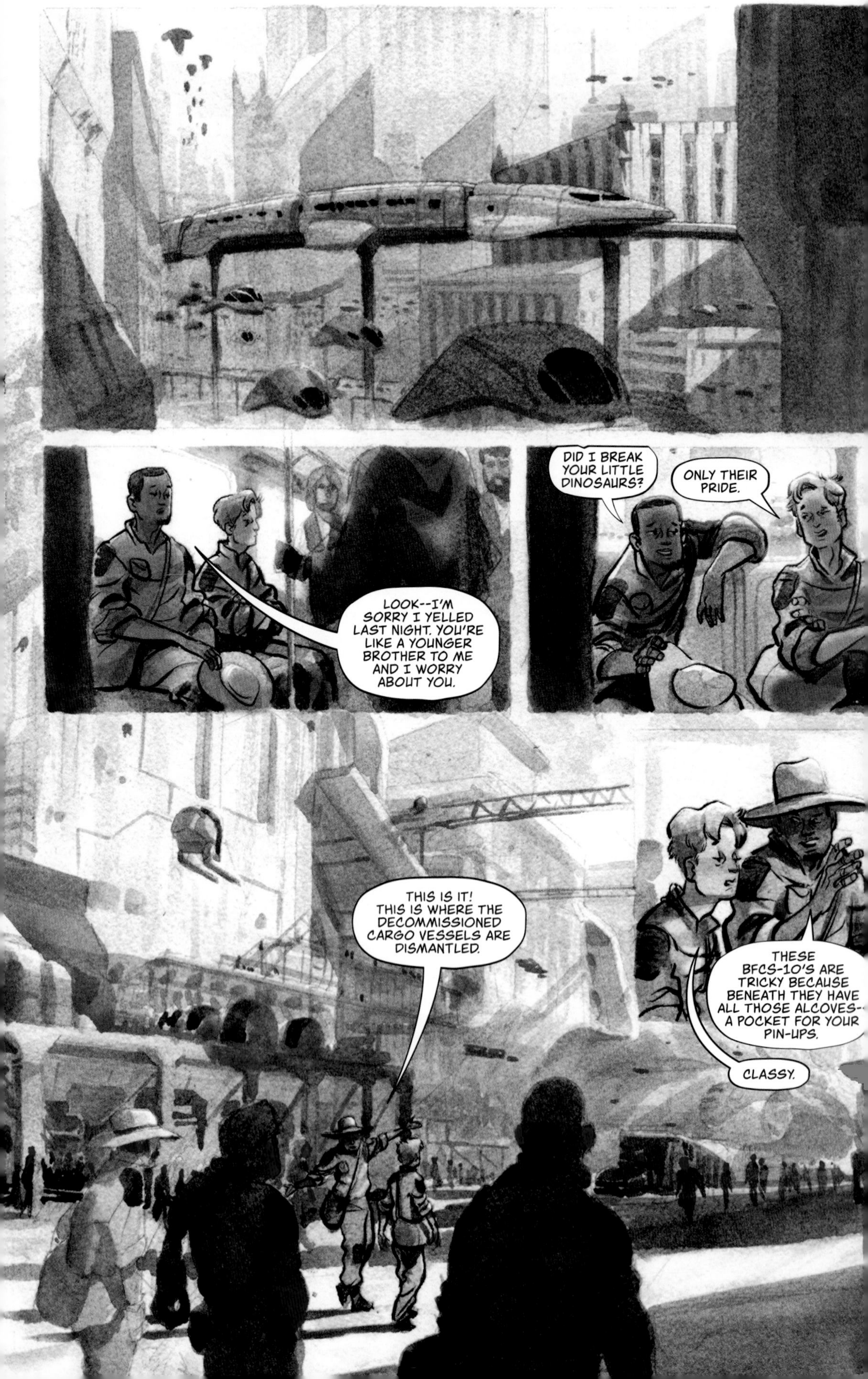
LOOK--I'M SORRY I YELLED LAST NIGHT. YOU'RE LIKE A YOUNGER BROTHER TO ME AND I WORRY ABOUT YOU.
DID I BREAK YOUR LITTLE DINOSAURS?
ONLY THEIR PRIDE.
THIS IS IT! THIS IS WHERE THE DECOMMISSIONED CARGO VESSELS ARE DISMANTLED.
THESE BFCS-10'S ARE TRICKY BECAUSE BENEATH THEY HAVE ALL THOSE ALCOVES--A POCKET FOR YOUR PIN-UPS.
CLASSY.

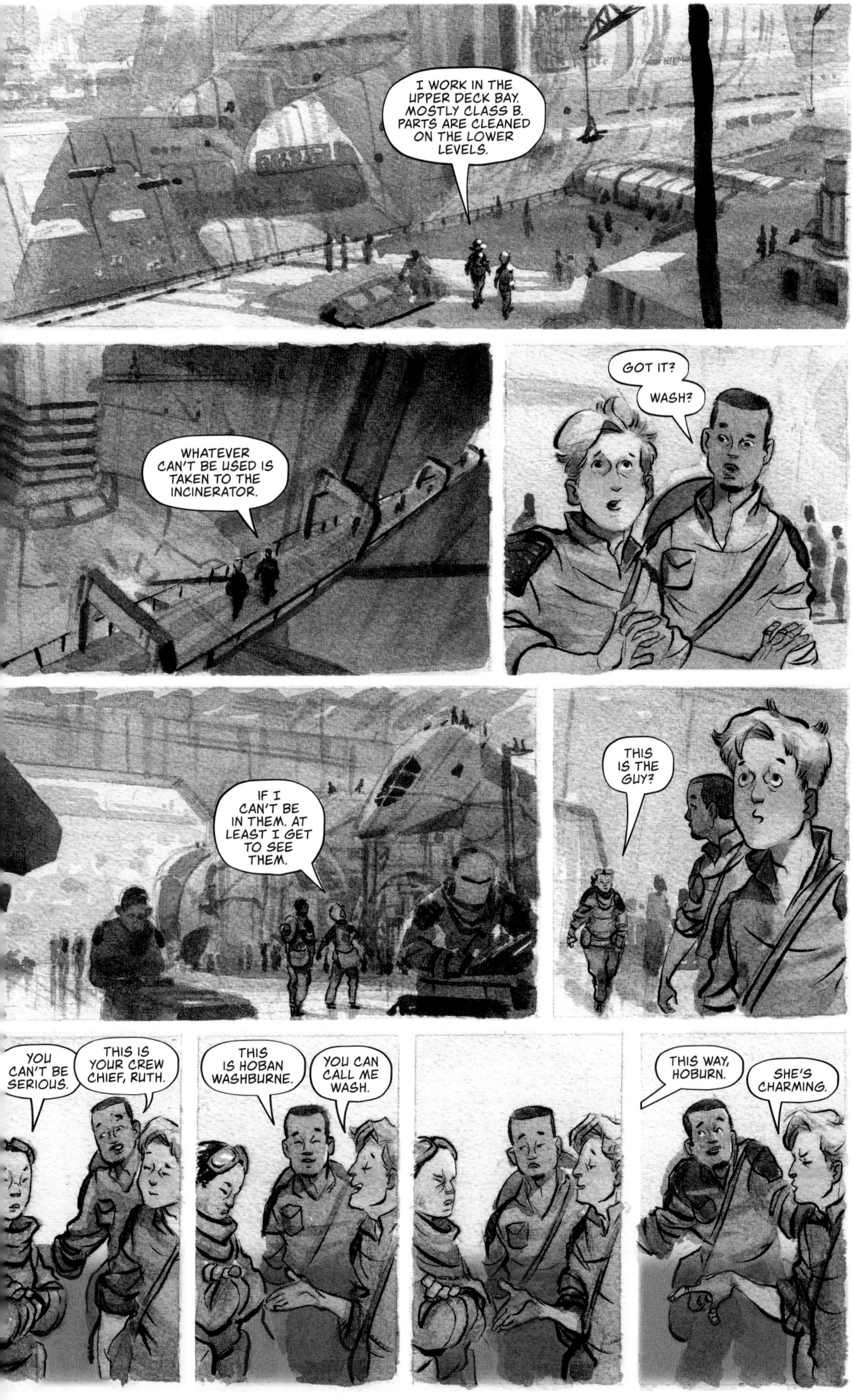
I WORK IN THE UPPER DECK BAY. MOSTLY CLASS B. PARTS ARE CLEANED ON THE LOWER LEVELS.
WHATEVER CAN'T BE USED IS TAKEN TO THE INCINERATOR.
GOT IT?
WASH?
IF I CAN'T BE IN THEM. AT LEAST I GET TO SEE THEM.
THIS IS THE GUY?
YOU CAN'T BE SERIOUS.
THIS IS YOUR CREW CHIEF, RUTH.
THIS IS HOBAN WASHBURNE.
YOU CAN CALL ME WASH.
THIS WAY, HOBURN.
SHE'S CHARMING.

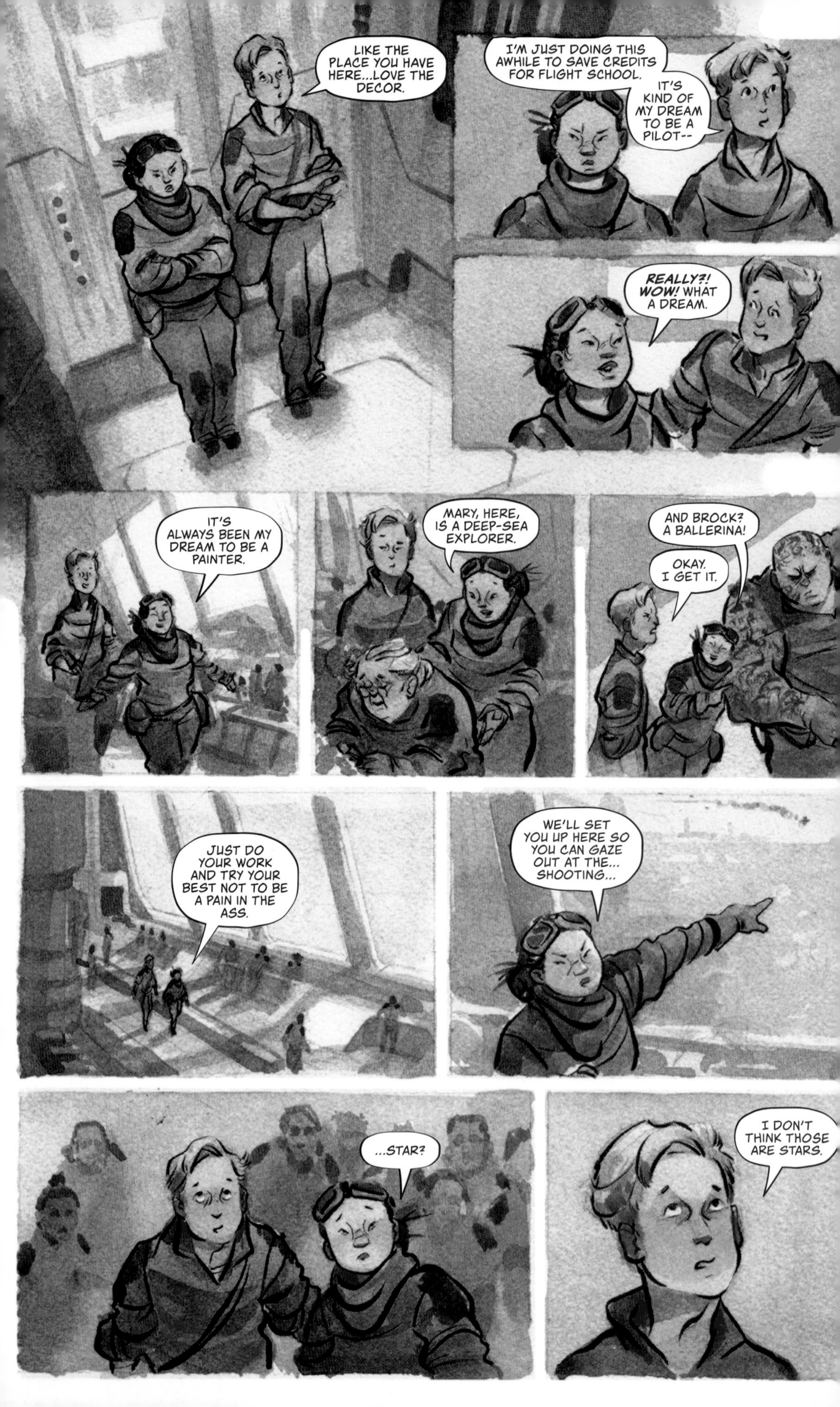
LIKE THE PLACE YOU HAVE HERE...LOVE THE DECOR.
I'M JUST DOING THIS AWHILE TO SAVE CREDITS FOR FLIGHT SCHOOL.
IT'S KIND OF MY DREAM TO BE A PILOT--
REALLY?! WOW! WHAT A DREAM.
IT'S ALWAYS BEEN MY DREAM TO BE A PAINTER.
MARY, HERE, IS A DEEP-SEA EXPLORER.
AND BROCK? A BALLERINA!
OKAY. I GET IT.
JUST DO YOUR WORK AND TRY YOUR BEST NOT TO BE A PAIN IN THE ASS.
WE'LL SET YOU UP HERE SO YOU CAN GAZE OUT AT THE... SHOOTING...
...STAR?
I DON'T THINK THOSE ARE STARS.

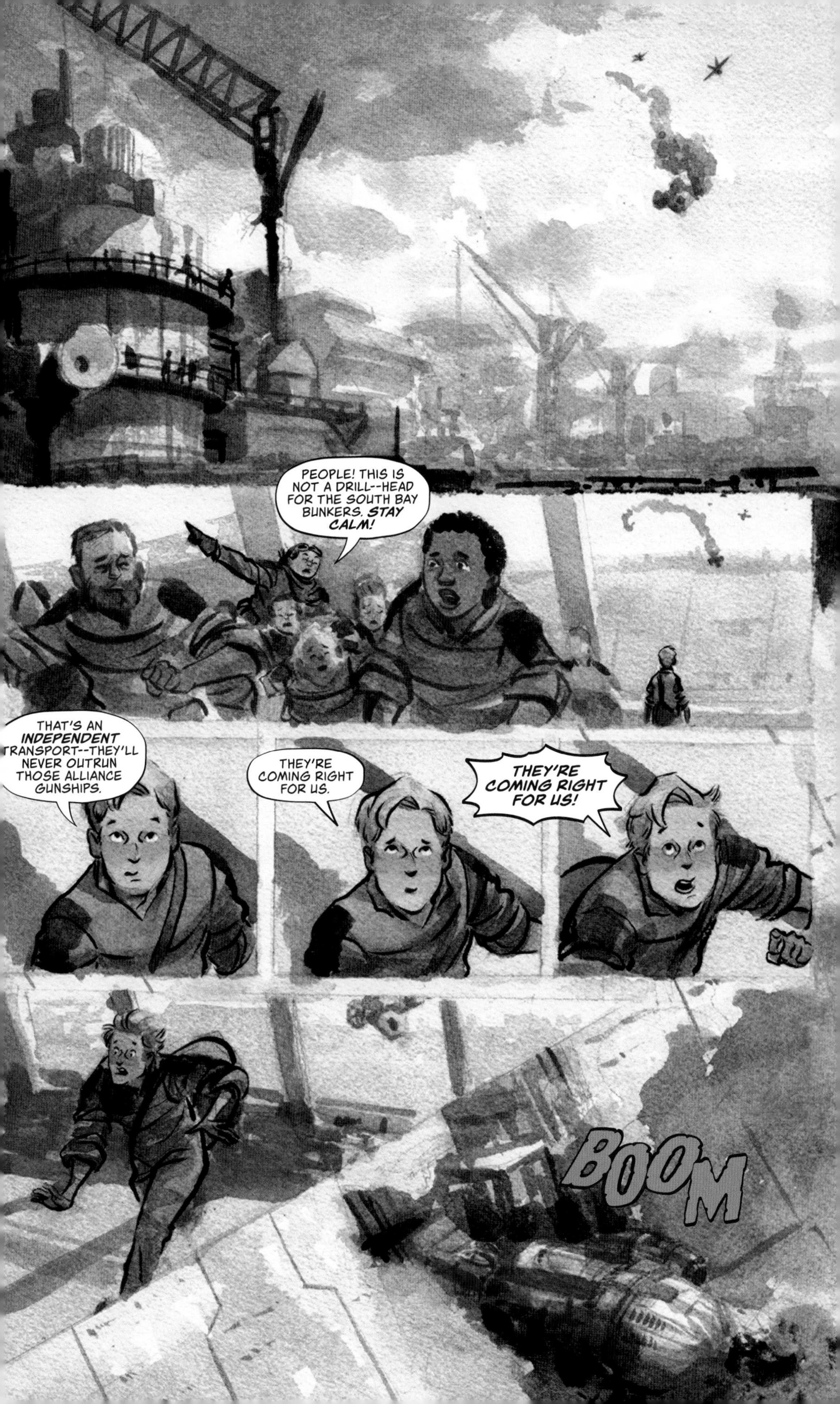
PEOPLE! THIS IS NOT A DRILL--HEAD FOR THE SOUTH BAY BUNKERS. STAY CALM!
THAT'S AN INDEPENDENT TRANSPORT--THEY'LL NEVER OUTRUN THOSE ALLIANCE GUNSHIPS.
THEY'RE COMING RIGHT FOR US.
THEY'RE COMING RIGHT FOR US!
BOOM

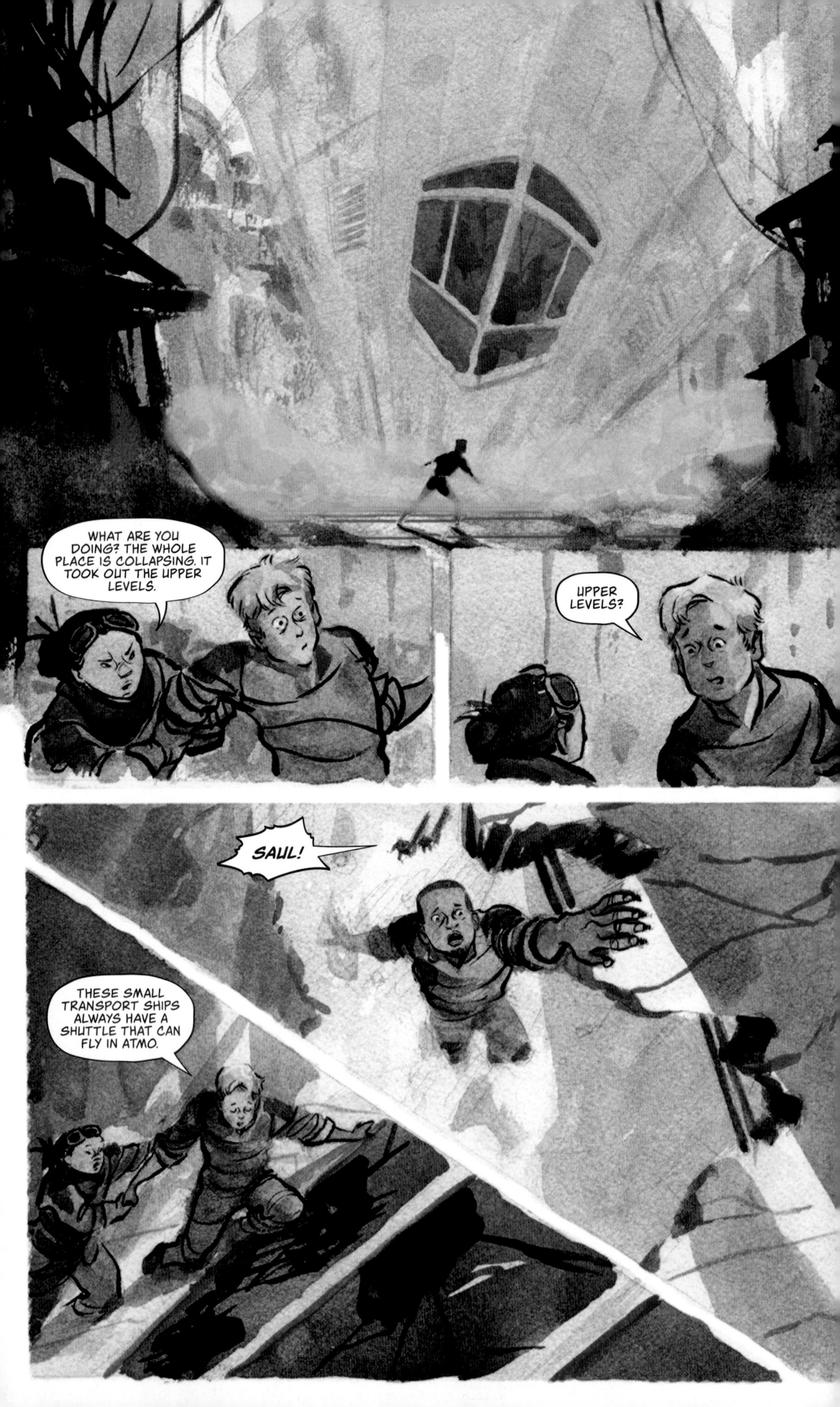
WHAT ARE YOU DOING? THE WHOLE PLACE IS COLLAPSING. IT TOOK OUT THE UPPER LEVELS.
UPPER LEVELS?
SAUL!
THESE SMALL TRANSPORT SHIPS ALWAYS HAVE A SHUTTLE THAT CAN FLY IN ATMO.

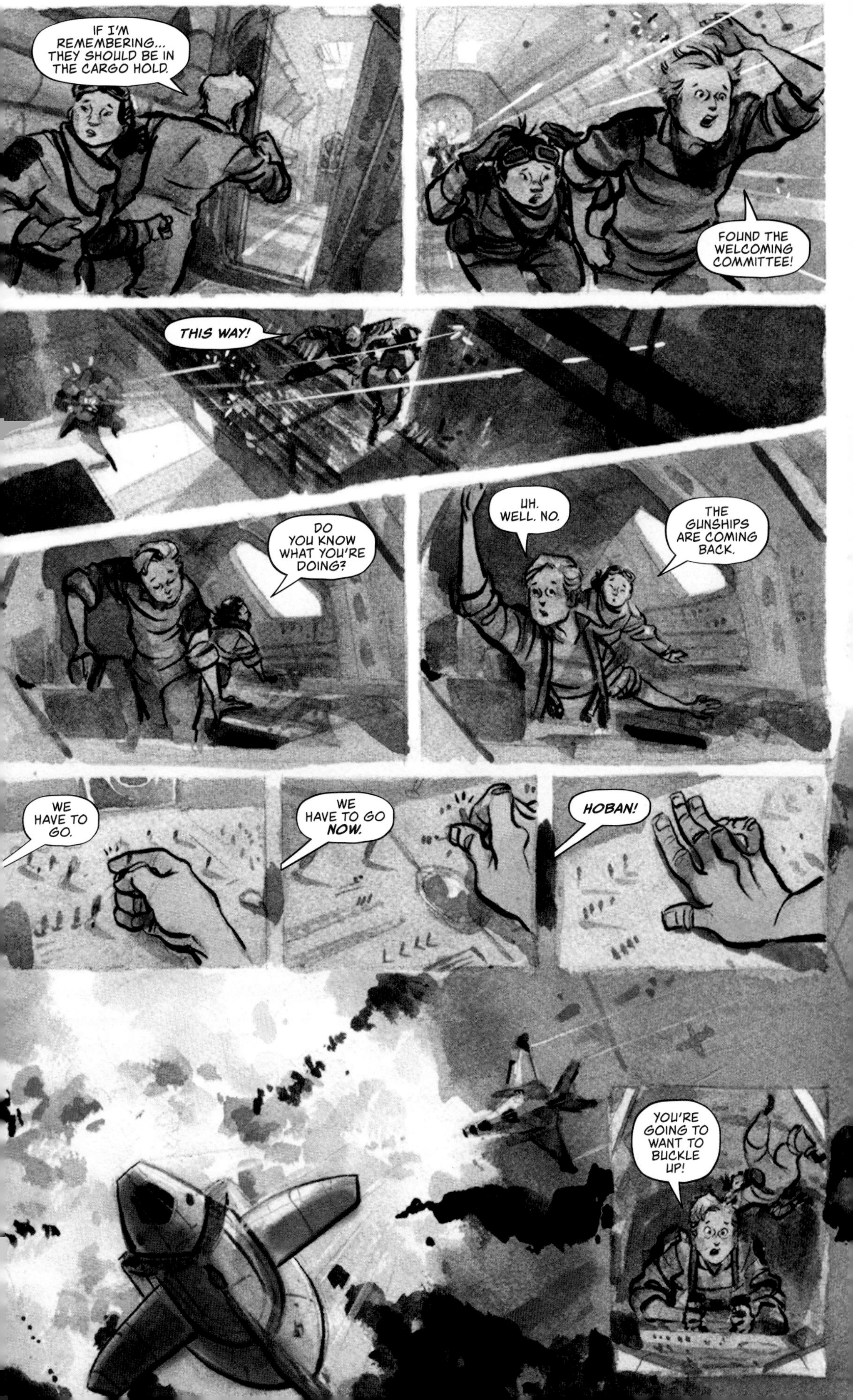
IF I'M REMEMBERING... THEY SHOULD BE IN THE CARGO HOLD.
FOUND THE WELCOMING COMMITTEE!
THIS WAY!
DO YOU KNOW WHAT YOU'RE DOING?
UH. WELL. NO.
THE GUNSHIPS ARE COMING BACK.
WE HAVE TO GO.
WE HAVE TO GO NOW.
HOBAN!
YOU'RE GOING TO WANT TO BUCKLE UP!

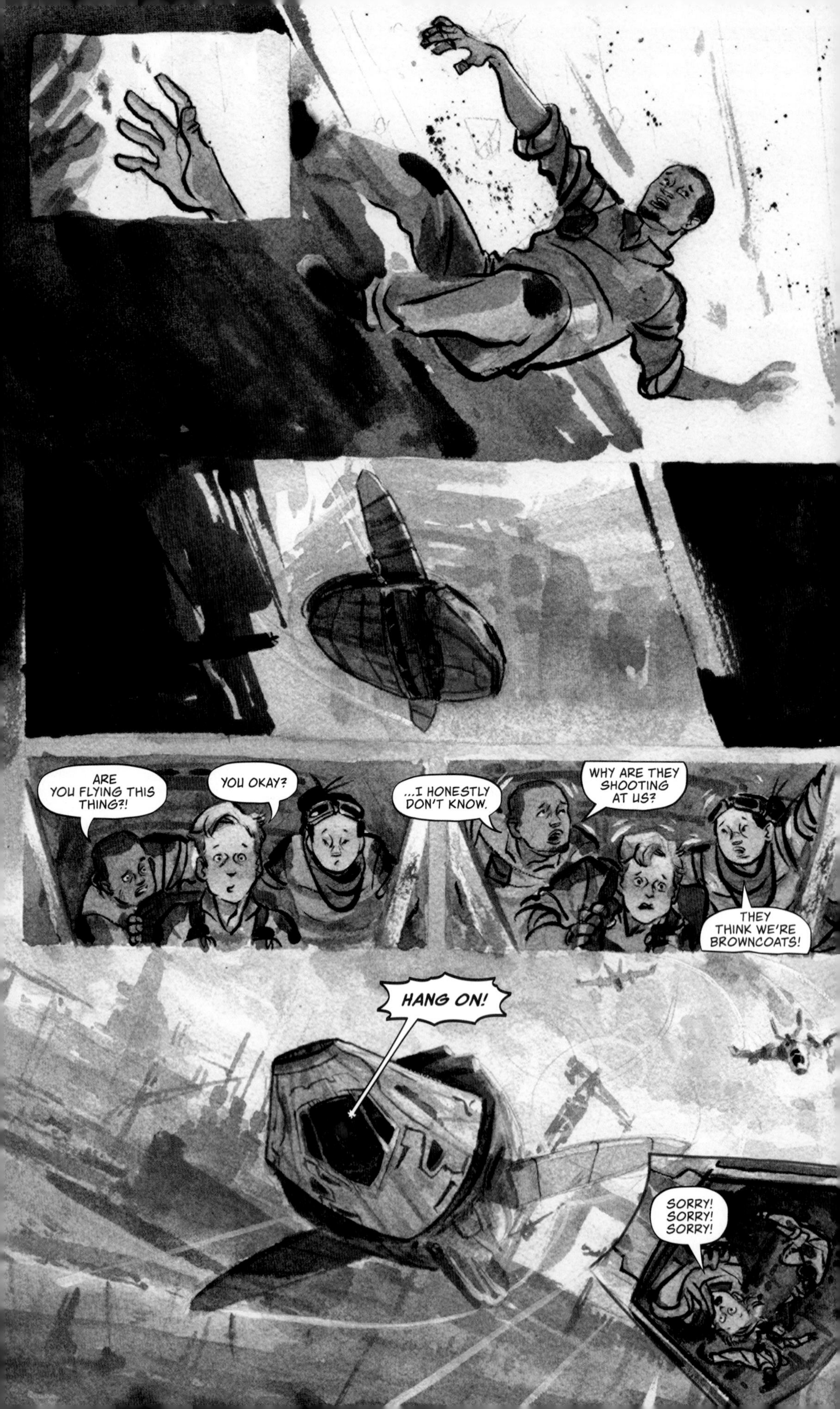
ARE YOU FLYING THIS THING?!
YOU OKAY?
...I HONESTLY DON'T KNOW.
WHY ARE THEY SHOOTING AT US?
THEY THINK WE'RE BROWNCOATS!
HANG ON!
SORRY! SORRY! SORRY!

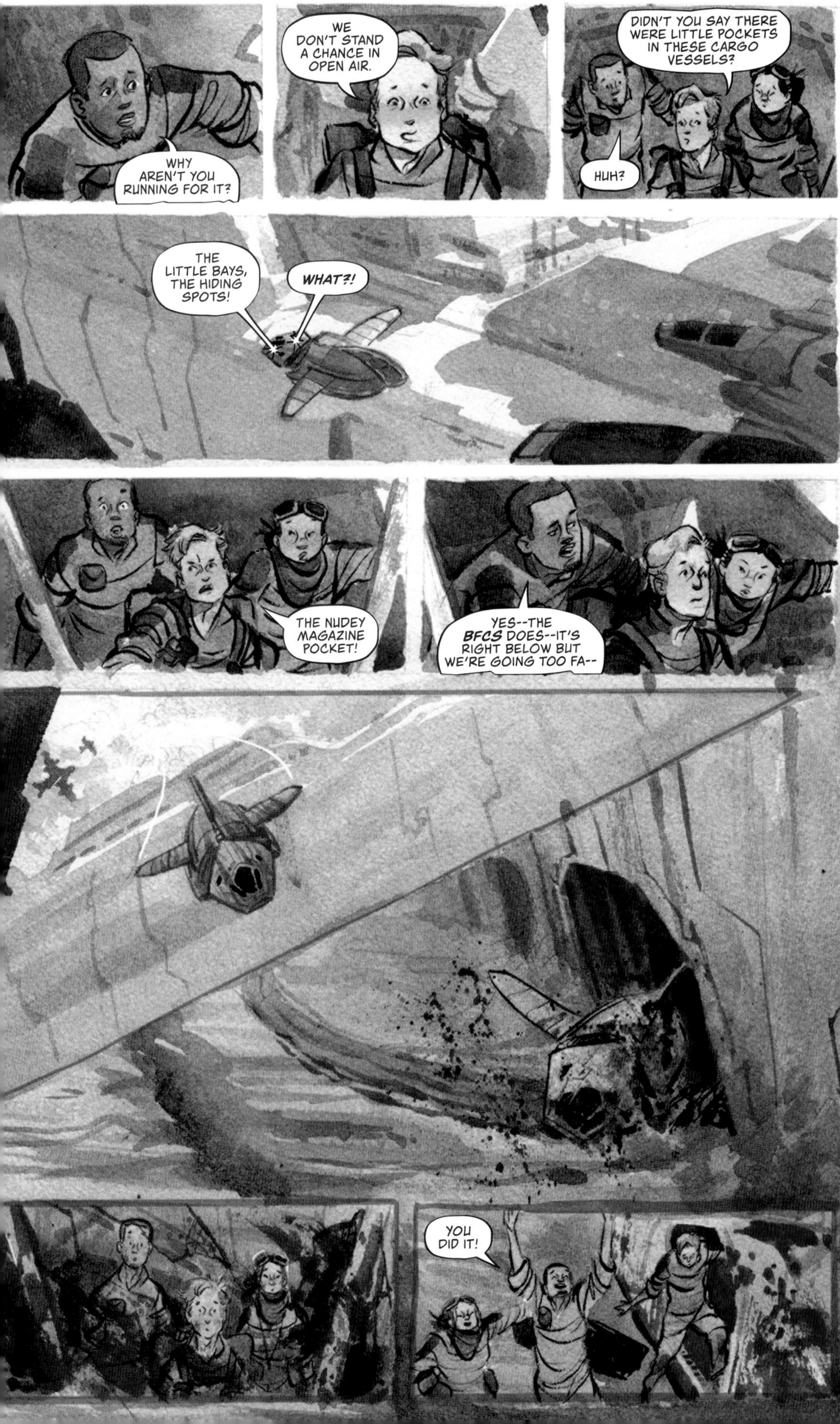
WHY AREN'T YOU RUNNING FOR IT?
WE DON'T STAND A CHANCE IN OPEN AIR.
DIDN'T YOU SAY THERE WERE LITTLE POCKETS IN THESE CARGO VESSELS?
HUH?
THE LITTLE BAYS, THE HIDING SPOTS!
WHAT?!
THE NUDEY MAGAZINE POCKET!
YES--THE BFCS DOES--IT'S RIGHT BELOW BUT WE'RE GOING TOO FA--
YOU DID IT!

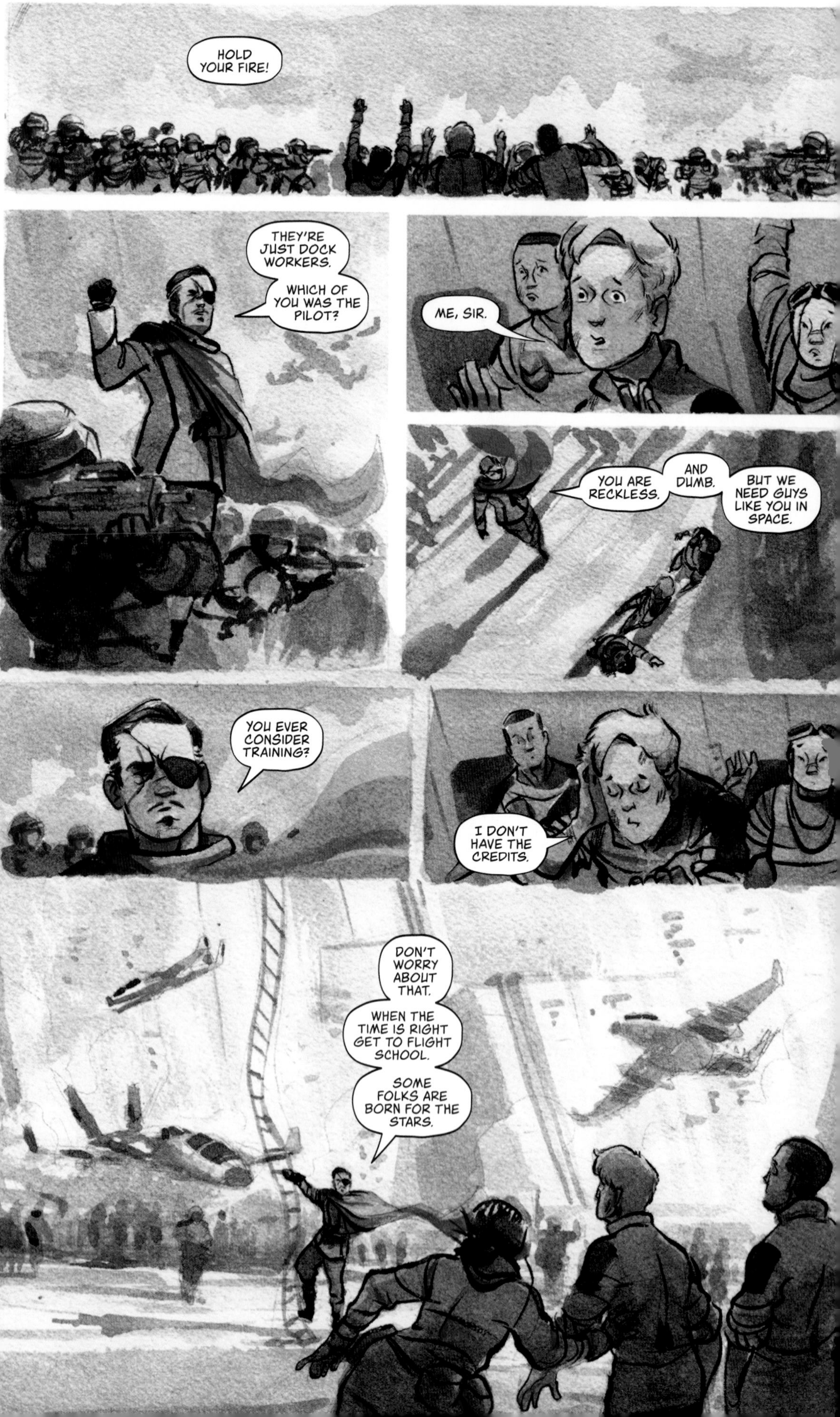
HOLD YOUR FIRE!
THEY'RE JUST DOCK WORKERS.
WHICH OF YOU WAS THE PILOT?
ME, SIR.
YOU ARE RECKLESS.
AND DUMB.
BUT WE NEED GUYS LIKE YOU IN SPACE.
YOU EVER CONSIDER TRAINING?
I DON'T HAVE THE CREDITS.
DON'T WORRY ABOUT THAT.
WHEN THE TIME IS RIGHT GET TO FLIGHT SCHOOL.
SOME FOLKS ARE BORN FOR THE STARS.

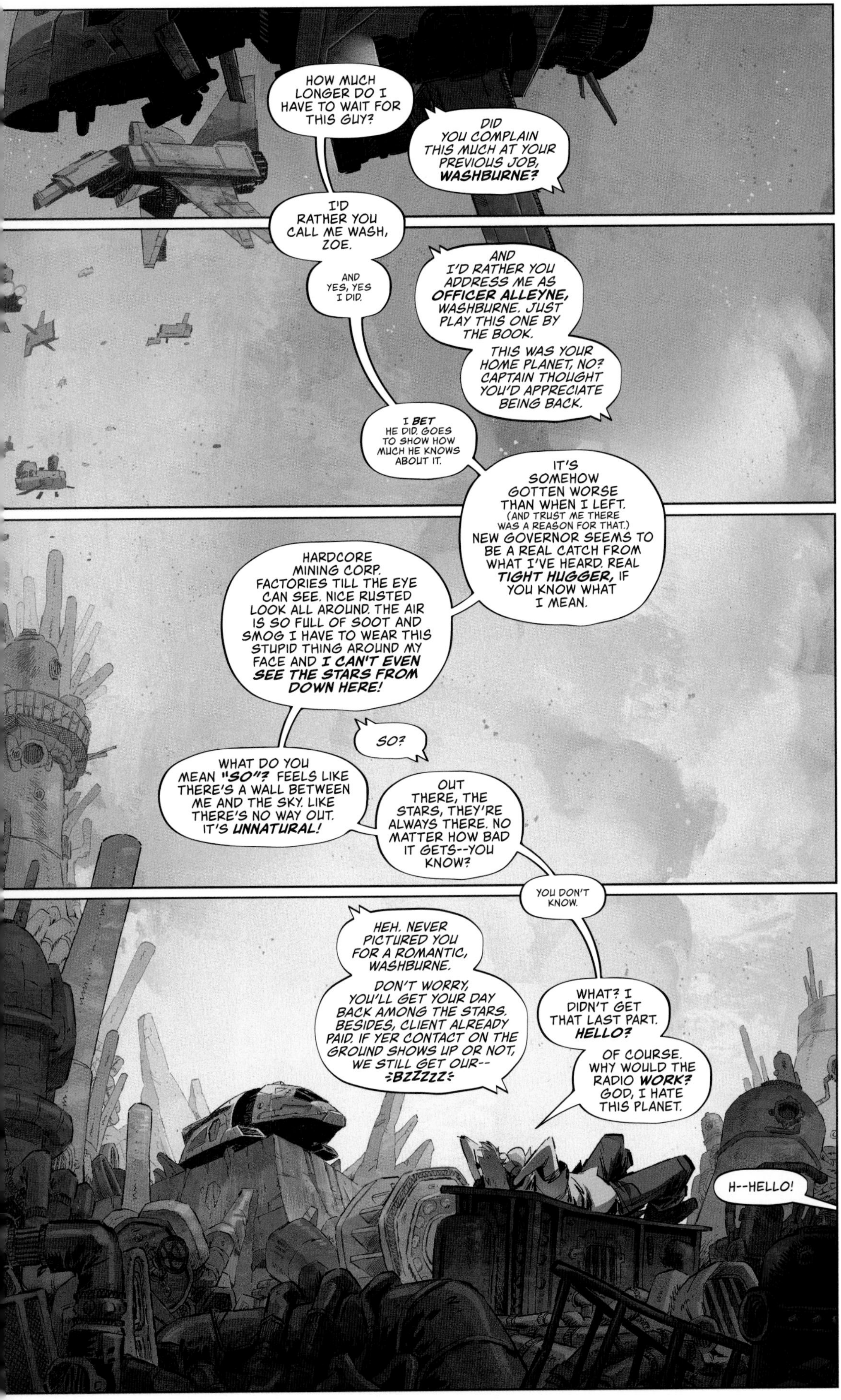
HOW MUCH LONGER DO I HAVE TO WAIT FOR THIS GUY?
DID YOU COMPLAIN THIS MUCH AT YOUR PREVIOUS JOB, WASHBURNE?
I'D RATHER YOU CALL ME WASH, ZOE.
AND YES, YES I DID.
AND I'D RATHER YOU ADDRESS ME AS OFFICER ALLEYNE, WASHBURNE. JUST PLAY THIS ONE BY THE BOOK.
THIS WAS YOUR HOME PLANET, NO? CAPTAIN THOUGHT YOU'D APPRECIATE BEING BACK.
I BET HE DID. GOES TO SHOW HOW MUCH HE KNOWS ABOUT IT.
IT'S SOMEHOW GOTTEN WORSE THAN WHEN I LEFT. (AND TRUST ME THERE WAS A REASON FOR THAT.) NEW GOVERNOR SEEMS TO BE A REAL CATCH FROM WHAT I'VE HEARD. REAL TIGHT HUGGER, IF YOU KNOW WHAT I MEAN.
HARDCORE MINING CORP. FACTORIES TILL THE EYE CAN SEE. NICE RUSTED LOOK ALL AROUND. THE AIR IS SO FULL OF SOOT AND SMOG I HAVE TO WEAR THIS STUPID THING AROUND MY FACE AND I CAN'T EVEN SEE THE STARS FROM DOWN HERE!
SO?
WHAT DO YOU MEAN "SO"? FEELS LIKE THERE'S A WALL BETWEEN ME AND THE SKY. LIKE THERE'S NO WAY OUT. IT'S UNNATURAL!
OUT THERE, THE STARS, THEY'RE ALWAYS THERE. NO MATTER HOW BAD IT GETS--YOU KNOW?
YOU DON'T KNOW.
HEH. NEVER PICTURED YOU FOR A ROMANTIC, WASHBURNE.
DON'T WORRY, YOU'LL GET YOUR DAY BACK AMONG THE STARS. BESIDES, CLIENT ALREADY PAID. IF YER CONTACT ON THE GROUND SHOWS UP OR NOT, WE STILL GET OUR-- ≈BZZZZZ≈
WHAT? I DIDN'T GET THAT LAST PART. HELLO?
OF COURSE. WHY WOULD THE RADIO WORK? GOD, I HATE THIS PLANET.
H--HELLO!

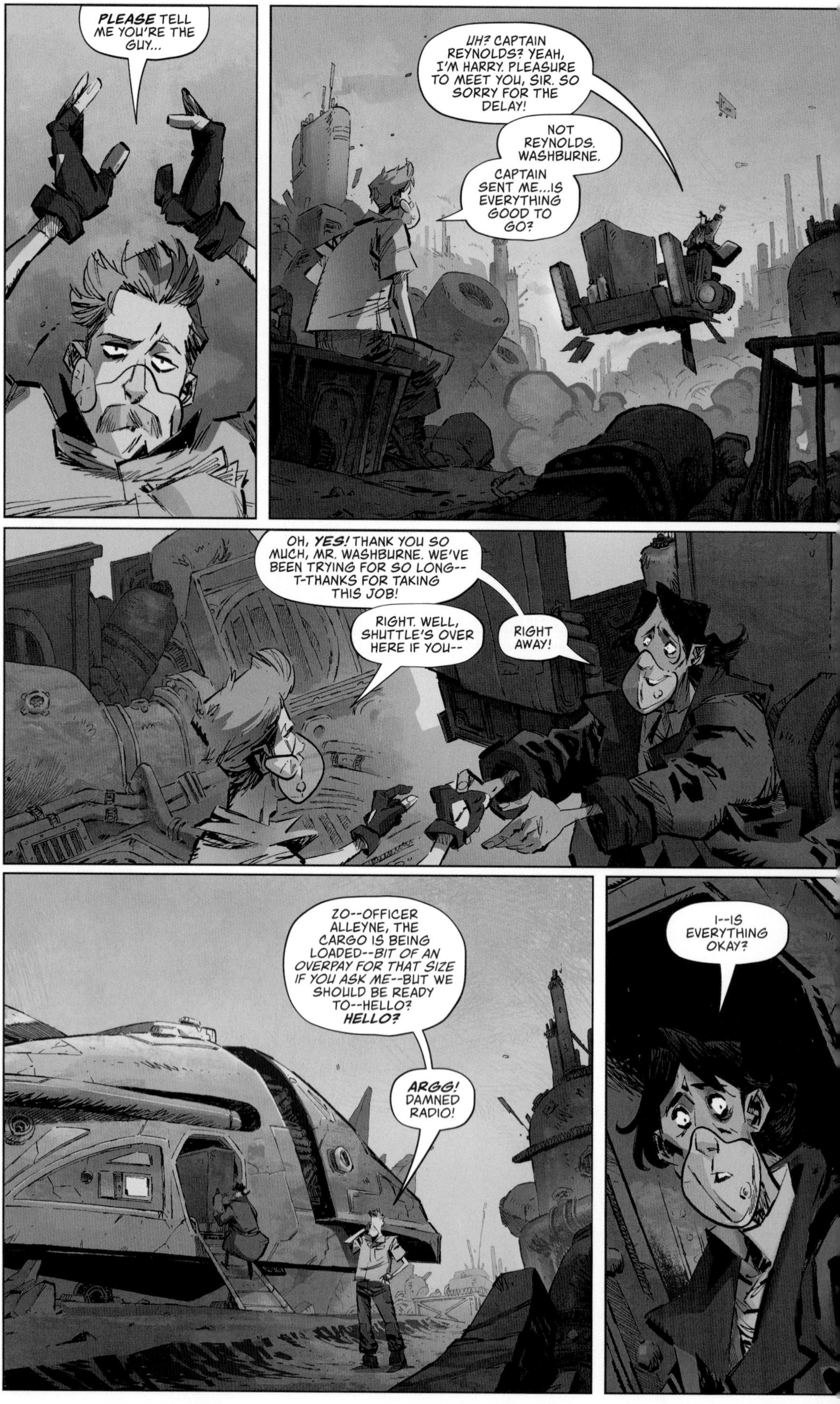
PLEASE TELL ME YOU'RE THE GUY...
UH? CAPTAIN REYNOLDS? YEAH, I'M HARRY. PLEASURE TO MEET YOU, SIR. SO SORRY FOR THE DELAY!
NOT REYNOLDS. WASHBURNE.
CAPTAIN SENT ME...IS EVERYTHING GOOD TO GO?
OH, YES! THANK YOU SO MUCH, MR. WASHBURNE. WE'VE BEEN TRYING FOR SO LONG-- T-THANKS FOR TAKING THIS JOB!
RIGHT. WELL, SHUTTLE'S OVER HERE IF YOU--
RIGHT AWAY!
ZO--OFFICER ALLEYNE, THE CARGO IS BEING LOADED--BIT OF AN OVERPAY FOR THAT SIZE IF YOU ASK ME--BUT WE SHOULD BE READY TO--HELLO? HELLO?
ARGG! DAMNED RADIO!
I--IS EVERYTHING OKAY?

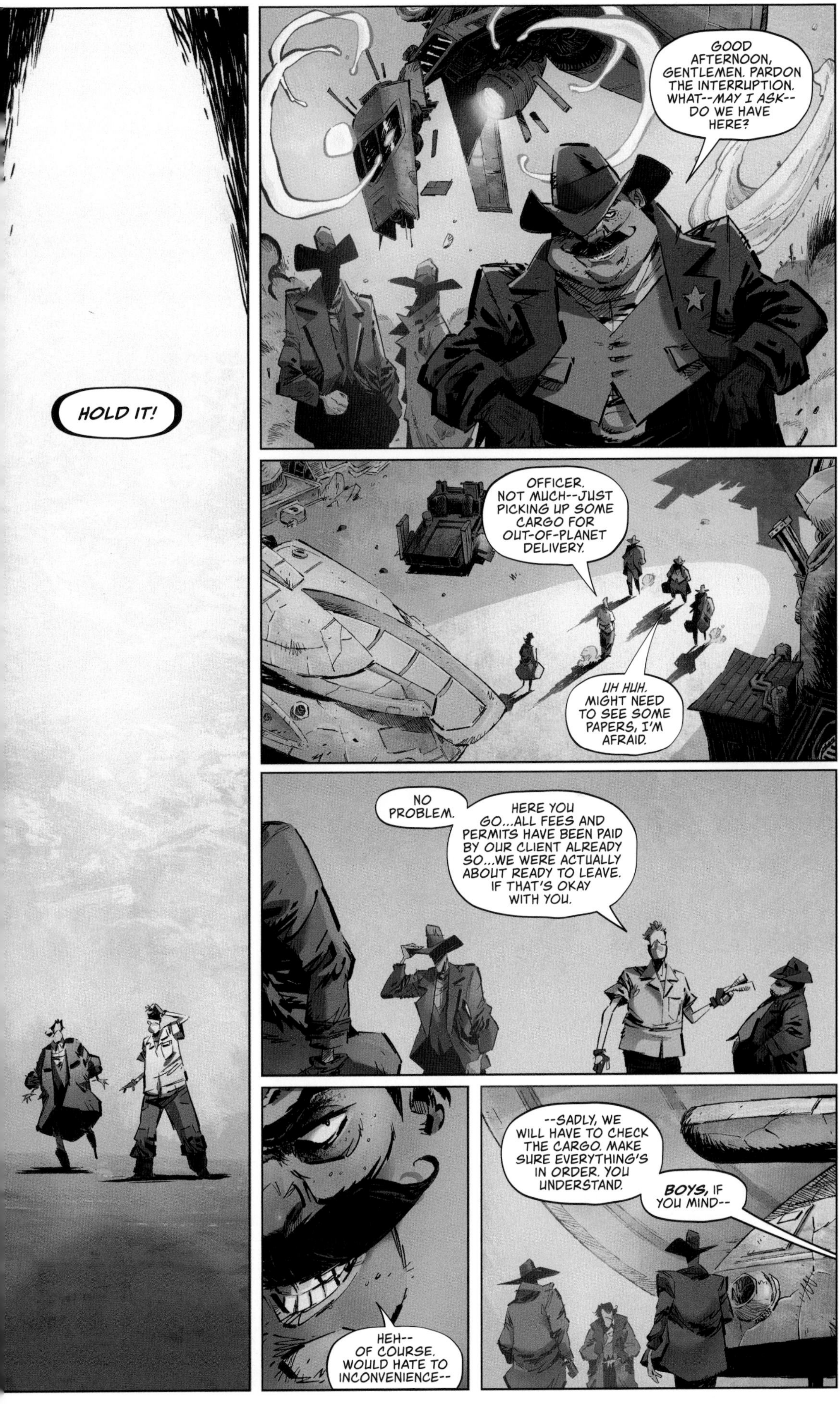
HOLD IT!
GOOD AFTERNOON, GENTLEMEN. PARDON THE INTERRUPTION. WHAT--MAY I ASK--DO WE HAVE HERE?
OFFICER. NOT MUCH--JUST PICKING UP SOME CARGO FOR OUT-OF-PLANET DELIVERY.
UH HUH. MIGHT NEED TO SEE SOME PAPERS, I'M AFRAID.
NO PROBLEM.
HERE YOU GO...ALL FEES AND PERMITS HAVE BEEN PAID BY OUR CLIENT ALREADY SO...WE WERE ACTUALLY ABOUT READY TO LEAVE. IF THAT'S OKAY WITH YOU.
HEH-- OF COURSE. WOULD HATE TO INCONVENIENCE--
--SADLY, WE WILL HAVE TO CHECK THE CARGO. MAKE SURE EVERYTHING'S IN ORDER. YOU UNDERSTAND.
BOYS, IF YOU MIND--

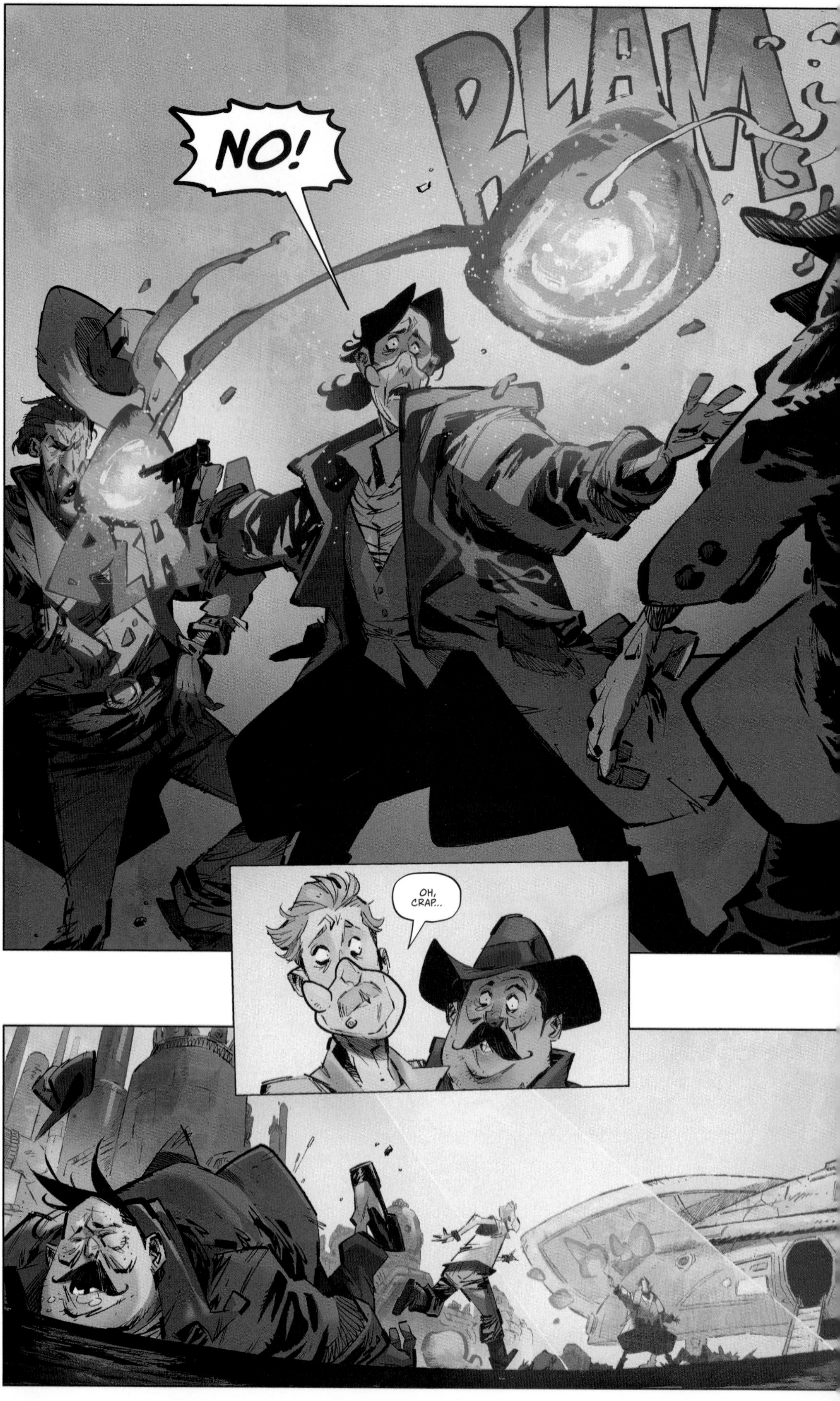
BLAM
NO!
OH, CRAP...

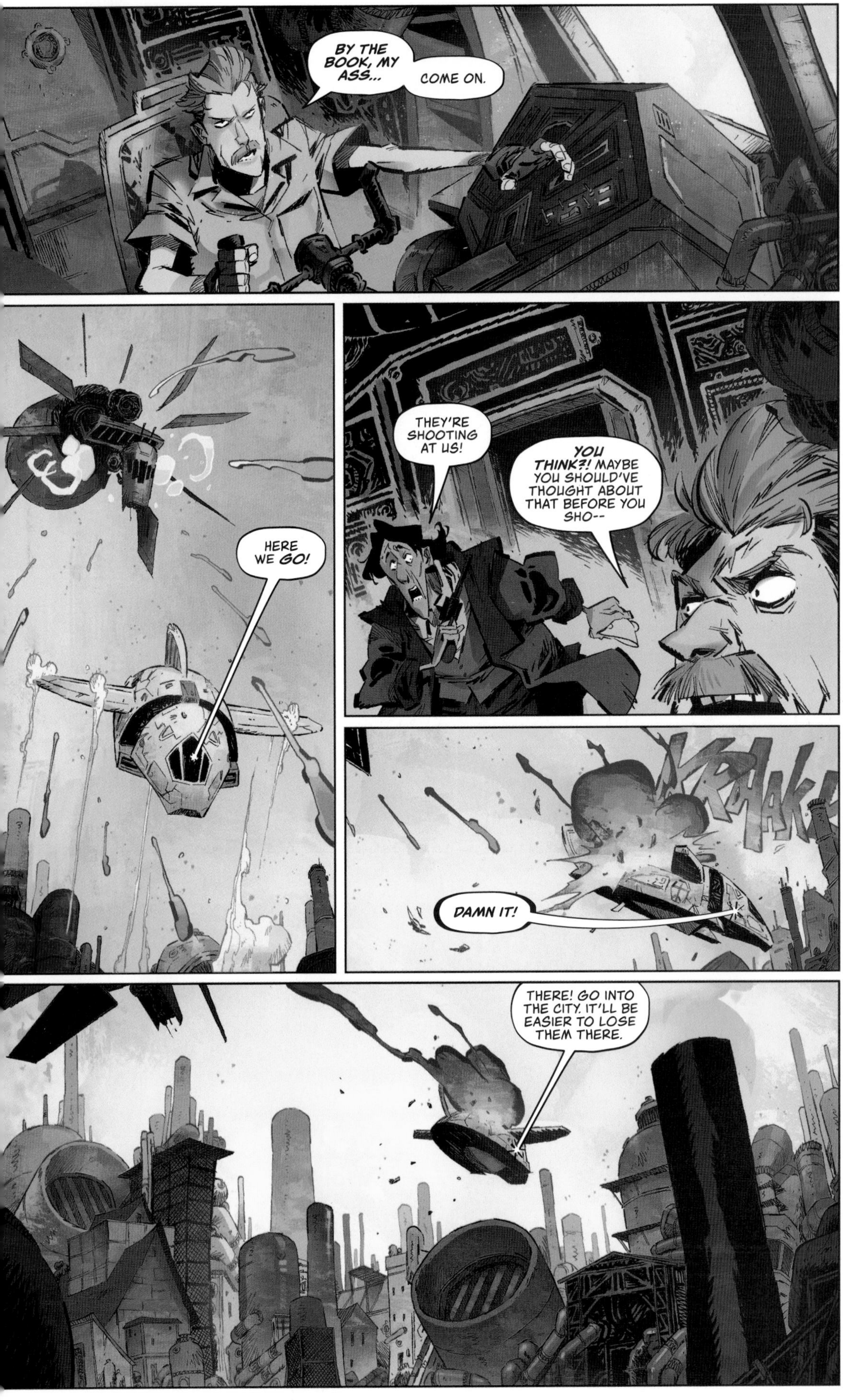

BY THE BOOK, MY ASS...
COME ON.
HERE WE GO!
THEY'RE SHOOTING AT US!
YOU THINK?! MAYBE YOU SHOULD'VE THOUGHT ABOUT THAT BEFORE YOU SHO--
DAMN IT!
THERE! GO INTO THE CITY. IT'LL BE EASIER TO LOSE THEM THERE.

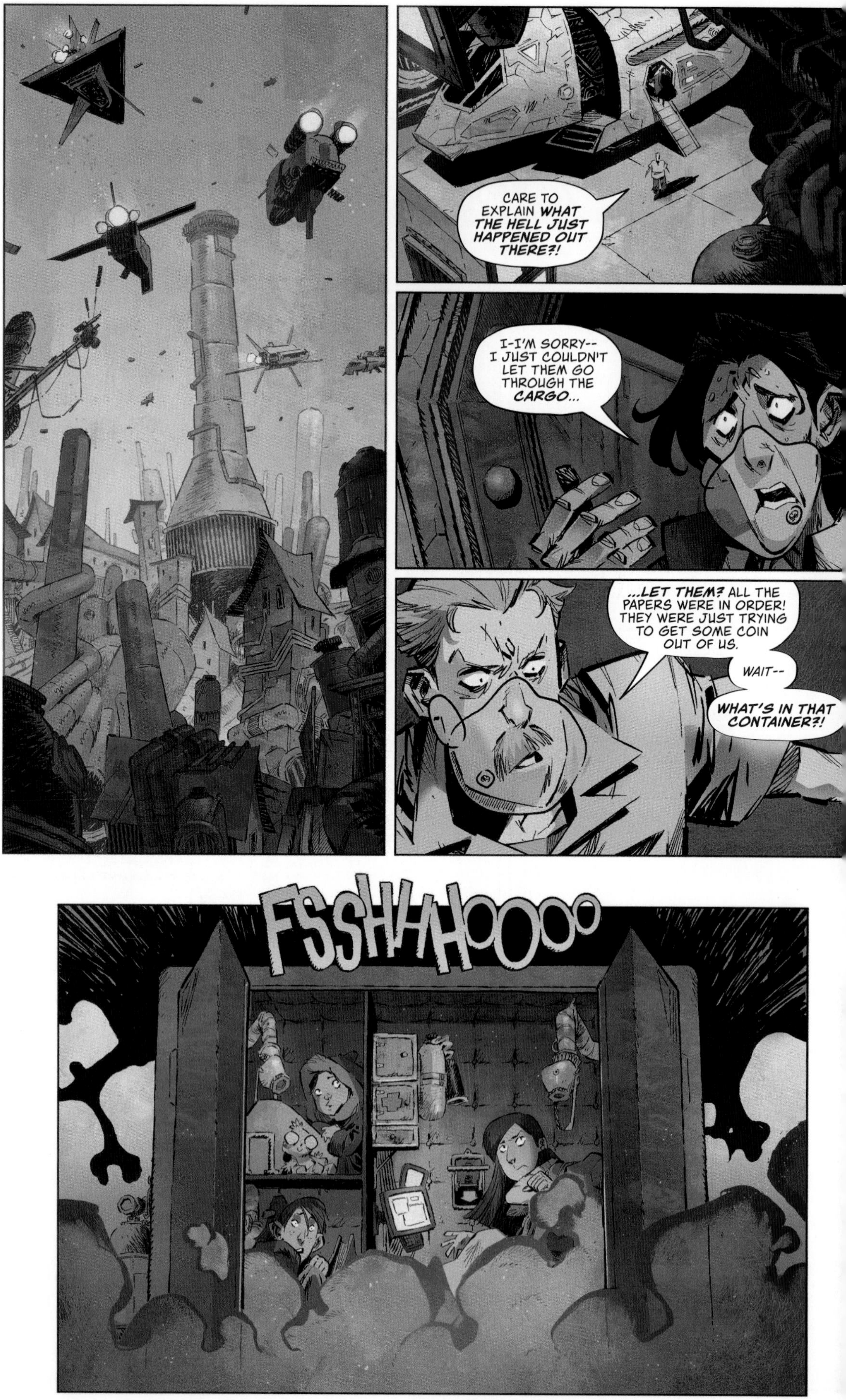
CARE TO EXPLAIN WHAT THE HELL JUST HAPPENED OUT THERE?!
I-I'M SORRY-- I JUST COULDN'T LET THEM GO THROUGH THE CARGO...
...LET THEM? ALL THE PAPERS WERE IN ORDER! THEY WERE JUST TRYING TO GET SOME COIN OUT OF US.
WAIT--
WHAT'S IN THAT CONTAINER?!
FSSHHHOOOO

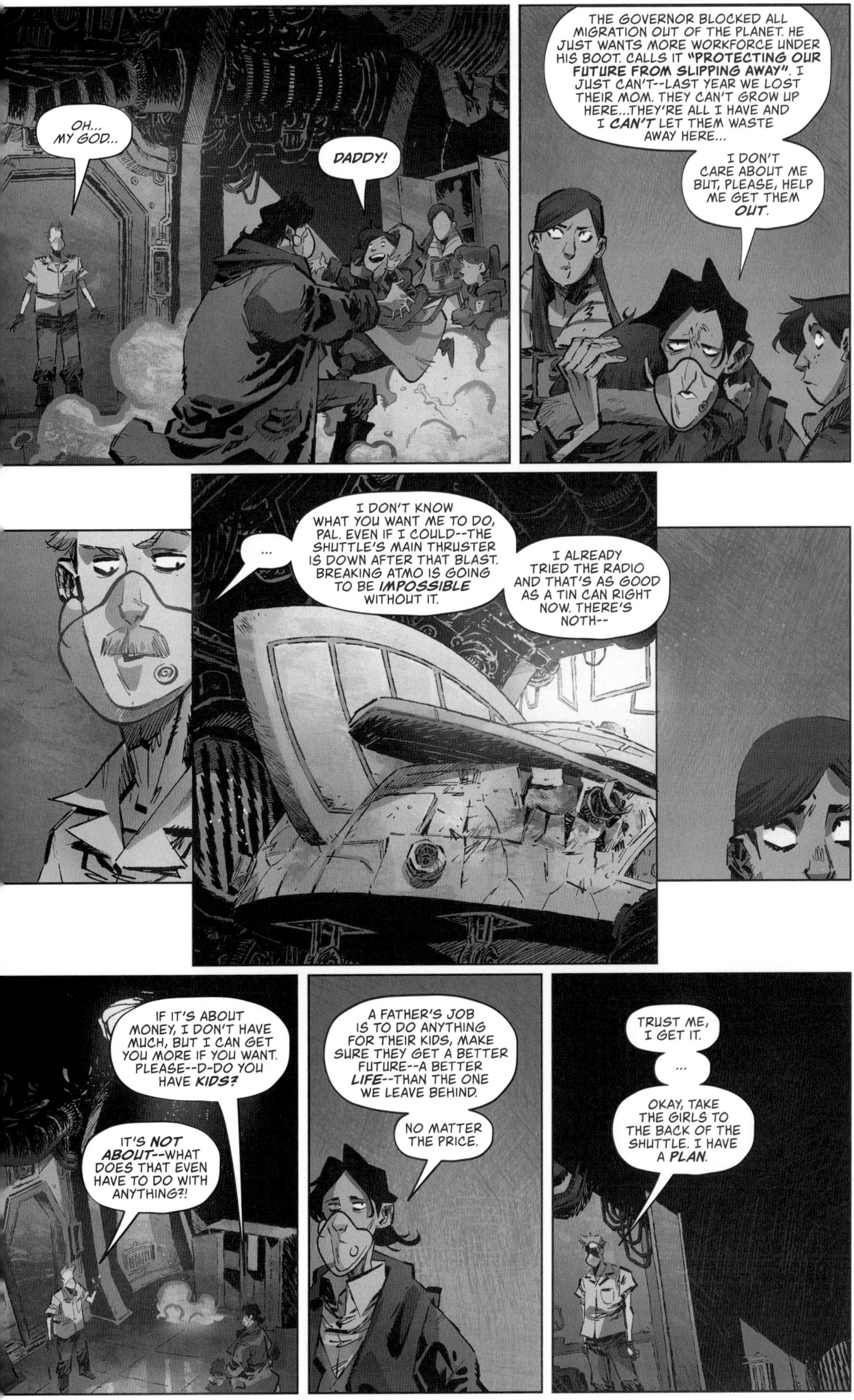
OH... MY GOD...
DADDY!
THE GOVERNOR BLOCKED ALL MIGRATION OUT OF THE PLANET. HE JUST WANTS MORE WORKFORCE UNDER HIS BOOT. CALLS IT **"PROTECTING OUR FUTURE FROM SLIPPING AWAY"**. I JUST CAN'T--LAST YEAR WE LOST THEIR MOM. THEY CAN'T GROW UP HERE...THEY'RE ALL I HAVE AND I ***CAN'T*** LET THEM WASTE AWAY HERE...
I DON'T CARE ABOUT ME BUT, PLEASE, HELP ME GET THEM ***OUT***.
...
I DON'T KNOW WHAT YOU WANT ME TO DO, PAL. EVEN IF I COULD--THE SHUTTLE'S MAIN THRUSTER IS DOWN AFTER THAT BLAST. BREAKING ATMO IS GOING TO BE ***IMPOSSIBLE*** WITHOUT IT.
I ALREADY TRIED THE RADIO AND THAT'S AS GOOD AS A TIN CAN RIGHT NOW. THERE'S NOTH--
IF IT'S ABOUT MONEY, I DON'T HAVE MUCH, BUT I CAN GET YOU MORE IF YOU WANT. PLEASE--D-DO YOU HAVE ***KIDS?***
IT'S ***NOT ABOUT***--WHAT DOES THAT EVEN HAVE TO DO WITH ANYTHING?!
A FATHER'S JOB IS TO DO ANYTHING FOR THEIR KIDS, MAKE SURE THEY GET A BETTER FUTURE--A BETTER ***LIFE***--THAN THE ONE WE LEAVE BEHIND.
NO MATTER THE PRICE.
TRUST ME, I GET IT.
...
OKAY, TAKE THE GIRLS TO THE BACK OF THE SHUTTLE. I HAVE A ***PLAN***.

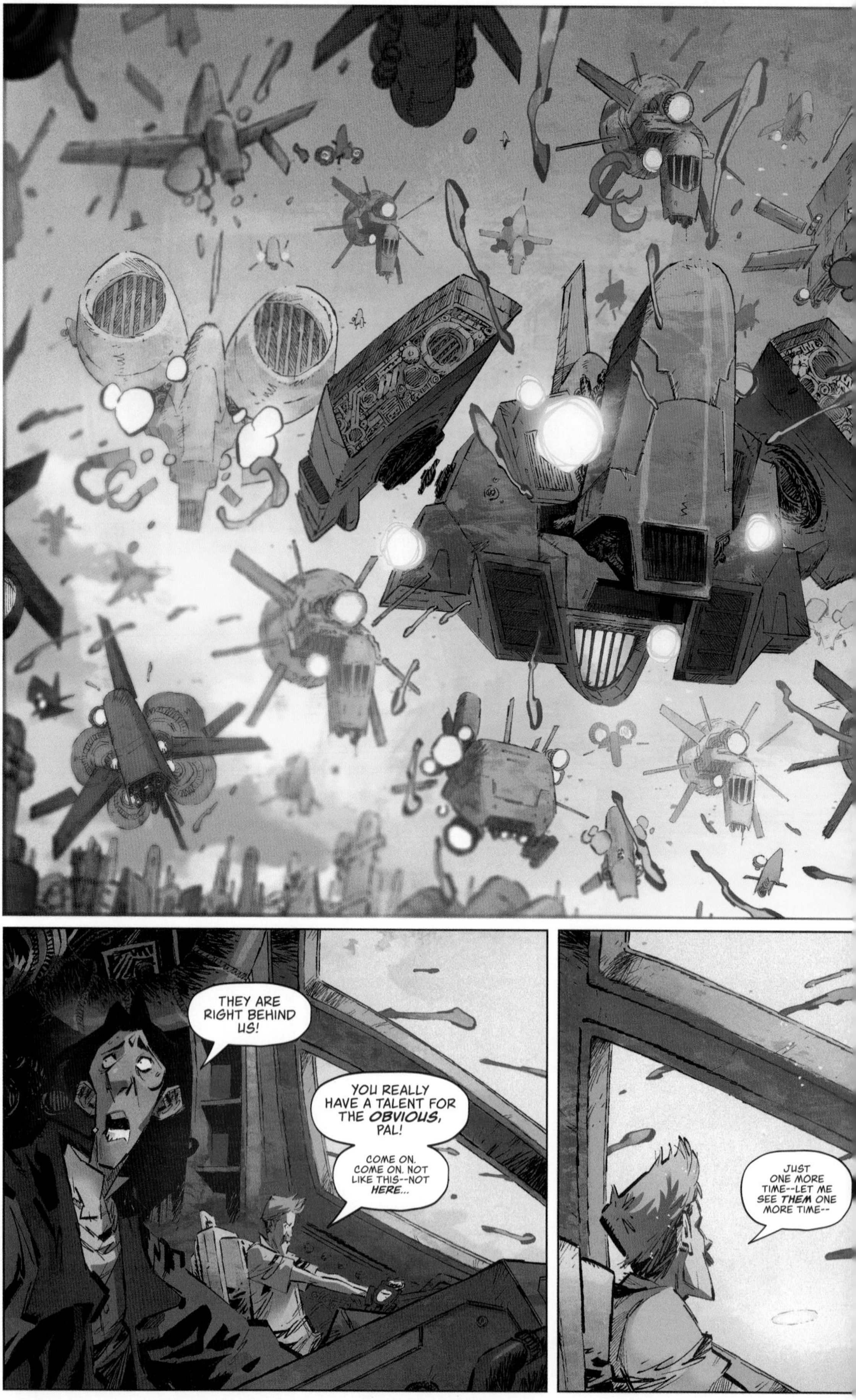
THEY ARE RIGHT BEHIND US!
YOU REALLY HAVE A TALENT FOR THE *OBVIOUS,* PAL!
COME ON. COME ON. NOT LIKE THIS--NOT *HERE...*
JUST ONE MORE TIME--LET ME SEE *THEM* ONE MORE TIME--

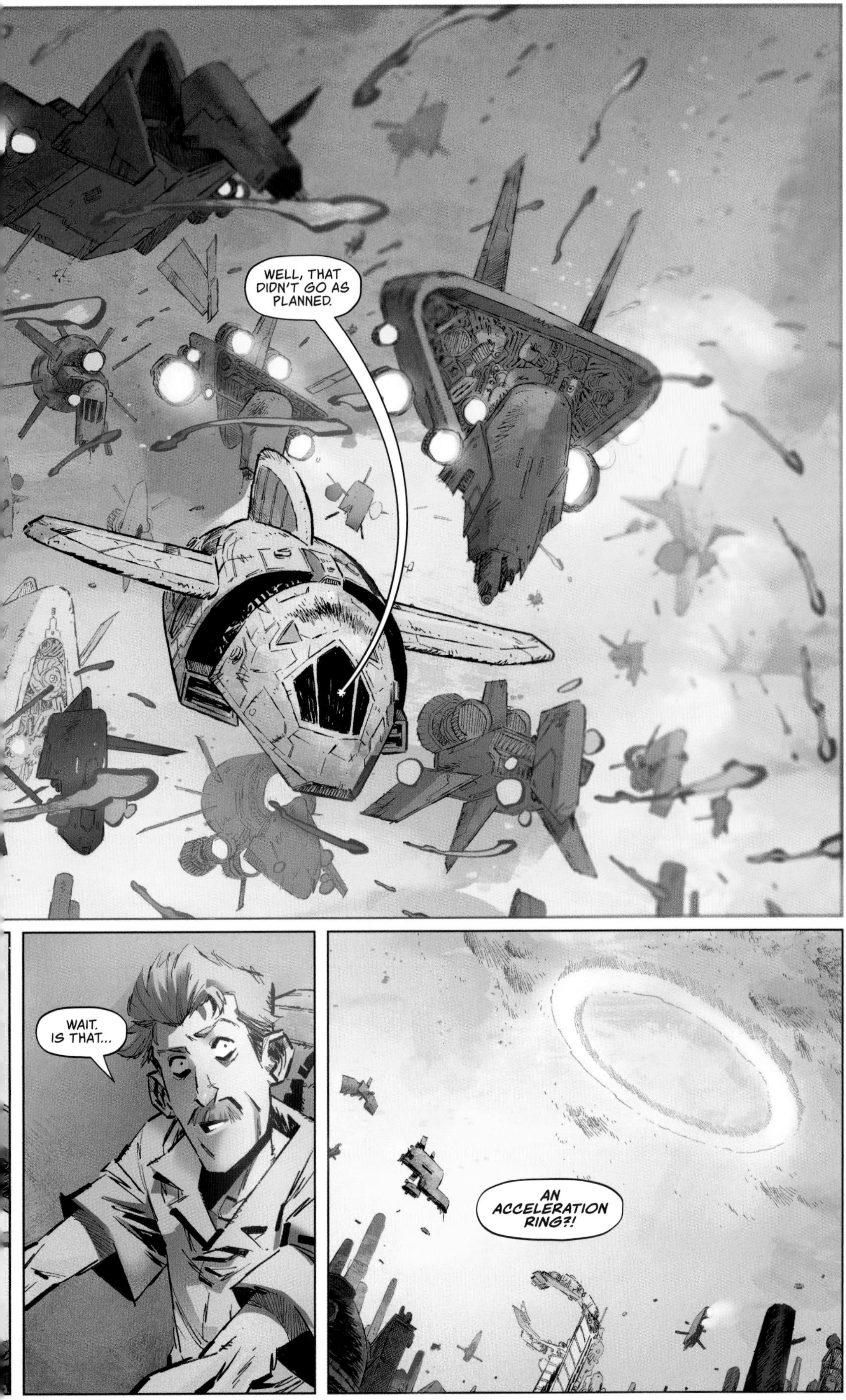
WELL, THAT DIDN'T GO AS PLANNED.
WAIT. IS THAT...
AN ACCELERATION RING?!

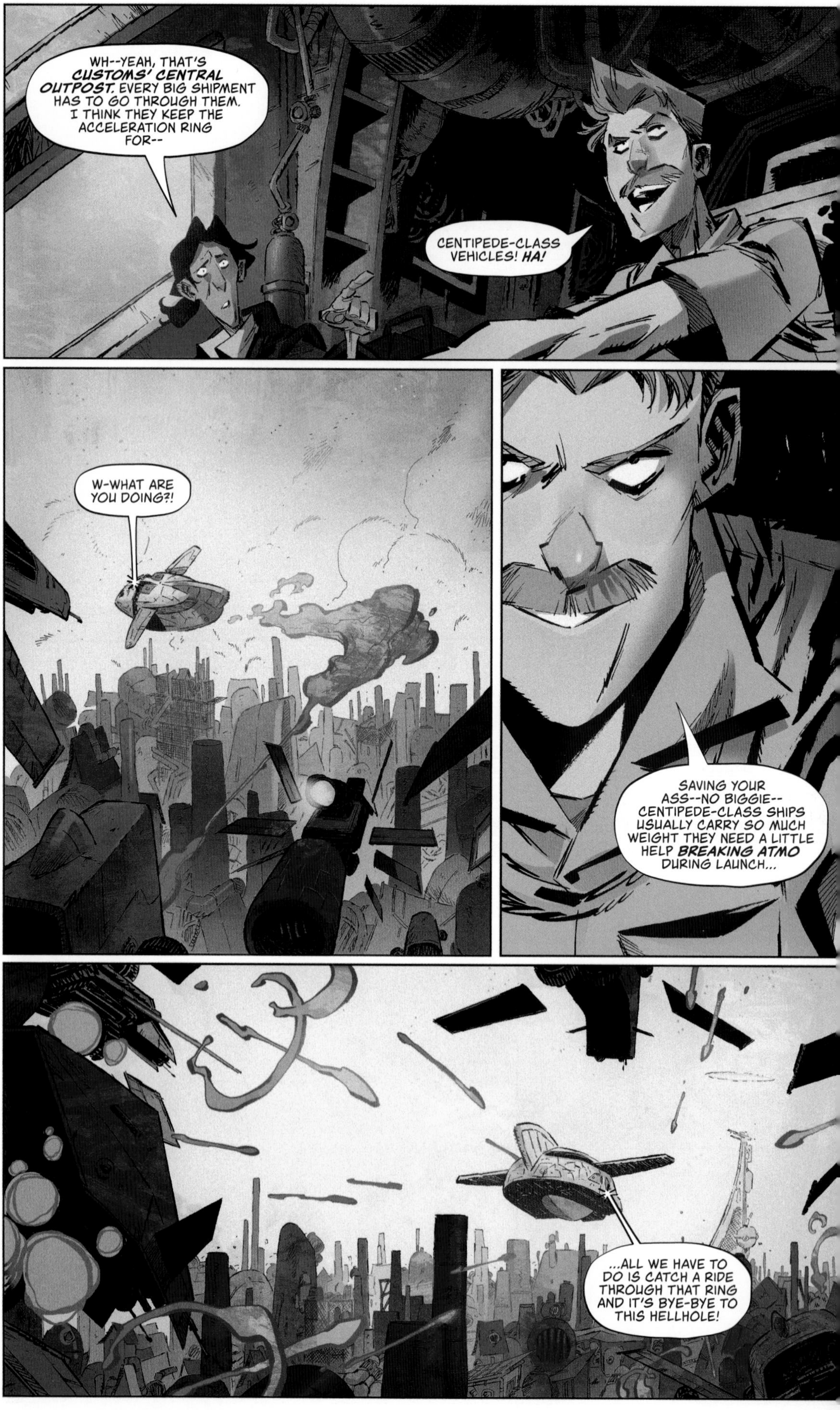

WH--YEAH, THAT'S CUSTOMS' CENTRAL OUTPOST. EVERY BIG SHIPMENT HAS TO GO THROUGH THEM. I THINK THEY KEEP THE ACCELERATION RING FOR--
CENTIPEDE-CLASS VEHICLES! HA!
W-WHAT ARE YOU DOING?!
SAVING YOUR ASS--NO BIGGIE-- CENTIPEDE-CLASS SHIPS USUALLY CARRY SO MUCH WEIGHT THEY NEED A LITTLE HELP BREAKING ATMO DURING LAUNCH...
...ALL WE HAVE TO DO IS CATCH A RIDE THROUGH THAT RING AND IT'S BYE-BYE TO THIS HELLHOLE!

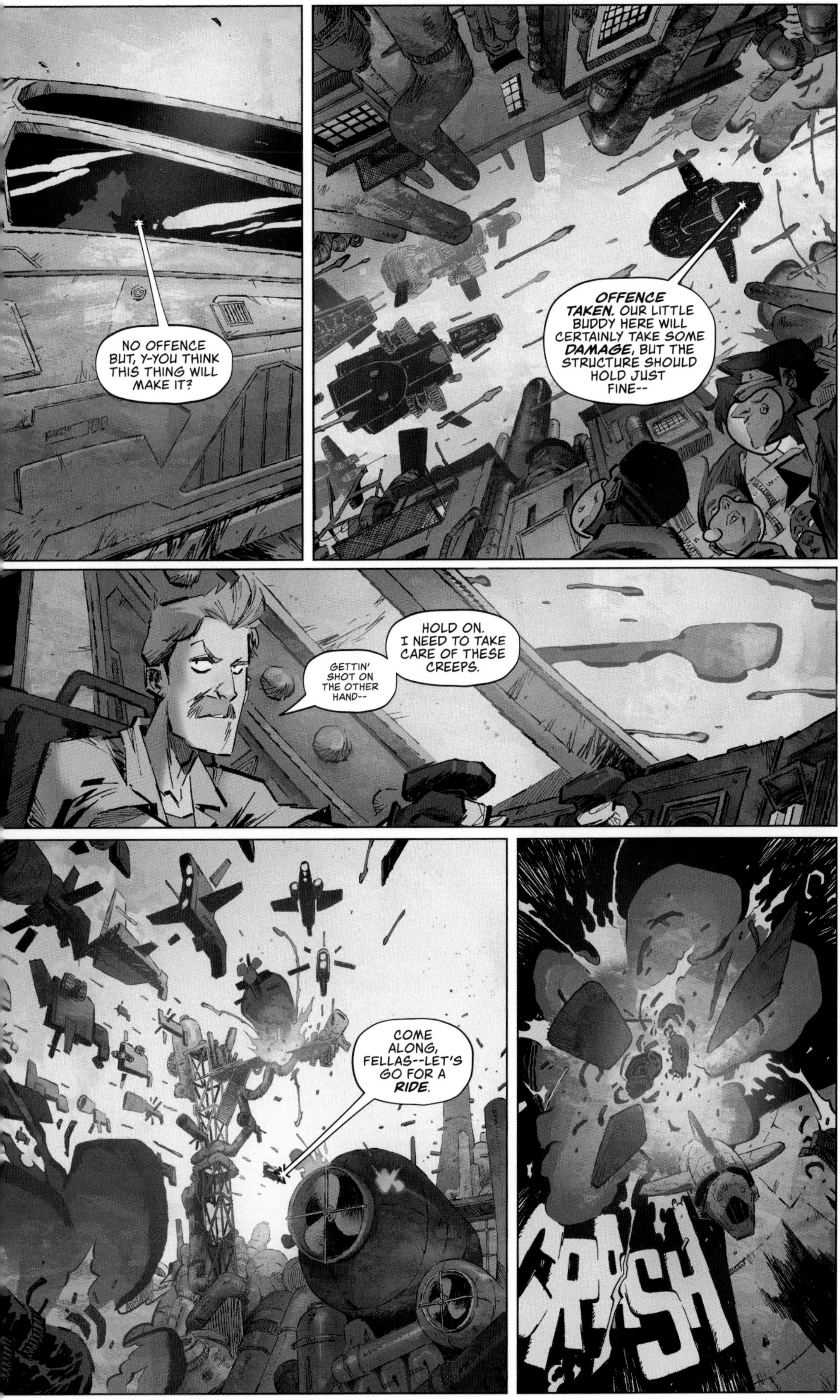
NO OFFENCE BUT, Y-YOU THINK THIS THING WILL MAKE IT?
OFFENCE TAKEN. OUR LITTLE BUDDY HERE WILL CERTAINLY TAKE SOME DAMAGE, BUT THE STRUCTURE SHOULD HOLD JUST FINE--
GETTIN' SHOT ON THE OTHER HAND--
HOLD ON. I NEED TO TAKE CARE OF THESE CREEPS.
COME ALONG, FELLAS--LET'S GO FOR A RIDE.
CRASH

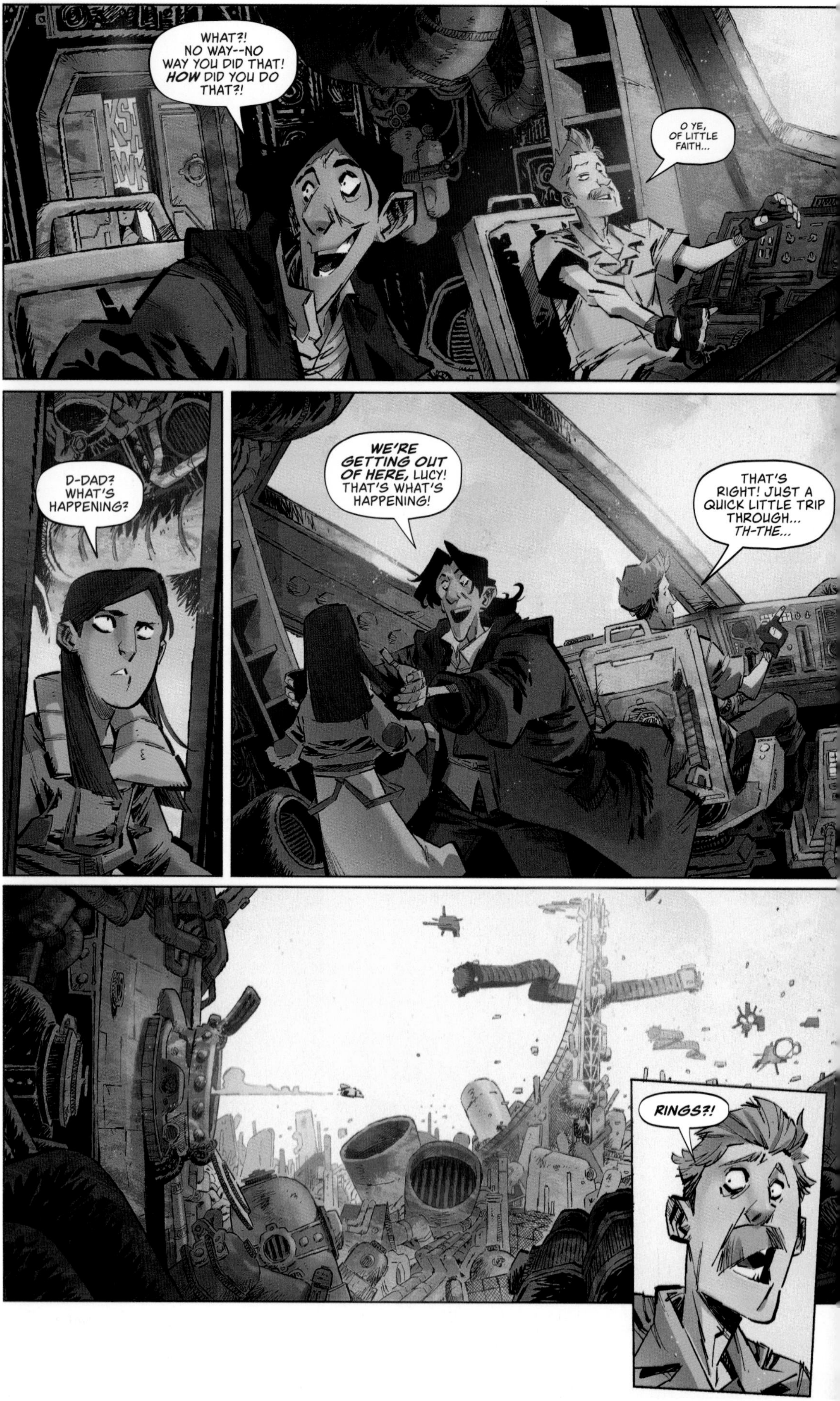

WHAT?! NO WAY--NO WAY YOU DID THAT! HOW DID YOU DO THAT?!
O YE, OF LITTLE FAITH...
D-DAD? WHAT'S HAPPENING?
WE'RE GETTING OUT OF HERE, LUCY! THAT'S WHAT'S HAPPENING!
THAT'S RIGHT! JUST A QUICK LITTLE TRIP THROUGH... TH-THE...
RINGS?!

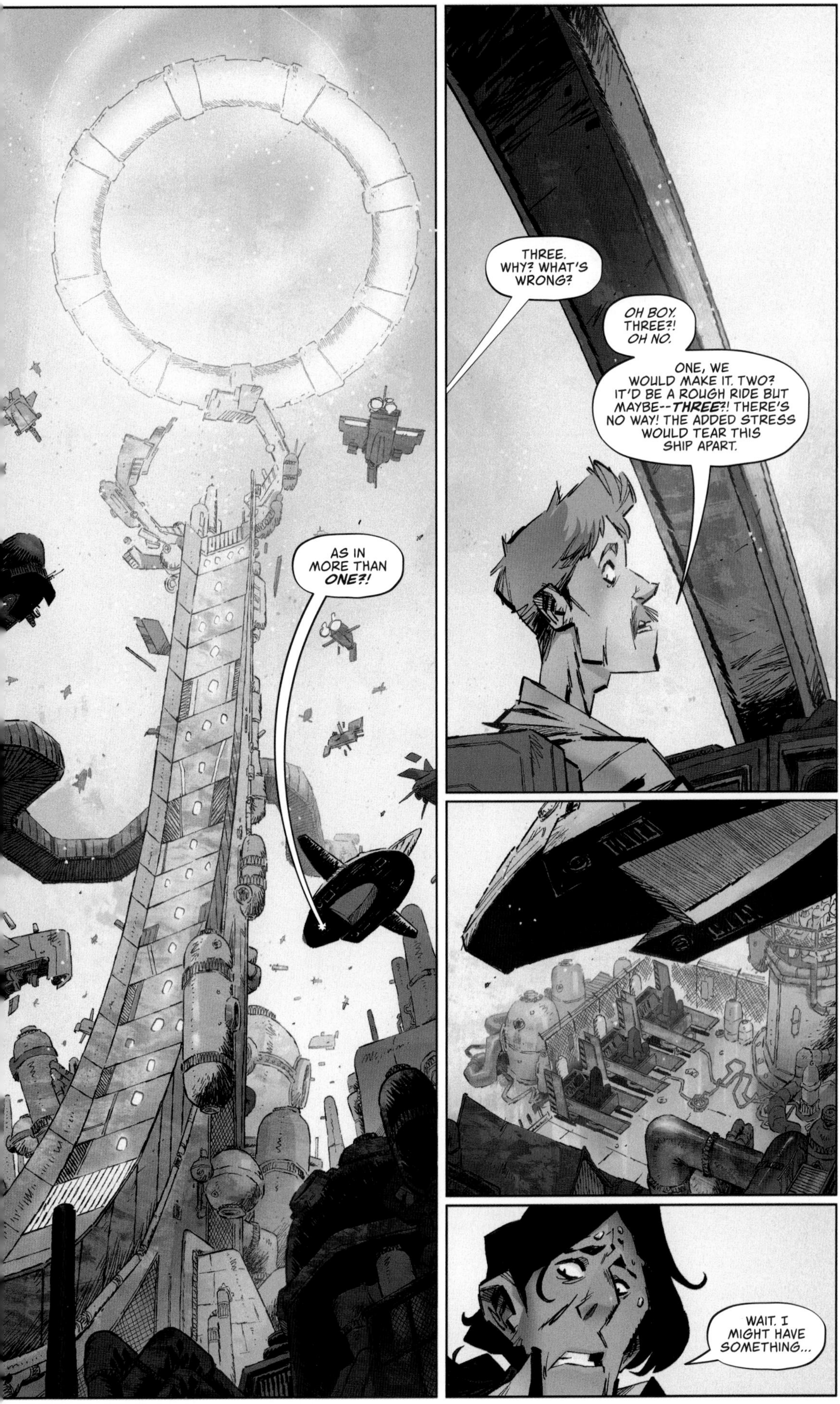
AS IN MORE THAN ONE?!
THREE. WHY? WHAT'S WRONG?
OH BOY. THREE?! OH NO.
ONE, WE WOULD MAKE IT. TWO? IT'D BE A ROUGH RIDE BUT MAYBE--THREE?! THERE'S NO WAY! THE ADDED STRESS WOULD TEAR THIS SHIP APART.
WAIT. I MIGHT HAVE SOMETHING...

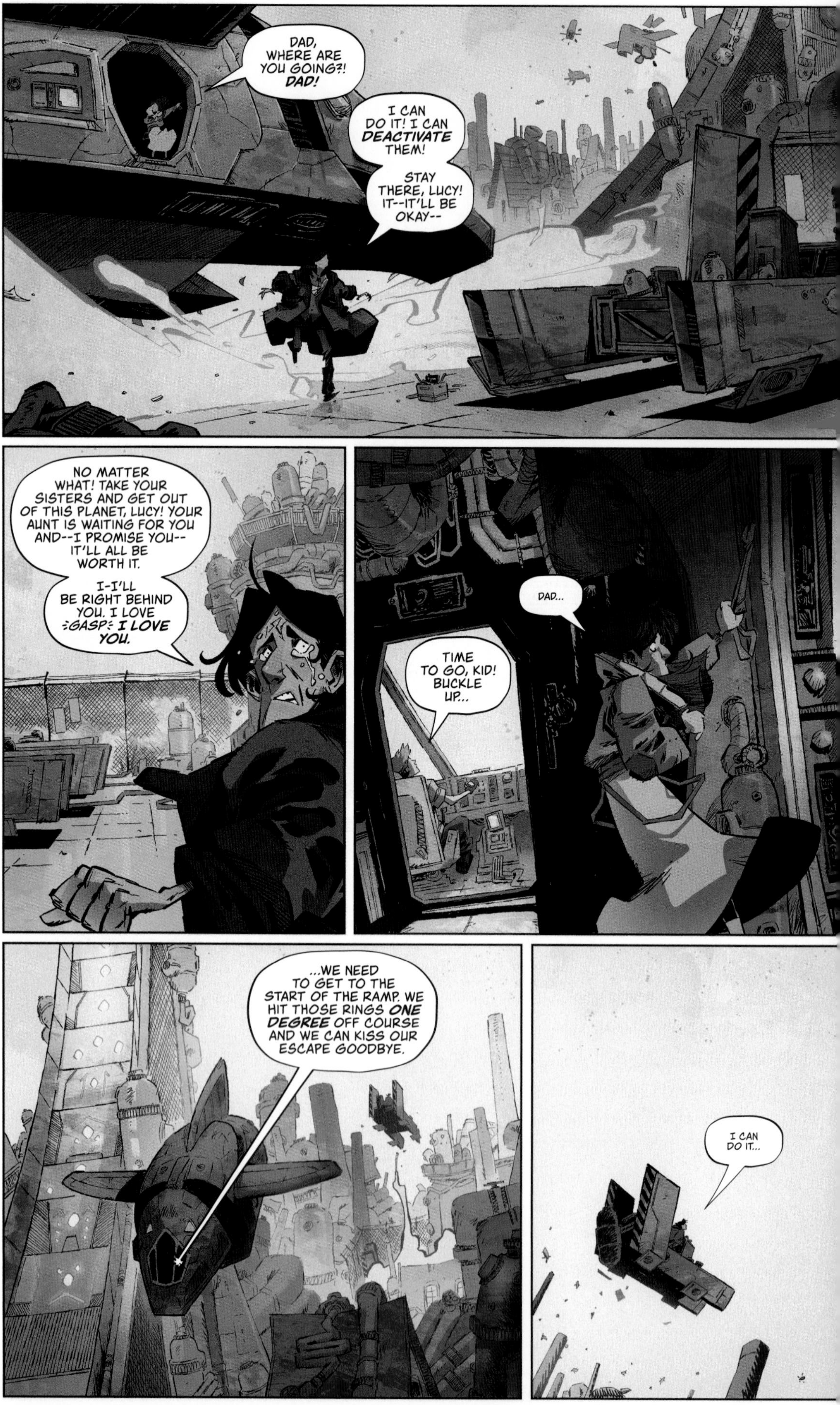

DAD, WHERE ARE YOU GOING?! **DAD!**
I CAN DO IT! I CAN ***DEACTIVATE*** THEM!
STAY THERE, LUCY! IT--IT'LL BE OKAY--
NO MATTER WHAT! TAKE YOUR SISTERS AND GET OUT OF THIS PLANET, LUCY! YOUR AUNT IS WAITING FOR YOU AND--I PROMISE YOU--IT'LL ALL BE WORTH IT.
I-I'LL BE RIGHT BEHIND YOU. I LOVE ~~GASP~~ ***I LOVE YOU.***
DAD...
TIME TO GO, KID! BUCKLE UP...
...WE NEED TO GET TO THE START OF THE RAMP. WE HIT THOSE RINGS ***ONE DEGREE*** OFF COURSE AND WE CAN KISS OUR ESCAPE GOODBYE.
I CAN DO IT...

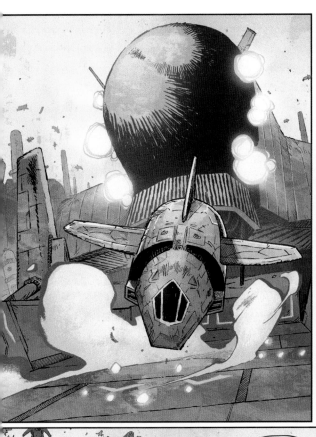

HEY--IT'LL BE OKAY, KID. HE'S JUST TRYING TO DO WHAT'S BEST FOR YOU THREE. I'M SURE YOU'LL--

AAAND *WE HAVE TO GO!*

CRAP. HARRY... HOPE YOU HAD ENOUGH TIME, PAL. *REALLY, REALLY DO.*

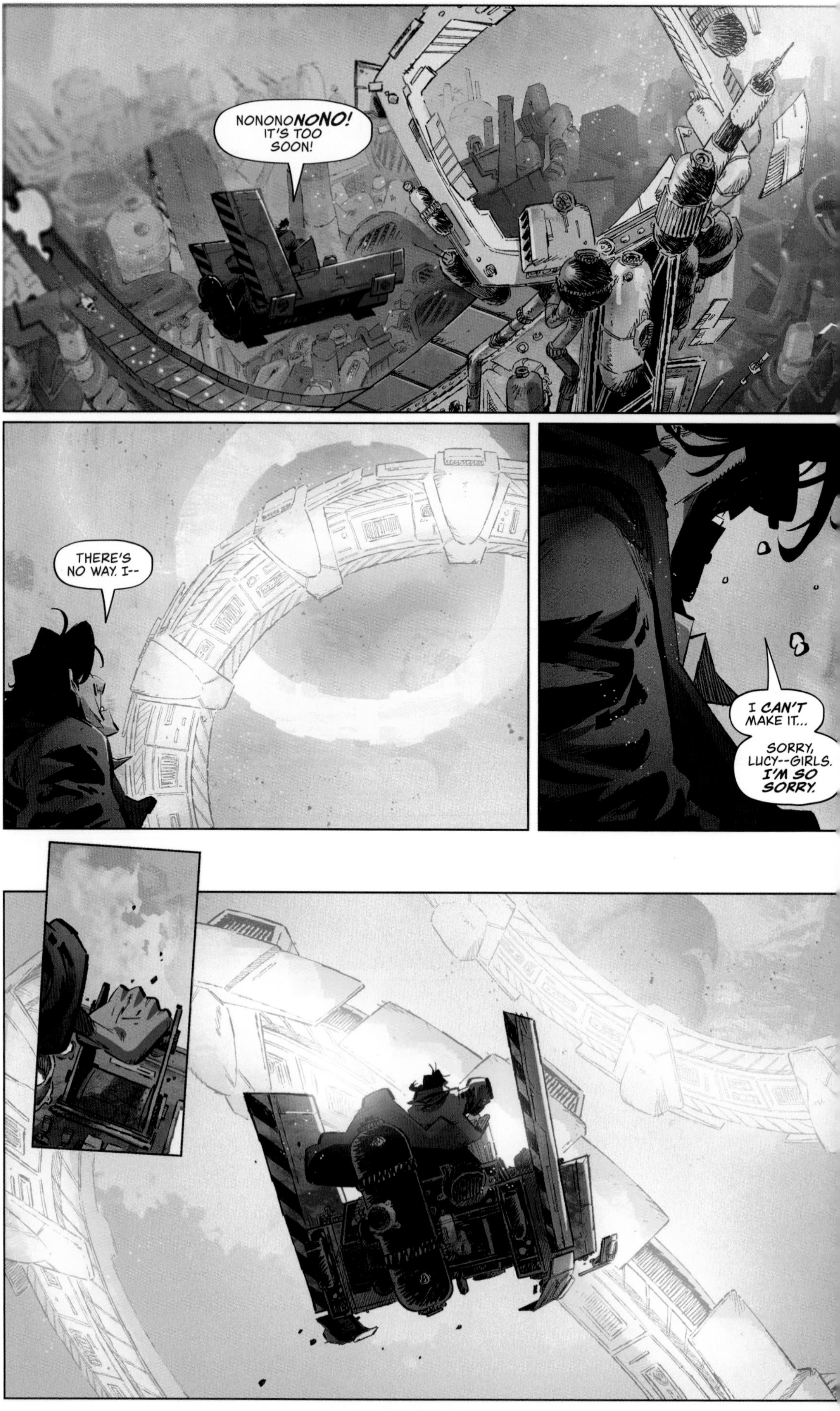
NONONONONO! IT'S TOO SOON!
THERE'S NO WAY. I--
I CAN'T MAKE IT...
SORRY, LUCY--GIRLS. I'M SO SORRY.

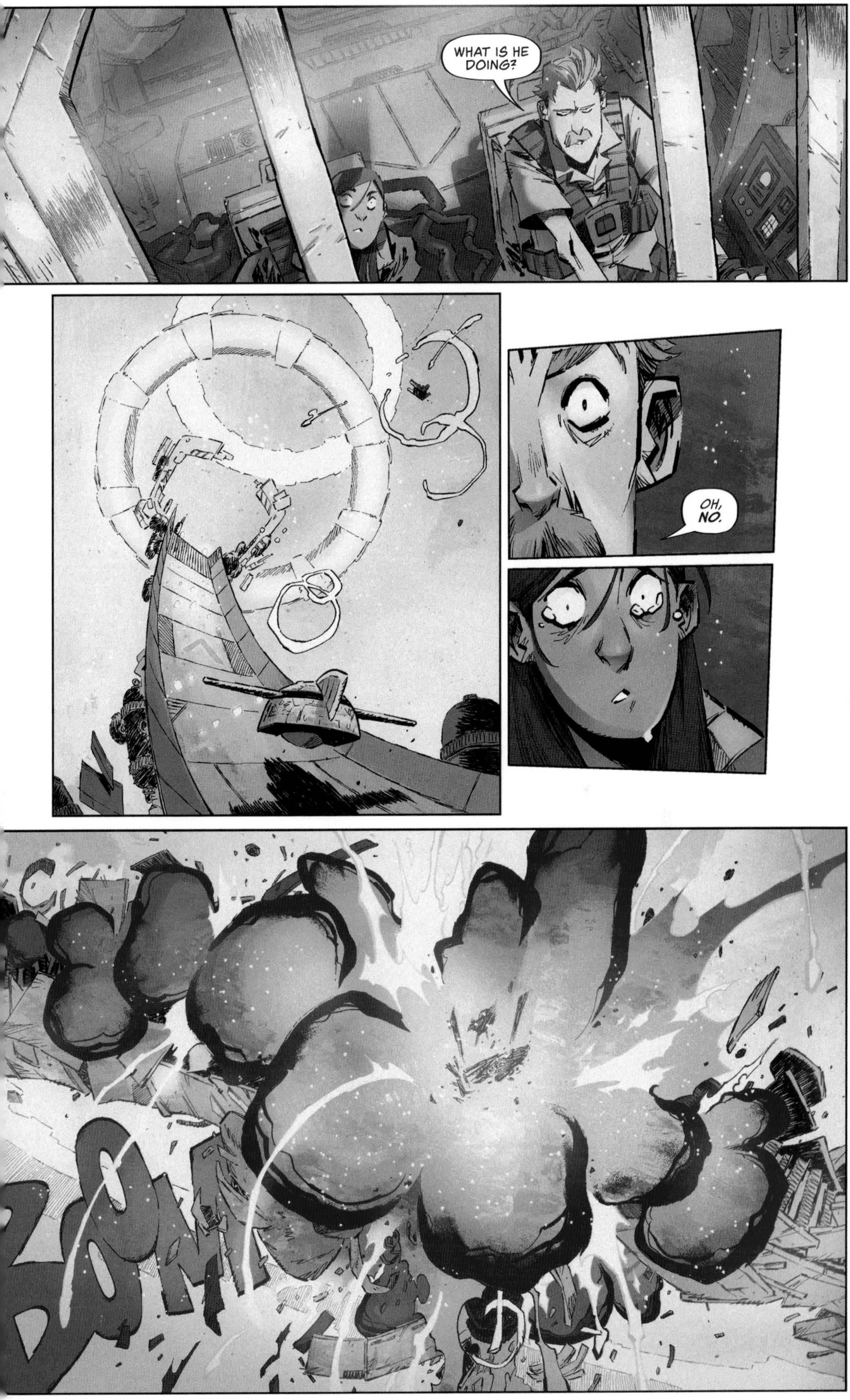

WHAT IS HE DOING?
OH, NO.
BOOM!

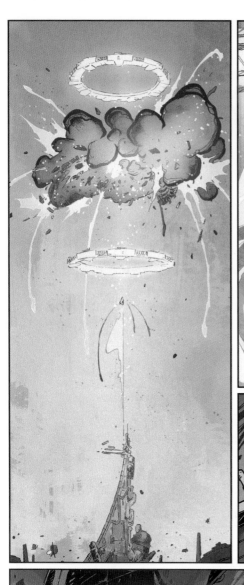

ARRRRGHHH!!!

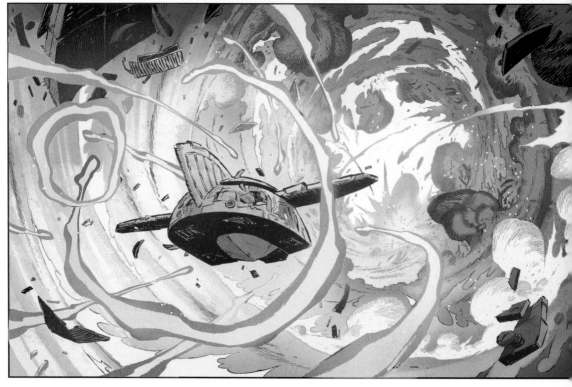

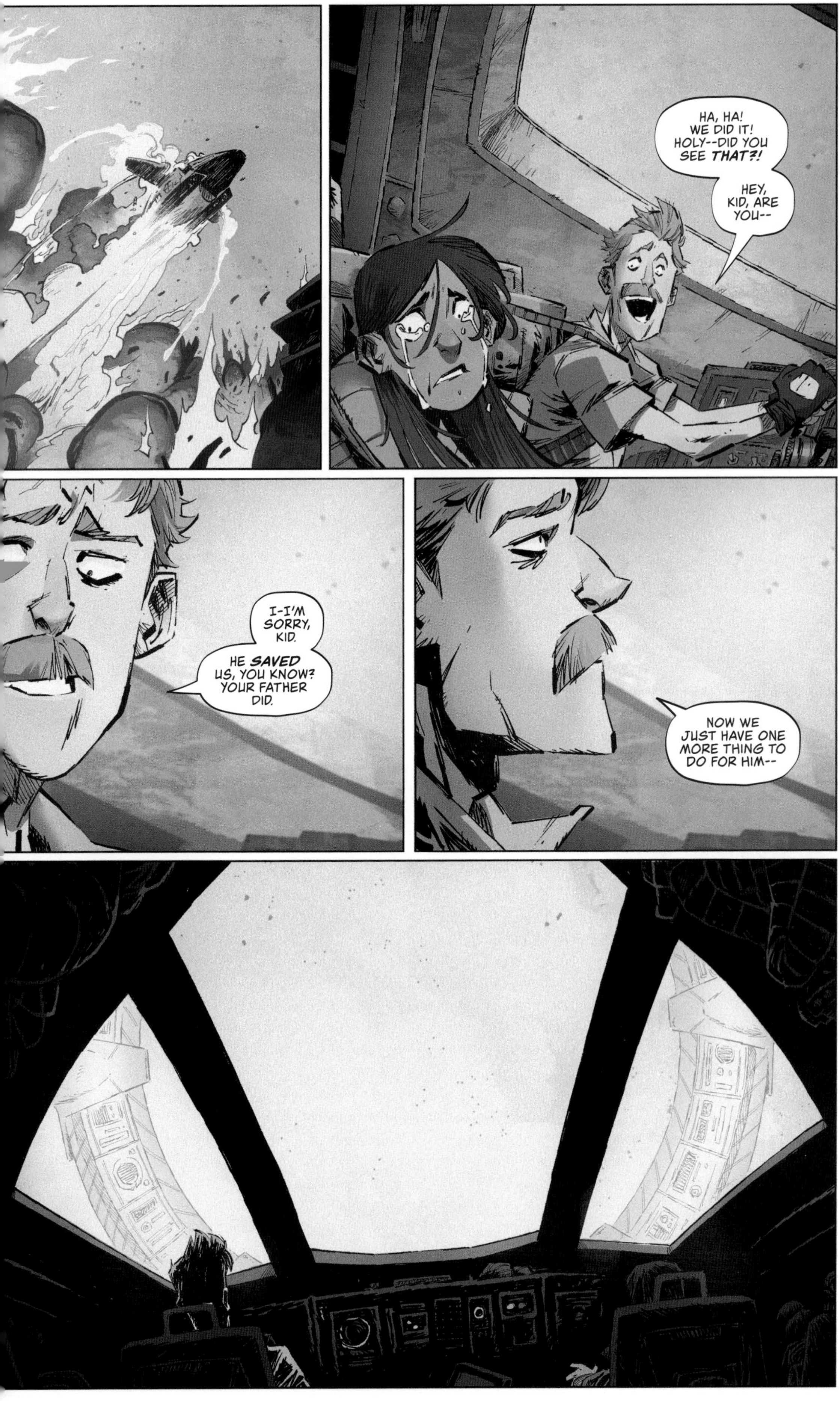
HA, HA! WE DID IT! HOLY--DID YOU SEE THAT?!
HEY, KID, ARE YOU--
I-I'M SORRY, KID.
HE SAVED US, YOU KNOW? YOUR FATHER DID.
NOW WE JUST HAVE ONE MORE THING TO DO FOR HIM--

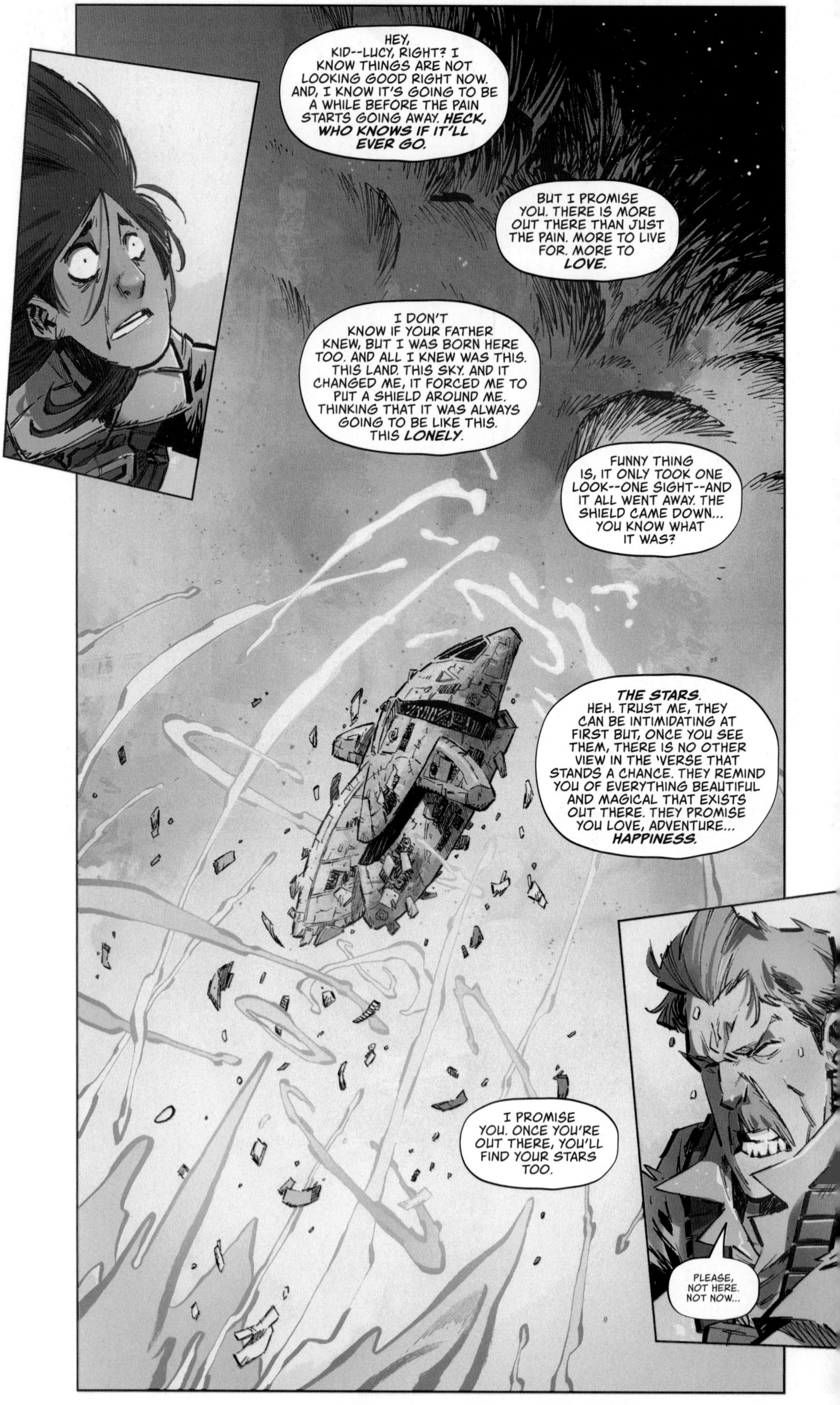
HEY, KID--LUCY, RIGHT? I KNOW THINGS ARE NOT LOOKING GOOD RIGHT NOW. AND, I KNOW IT'S GOING TO BE A WHILE BEFORE THE PAIN STARTS GOING AWAY. HECK, WHO KNOWS IF IT'LL EVER GO.
BUT I PROMISE YOU. THERE IS MORE OUT THERE THAN JUST THE PAIN. MORE TO LIVE FOR. MORE TO LOVE.
I DON'T KNOW IF YOUR FATHER KNEW, BUT I WAS BORN HERE TOO. AND ALL I KNEW WAS THIS. THIS LAND. THIS SKY. AND IT CHANGED ME, IT FORCED ME TO PUT A SHIELD AROUND ME. THINKING THAT IT WAS ALWAYS GOING TO BE LIKE THIS. THIS LONELY.
FUNNY THING IS, IT ONLY TOOK ONE LOOK--ONE SIGHT--AND IT ALL WENT AWAY. THE SHIELD CAME DOWN... YOU KNOW WHAT IT WAS?
THE STARS. HEH. TRUST ME, THEY CAN BE INTIMIDATING AT FIRST BUT, ONCE YOU SEE THEM, THERE IS NO OTHER VIEW IN THE 'VERSE THAT STANDS A CHANCE. THEY REMIND YOU OF EVERYTHING BEAUTIFUL AND MAGICAL THAT EXISTS OUT THERE. THEY PROMISE YOU LOVE, ADVENTURE... HAPPINESS.
I PROMISE YOU. ONCE YOU'RE OUT THERE, YOU'LL FIND YOUR STARS TOO.
PLEASE, NOT HERE. NOT NOW...

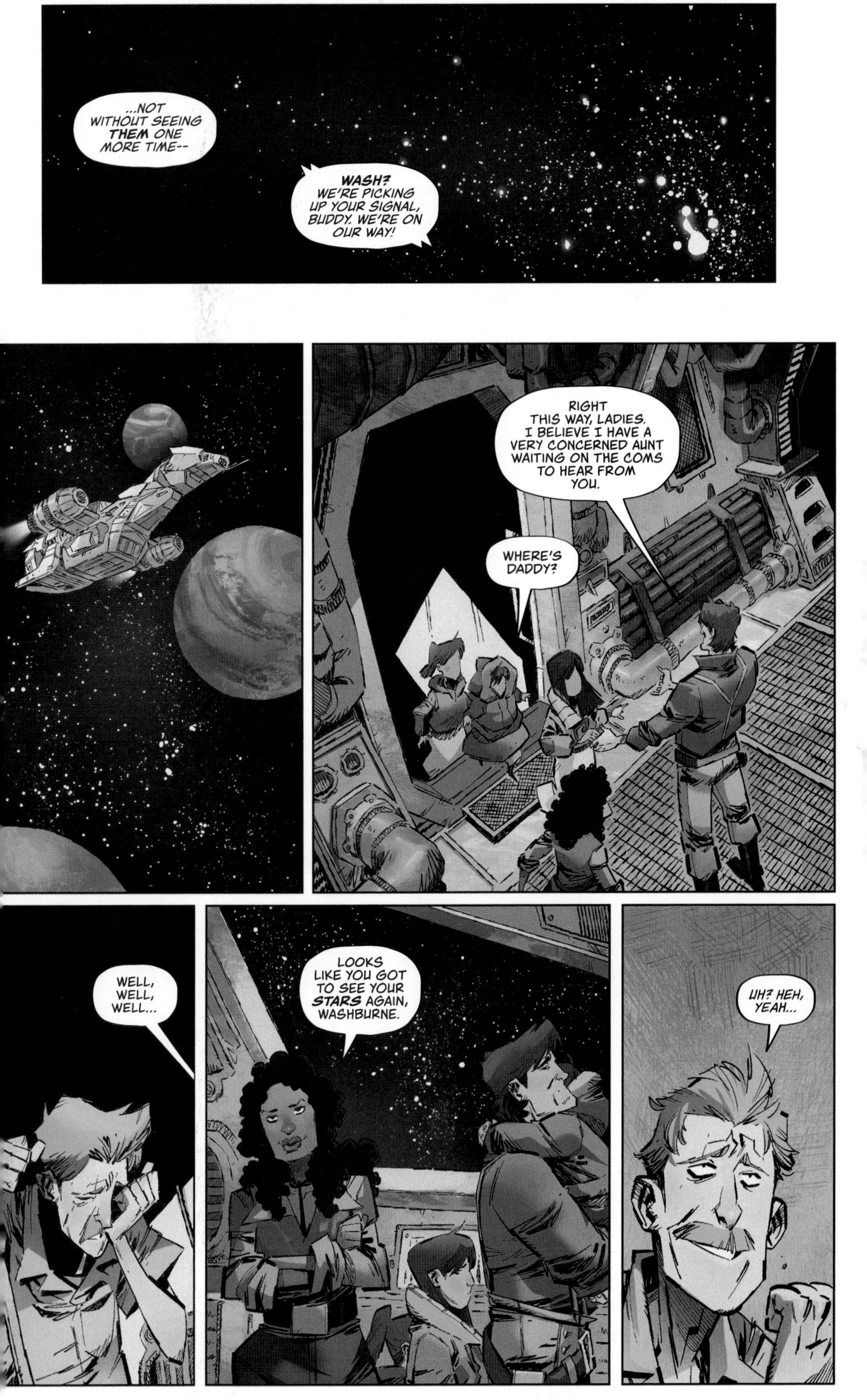
...NOT WITHOUT SEEING **THEM** ONE MORE TIME--
WASH? WE'RE PICKING UP YOUR SIGNAL, BUDDY. WE'RE ON OUR WAY!
RIGHT THIS WAY, LADIES. I BELIEVE I HAVE A VERY CONCERNED AUNT WAITING ON THE COMS TO HEAR FROM YOU.
WHERE'S DADDY?
WELL, WELL, WELL...
LOOKS LIKE YOU GOT TO SEE YOUR **STARS** AGAIN, WASHBURNE.
UH? HEH, YEAH...

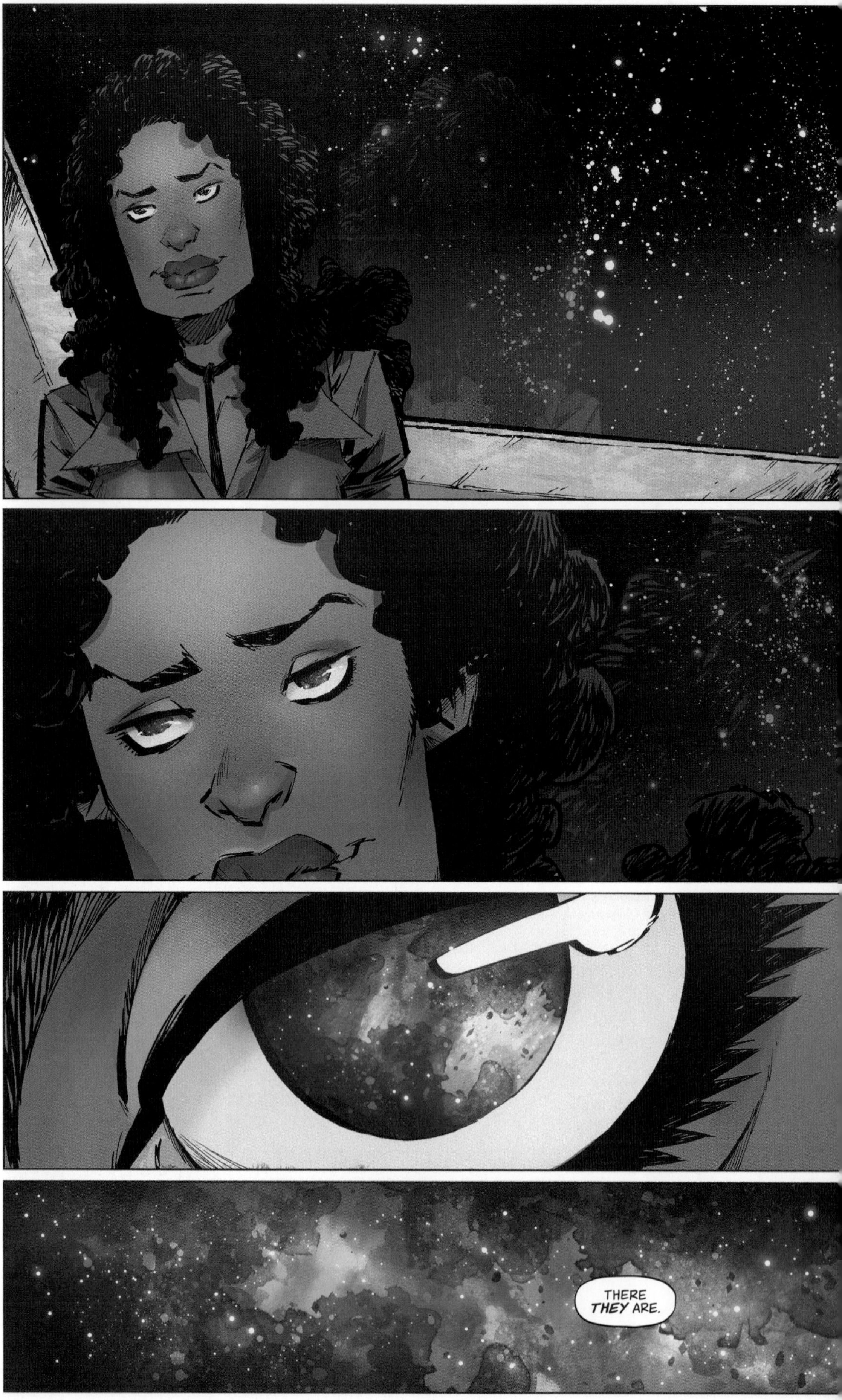
THERE THEY ARE.

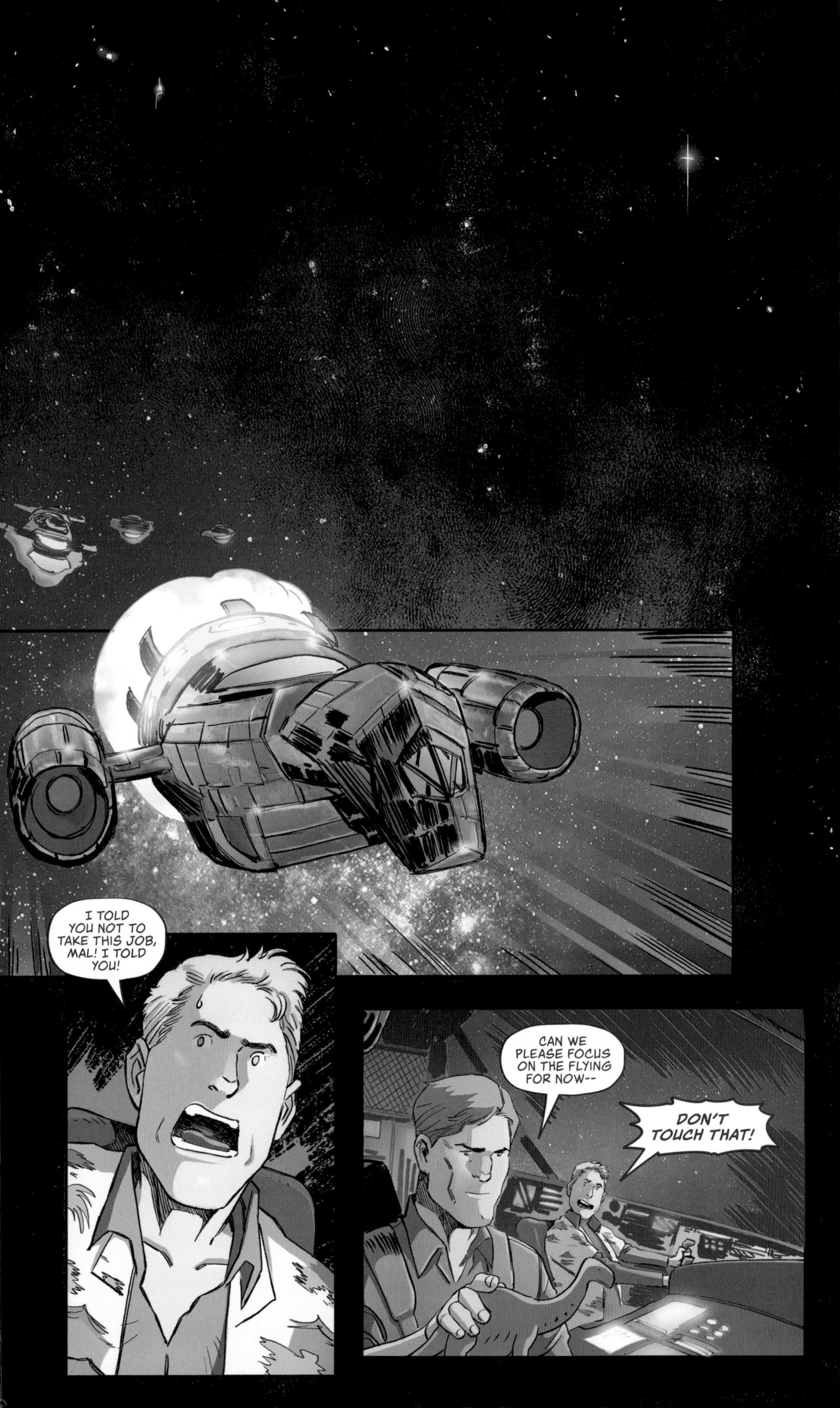
I TOLD YOU NOT TO TAKE THIS JOB, MAL! I TOLD YOU!
CAN WE PLEASE FOCUS ON THE FLYING FOR NOW--
DON'T TOUCH THAT!

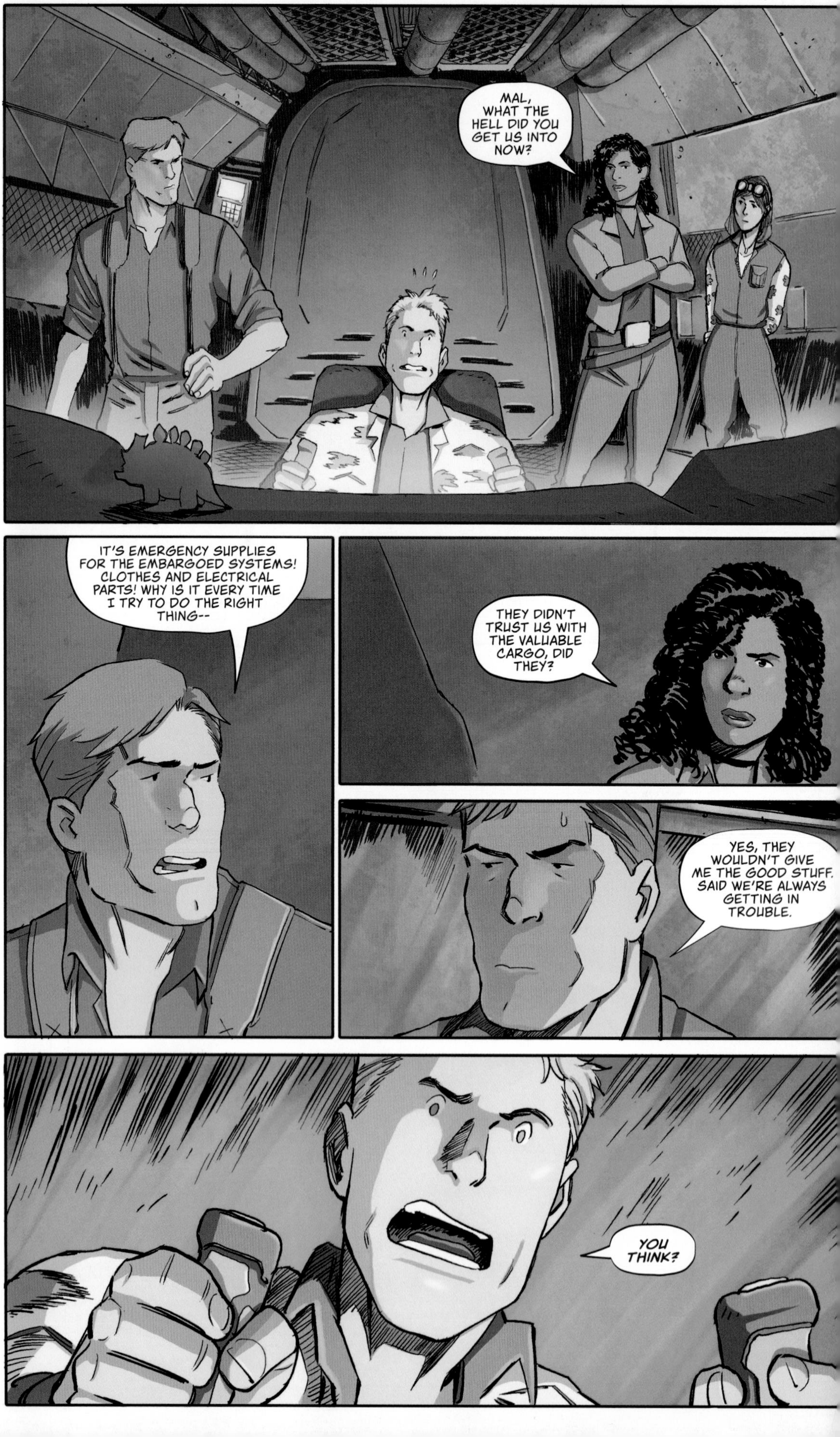
MAL, WHAT THE HELL DID YOU GET US INTO NOW?
IT'S EMERGENCY SUPPLIES FOR THE EMBARGOED SYSTEMS! CLOTHES AND ELECTRICAL PARTS! WHY IS IT EVERY TIME I TRY TO DO THE RIGHT THING--
THEY DIDN'T TRUST US WITH THE VALUABLE CARGO, DID THEY?
YES, THEY WOULDN'T GIVE ME THE GOOD STUFF. SAID WE'RE ALWAYS GETTING IN TROUBLE.
YOU THINK?

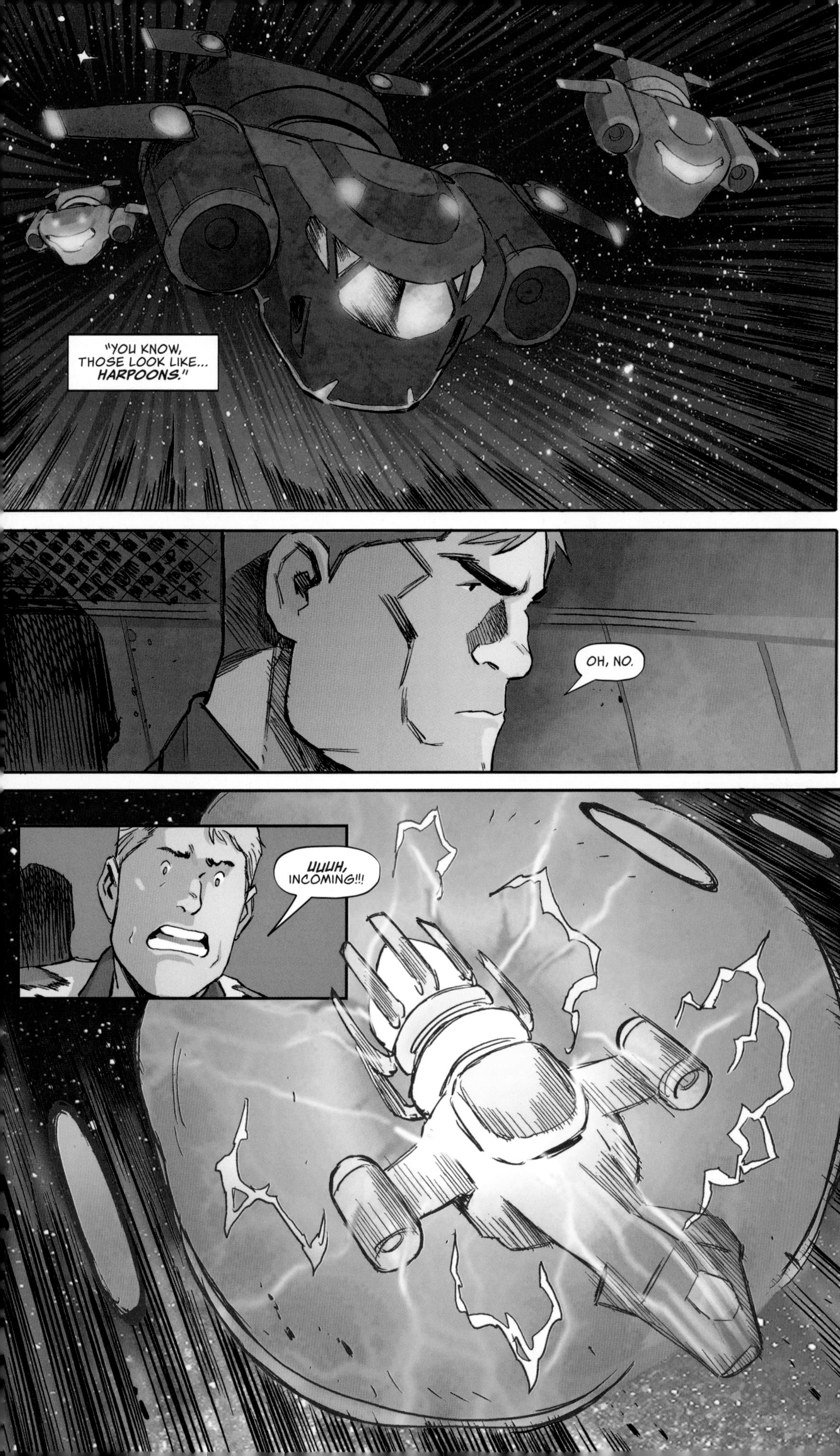
"YOU KNOW, THOSE LOOK LIKE... HARPOONS."
OH, NO.
UUUH, INCOMING!!!

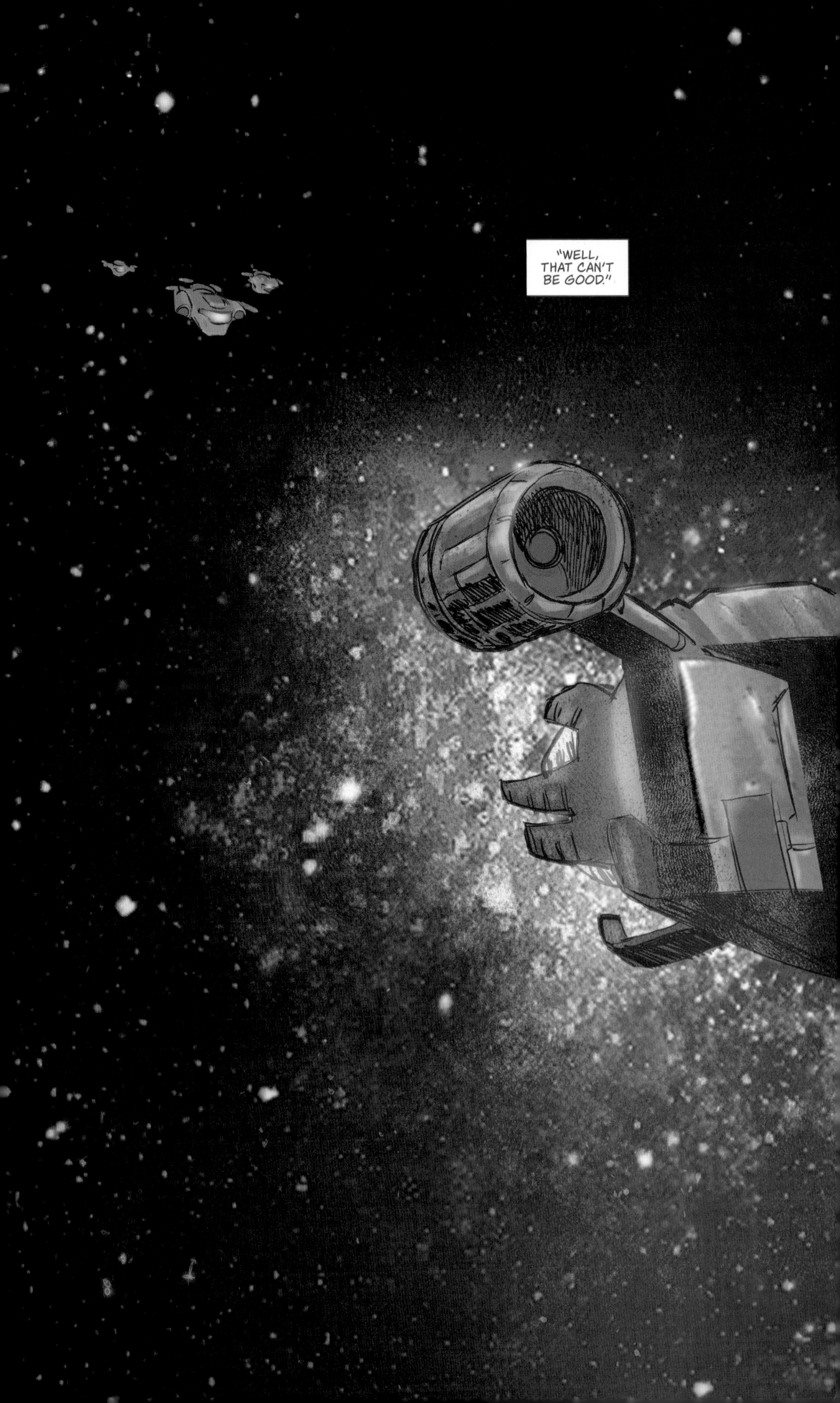
"WELL, THAT CAN'T BE GOOD."

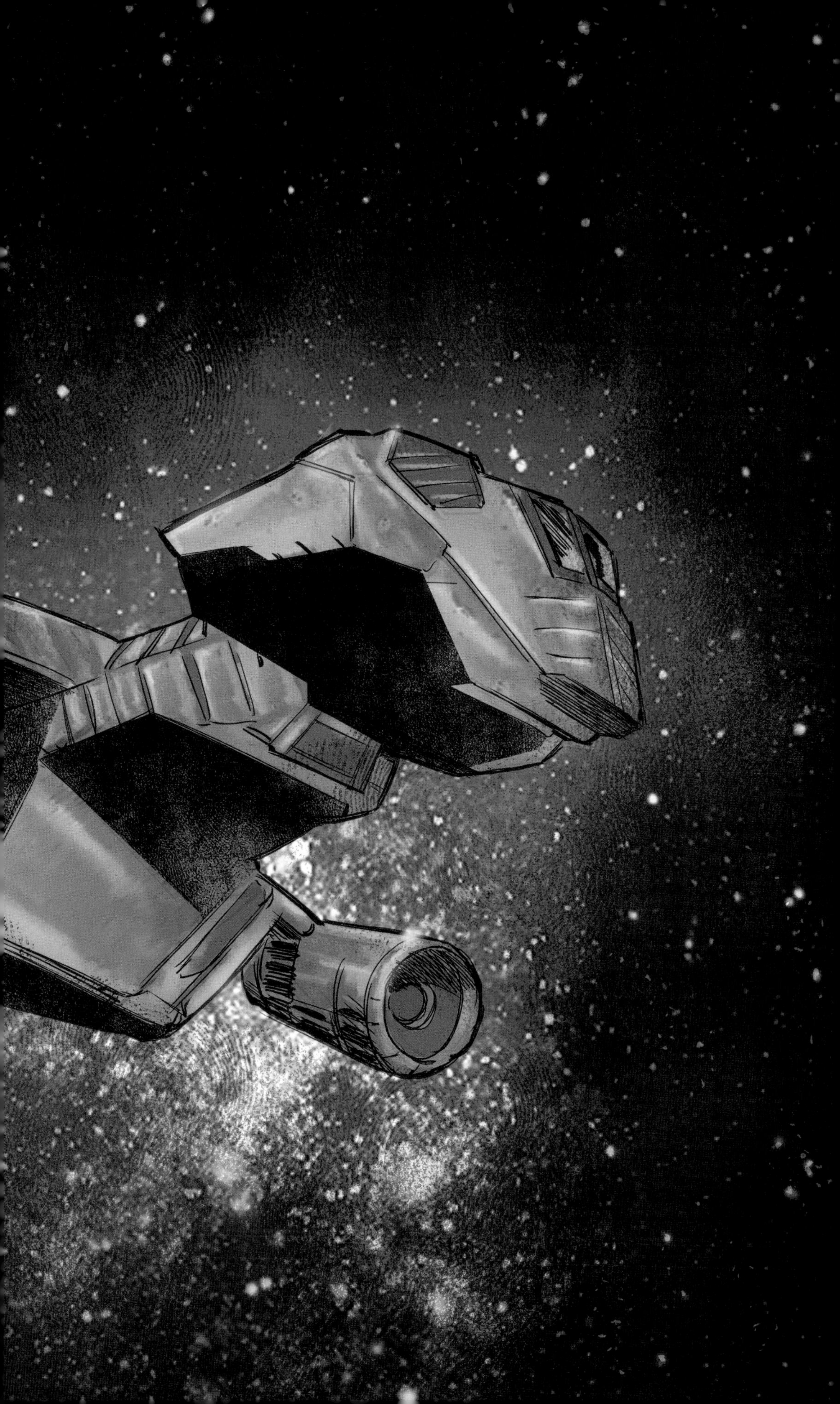

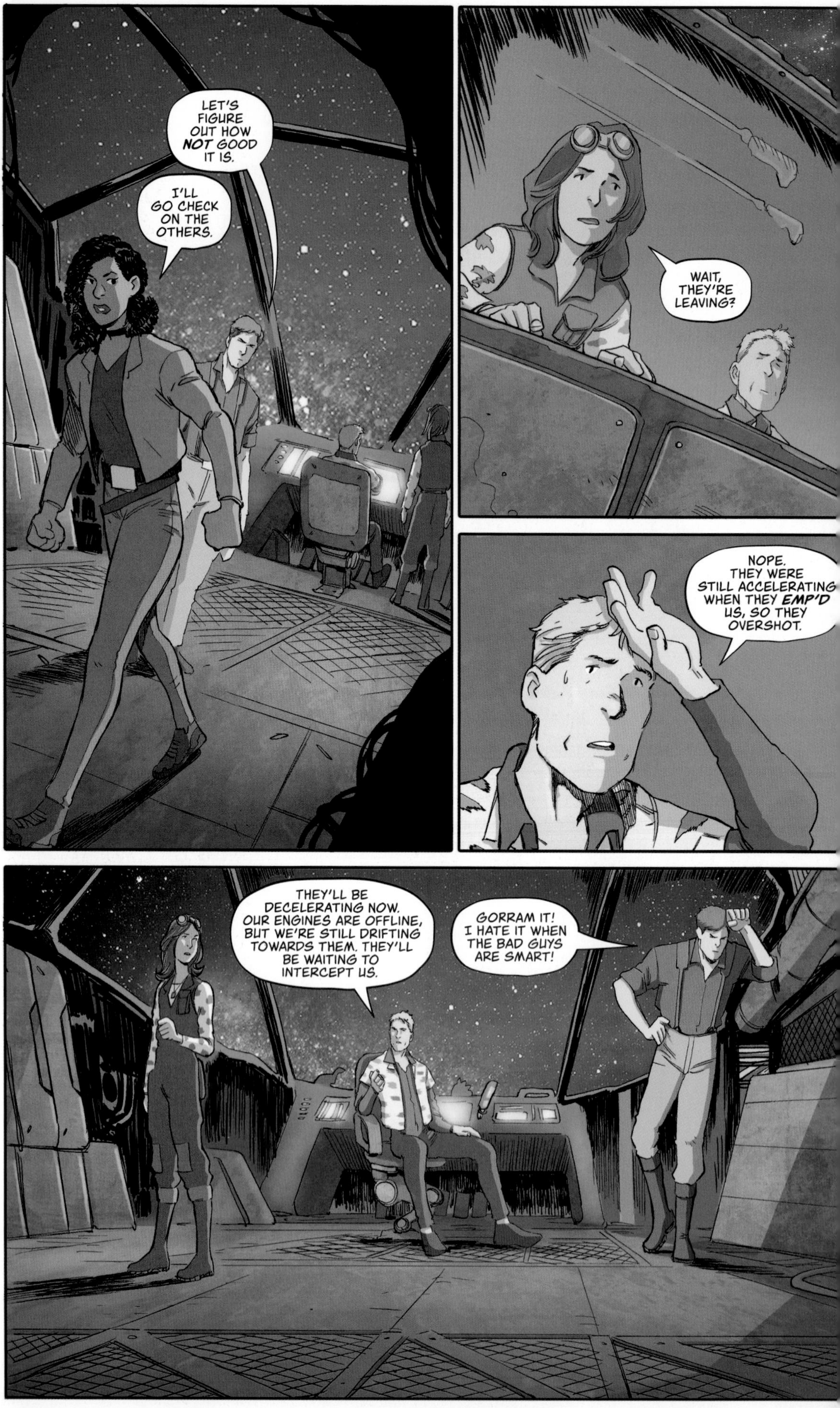

LET'S FIGURE OUT HOW NOT GOOD IT IS.
I'LL GO CHECK ON THE OTHERS.
WAIT, THEY'RE LEAVING?
NOPE. THEY WERE STILL ACCELERATING WHEN THEY EMP'D US, SO THEY OVERSHOT.
THEY'LL BE DECELERATING NOW. OUR ENGINES ARE OFFLINE, BUT WE'RE STILL DRIFTING TOWARDS THEM. THEY'LL BE WAITING TO INTERCEPT US.
GORRAM IT! I HATE IT WHEN THE BAD GUYS ARE SMART!

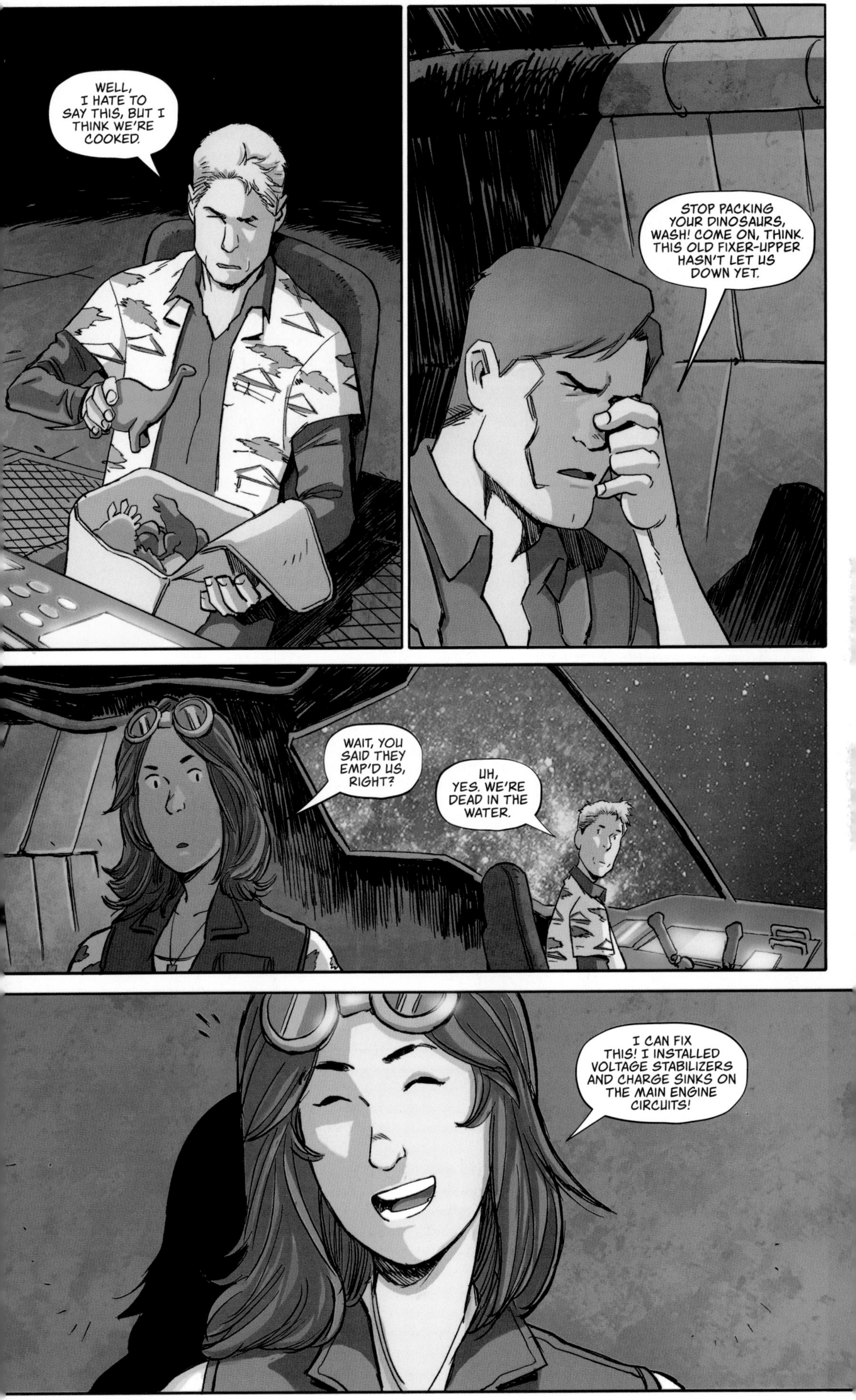

WELL, I HATE TO SAY THIS, BUT I THINK WE'RE COOKED.
STOP PACKING YOUR DINOSAURS, WASH! COME ON, THINK. THIS OLD FIXER-UPPER HASN'T LET US DOWN YET.
WAIT, YOU SAID THEY EMP'D US, RIGHT?
UH, YES. WE'RE DEAD IN THE WATER.
I CAN FIX THIS! I INSTALLED VOLTAGE STABILIZERS AND CHARGE SINKS ON THE MAIN ENGINE CIRCUITS!

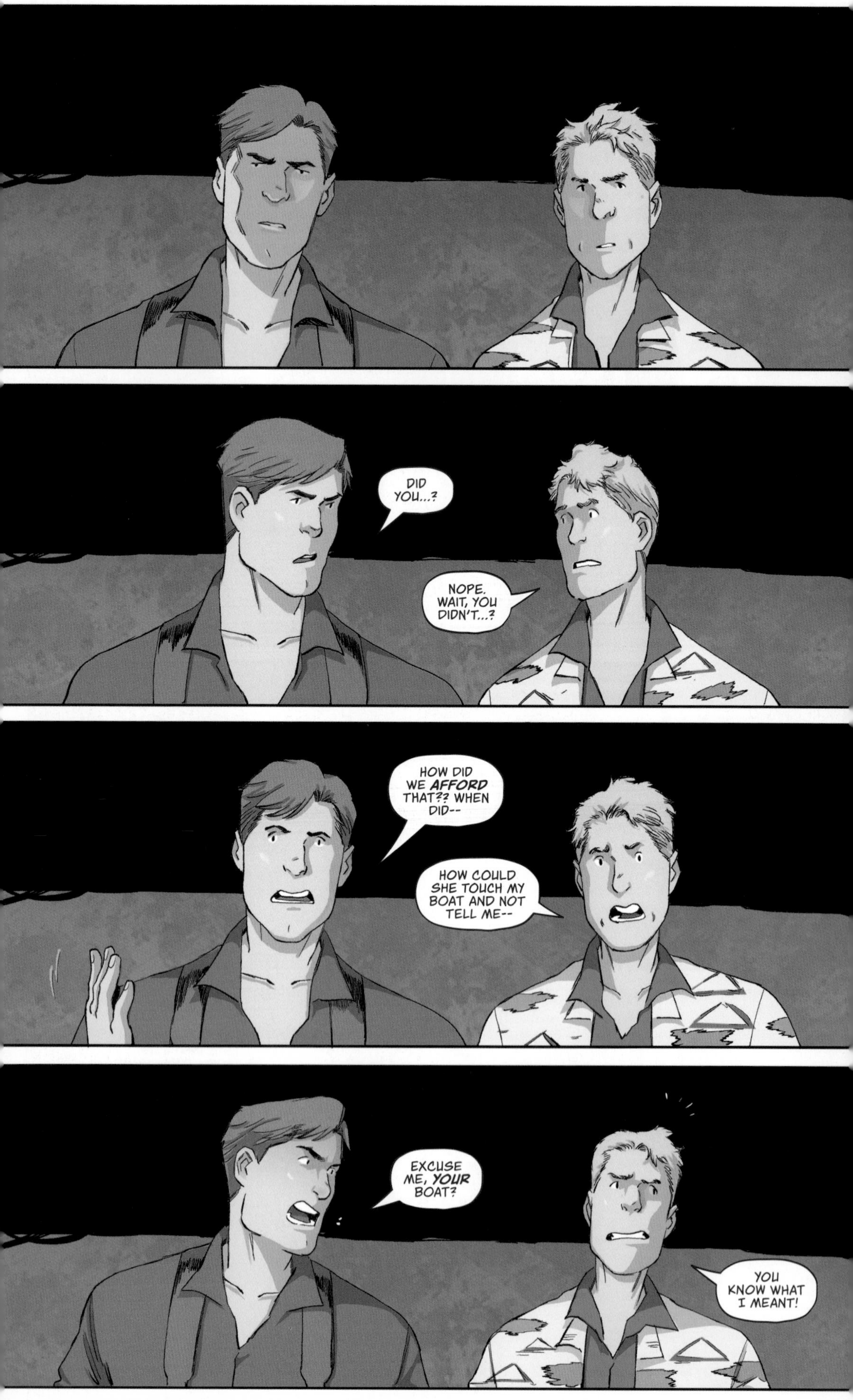
DID YOU...?
NOPE. WAIT, YOU DIDN'T...?
HOW DID WE **AFFORD** THAT?? WHEN DID--
HOW COULD SHE TOUCH MY BOAT AND NOT TELL ME--
EXCUSE ME, **YOUR** BOAT?
YOU KNOW WHAT I MEANT!

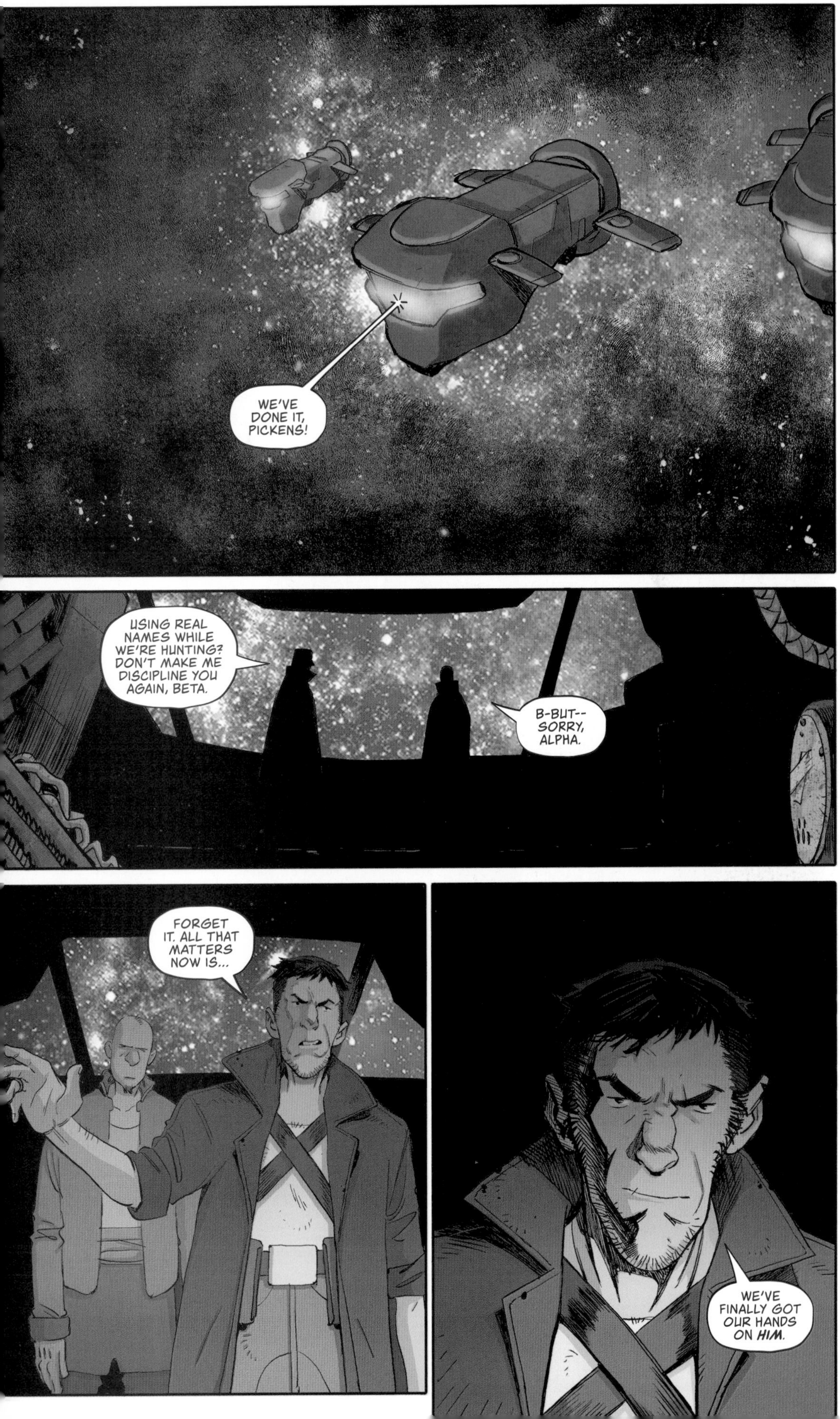
WE'VE DONE IT, PICKENS!
USING REAL NAMES WHILE WE'RE HUNTING? DON'T MAKE ME DISCIPLINE YOU AGAIN, BETA.
B-BUT-- SORRY, ALPHA.
FORGET IT. ALL THAT MATTERS NOW IS...
WE'VE FINALLY GOT OUR HANDS ON **HIM**.

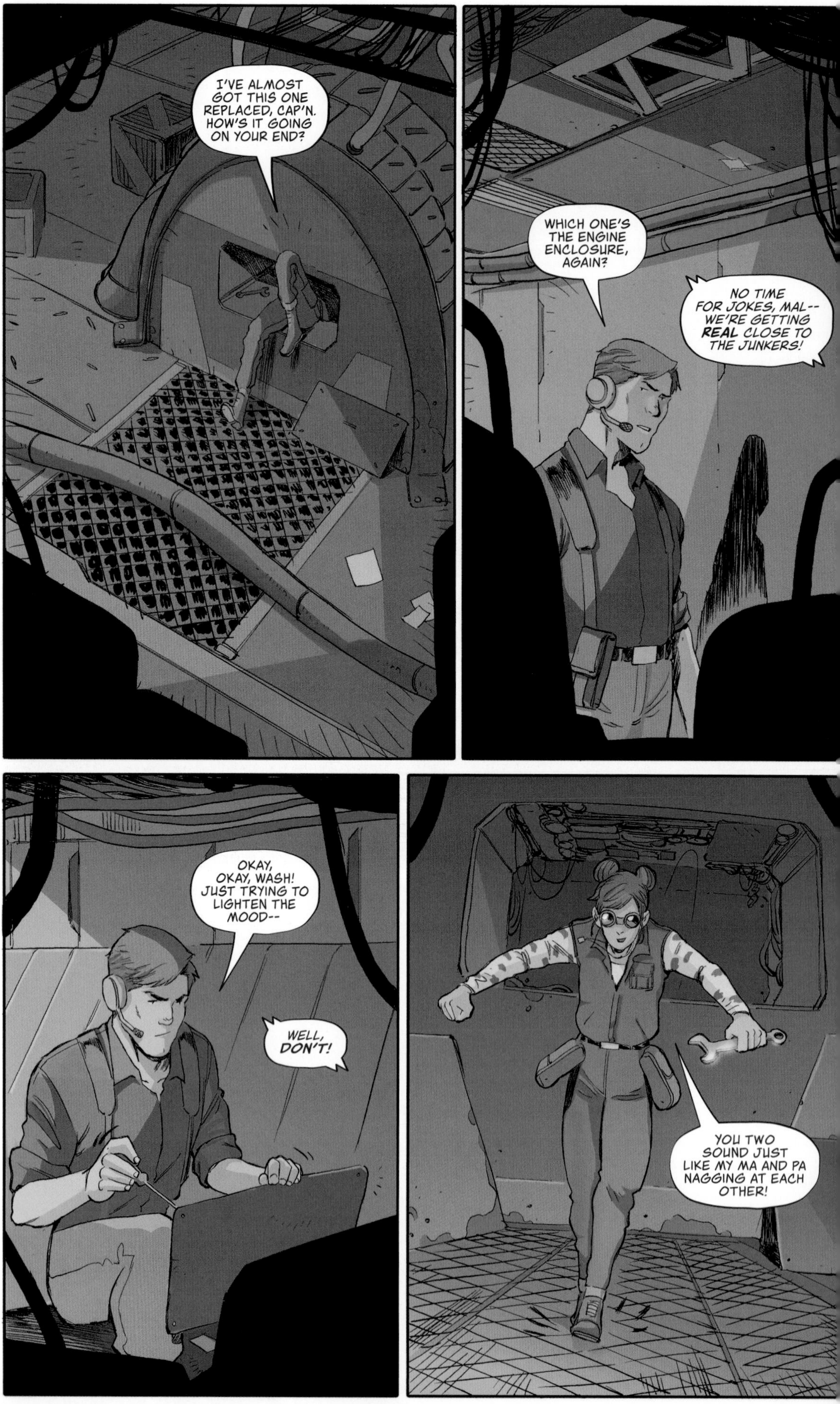
I'VE ALMOST GOT THIS ONE REPLACED, CAP'N. HOW'S IT GOING ON YOUR END?
WHICH ONE'S THE ENGINE ENCLOSURE, AGAIN?
NO TIME FOR JOKES, MAL-- WE'RE GETTING **REAL** CLOSE TO THE JUNKERS!
OKAY, OKAY, WASH! JUST TRYING TO LIGHTEN THE MOOD--
WELL, **DON'T**!
YOU TWO SOUND JUST LIKE MY MA AND PA NAGGING AT EACH OTHER!

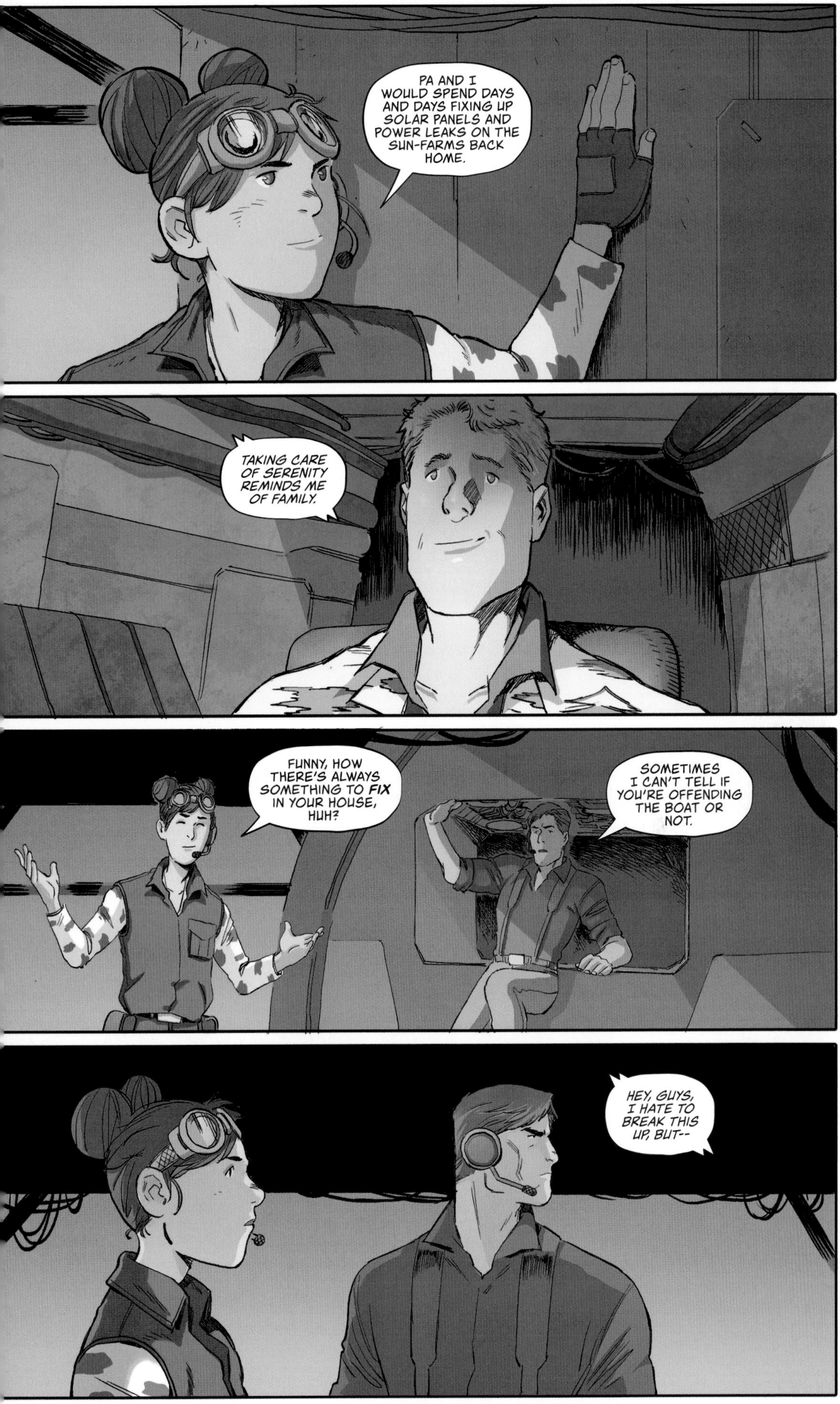
PA AND I WOULD SPEND DAYS AND DAYS FIXING UP SOLAR PANELS AND POWER LEAKS ON THE SUN-FARMS BACK HOME.
TAKING CARE OF SERENITY REMINDS ME OF FAMILY.
FUNNY, HOW THERE'S ALWAYS SOMETHING TO FIX IN YOUR HOUSE, HUH?
SOMETIMES I CAN'T TELL IF YOU'RE OFFENDING THE BOAT OR NOT.
HEY, GUYS, I HATE TO BREAK THIS UP, BUT--

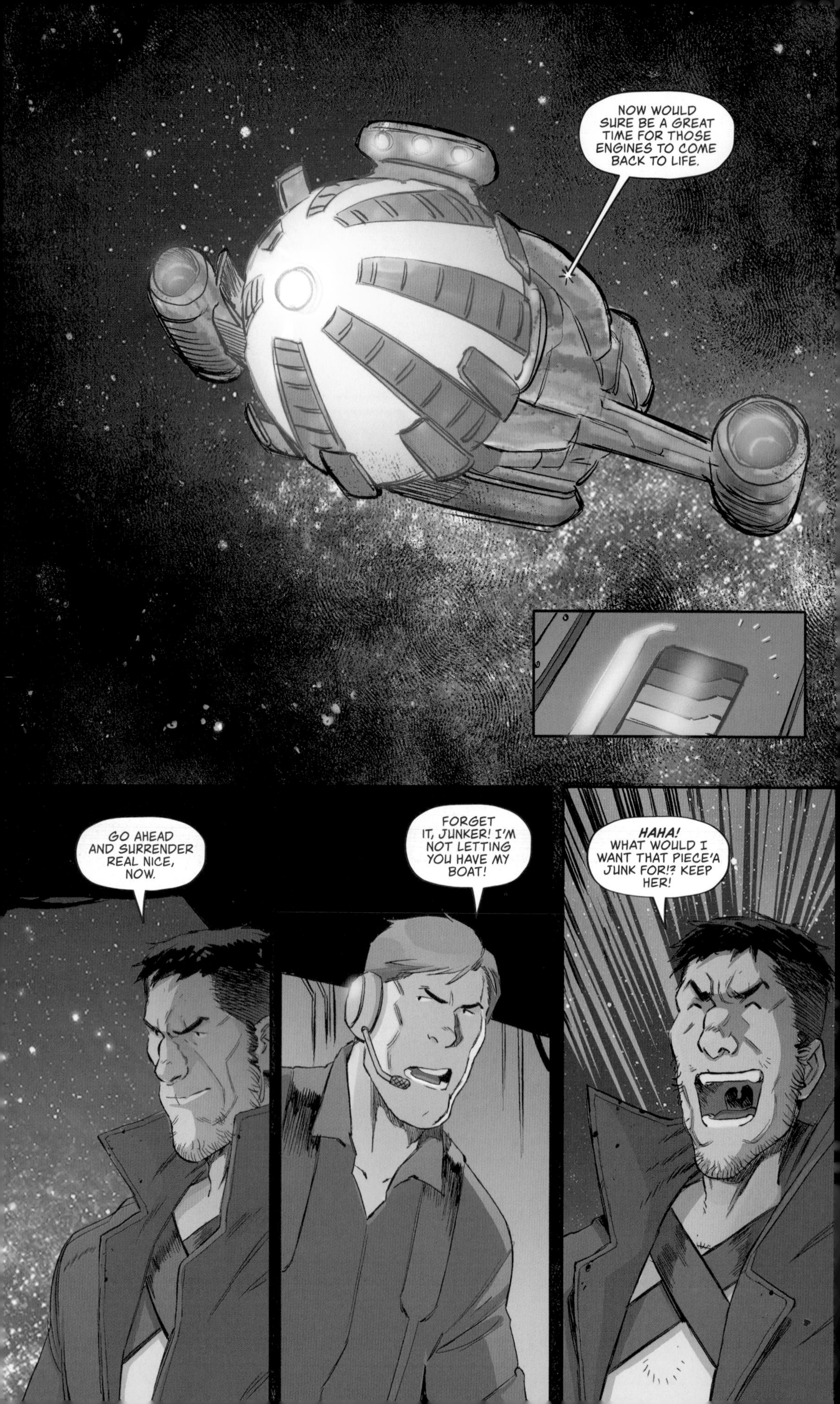
NOW WOULD SURE BE A GREAT TIME FOR THOSE ENGINES TO COME BACK TO LIFE.
GO AHEAD AND SURRENDER REAL NICE, NOW.
FORGET IT, JUNKER! I'M NOT LETTING YOU HAVE MY BOAT!
HAHA! WHAT WOULD I WANT THAT PIECE'A JUNK FOR!? KEEP HER!

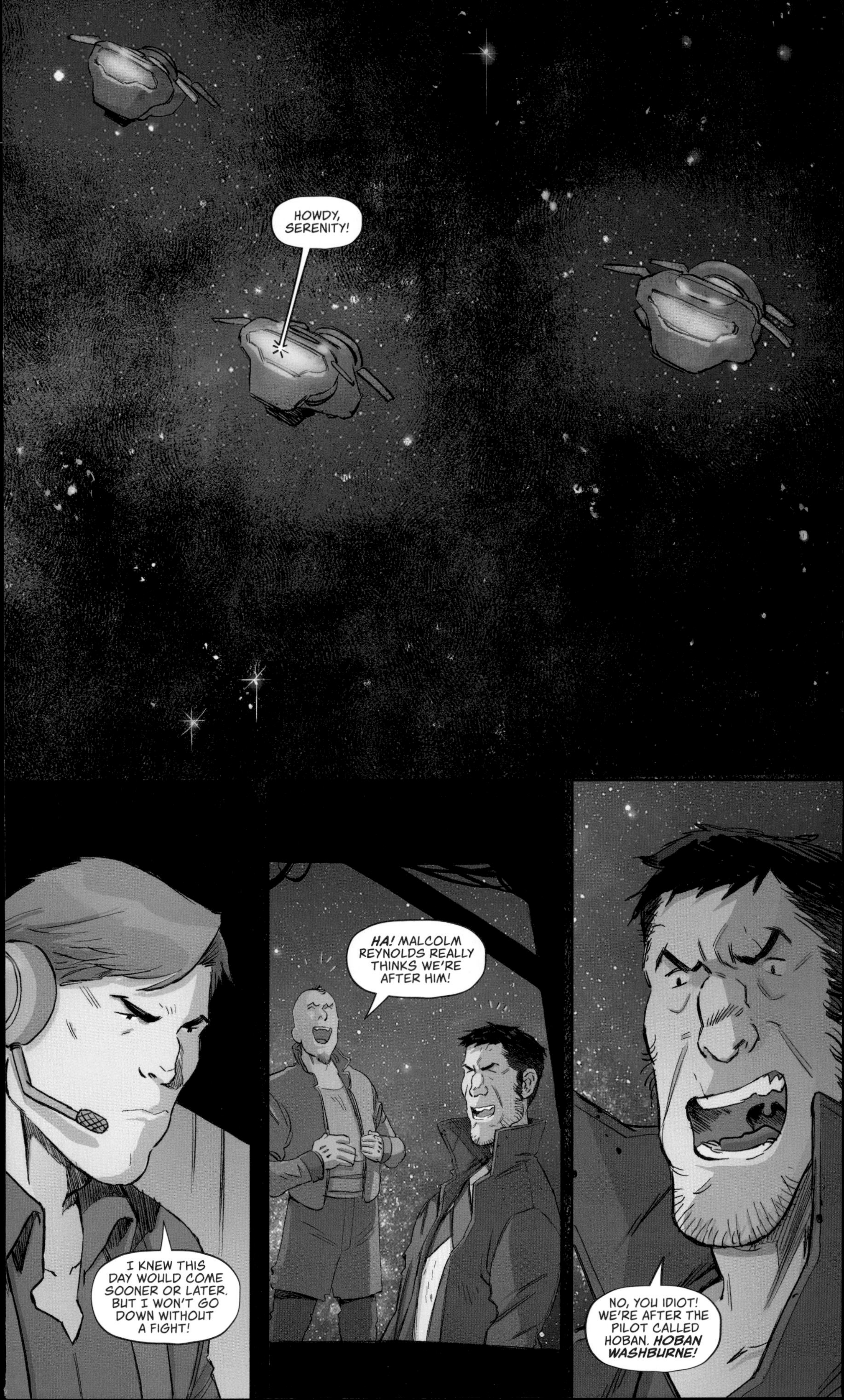
HOWDY, SERENITY!
I KNEW THIS DAY WOULD COME SOONER OR LATER. BUT I WON'T GO DOWN WITHOUT A FIGHT!
HA! MALCOLM REYNOLDS REALLY THINKS WE'RE AFTER HIM!
NO, YOU IDIOT! WE'RE AFTER THE PILOT CALLED HOBAN. HOBAN WASHBURNE!

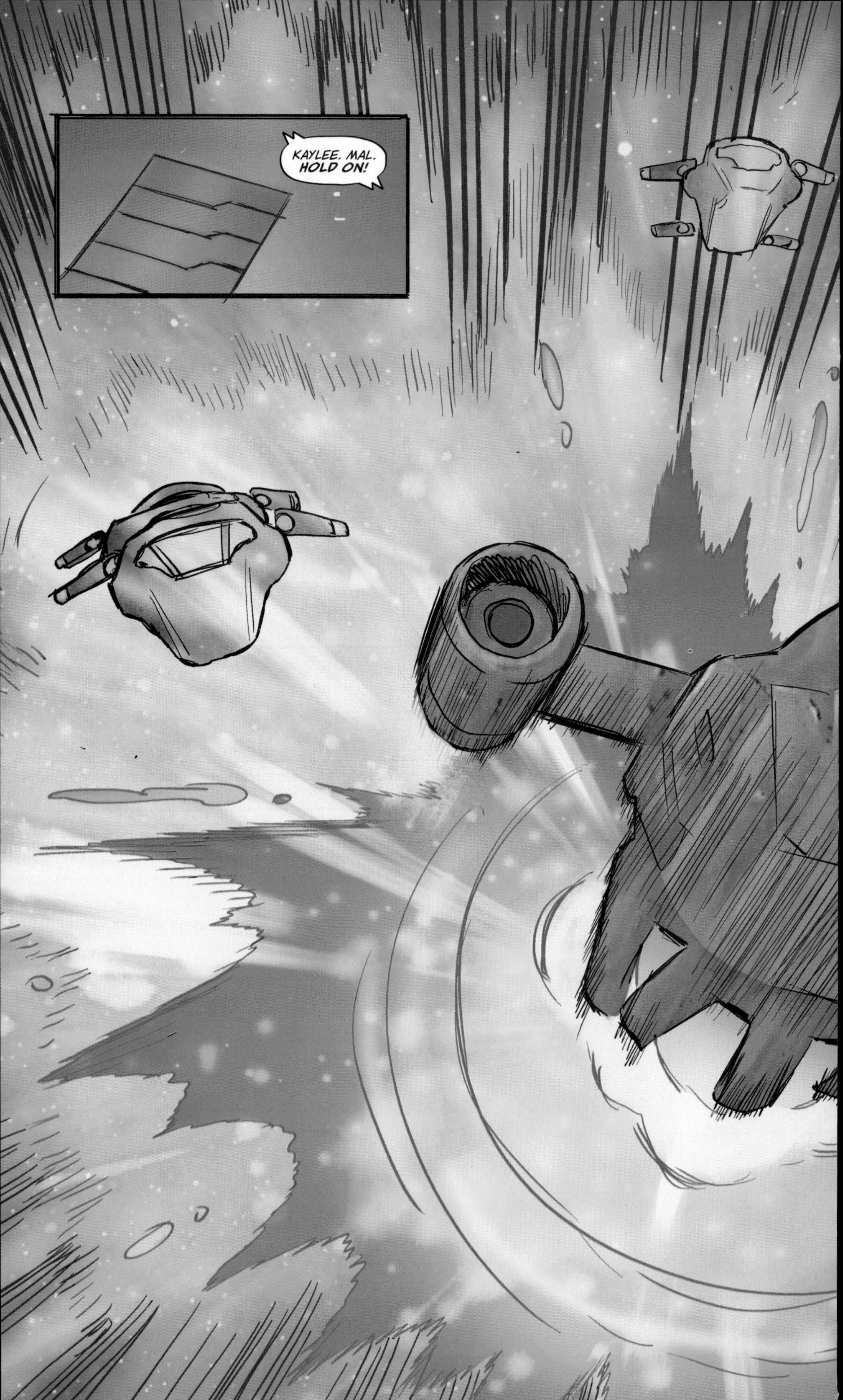
KAYLEE. MAL. HOLD ON!

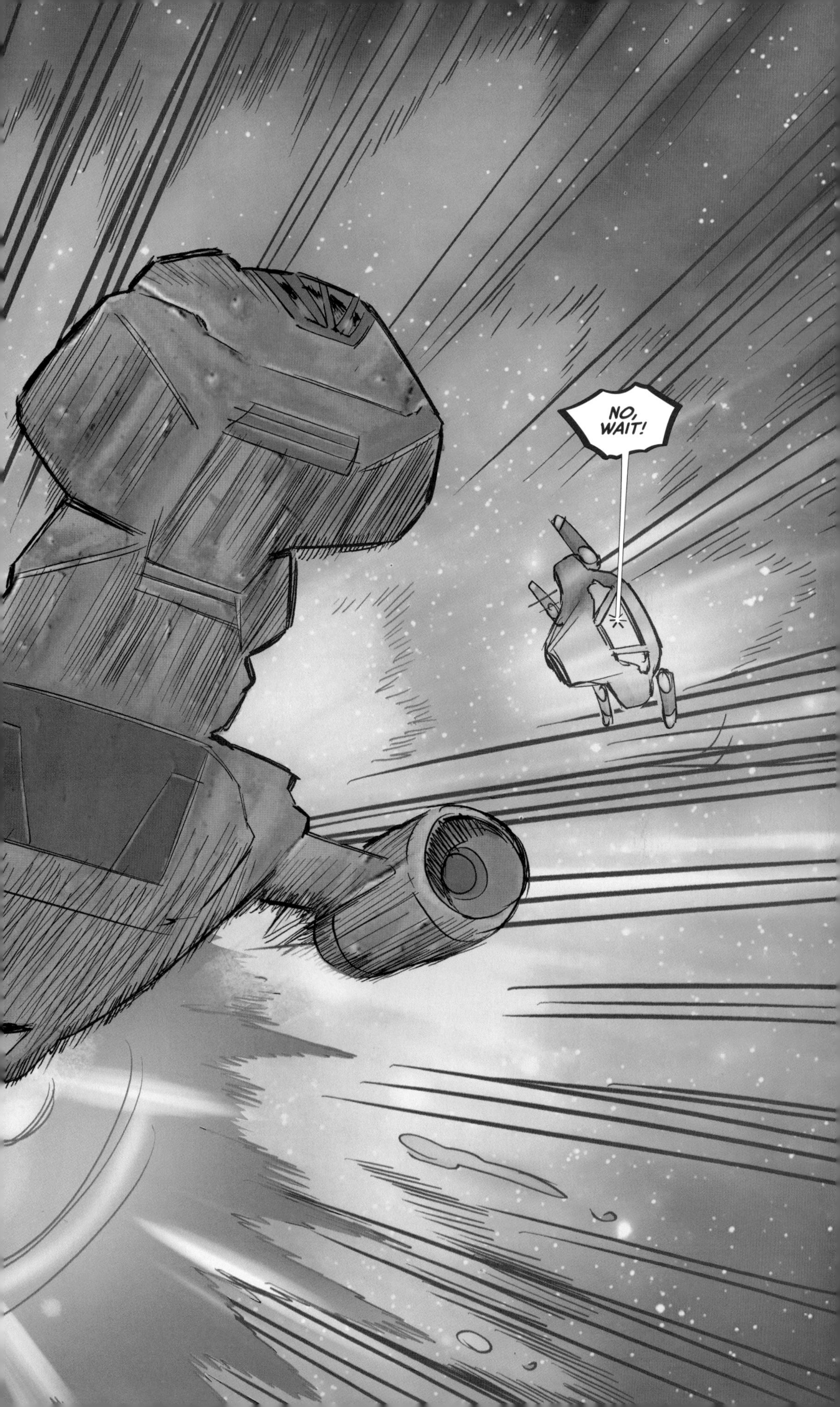
NO, WAIT!

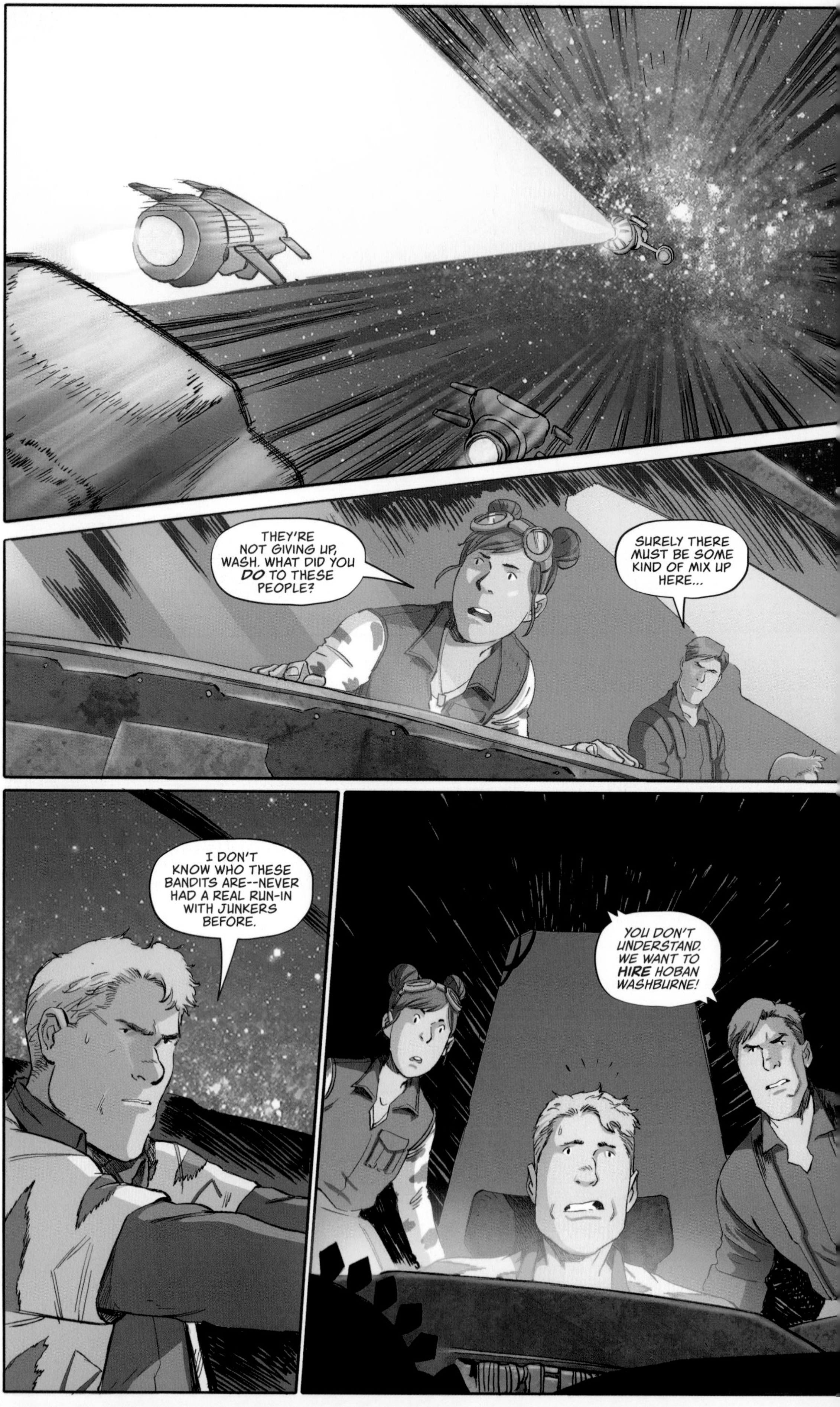
THEY'RE NOT GIVING UP, WASH. WHAT DID YOU DO TO THESE PEOPLE?
SURELY THERE MUST BE SOME KIND OF MIX UP HERE...
I DON'T KNOW WHO THESE BANDITS ARE--NEVER HAD A REAL RUN-IN WITH JUNKERS BEFORE.
YOU DON'T UNDERSTAND. WE WANT TO HIRE HOBAN WASHBURNE!

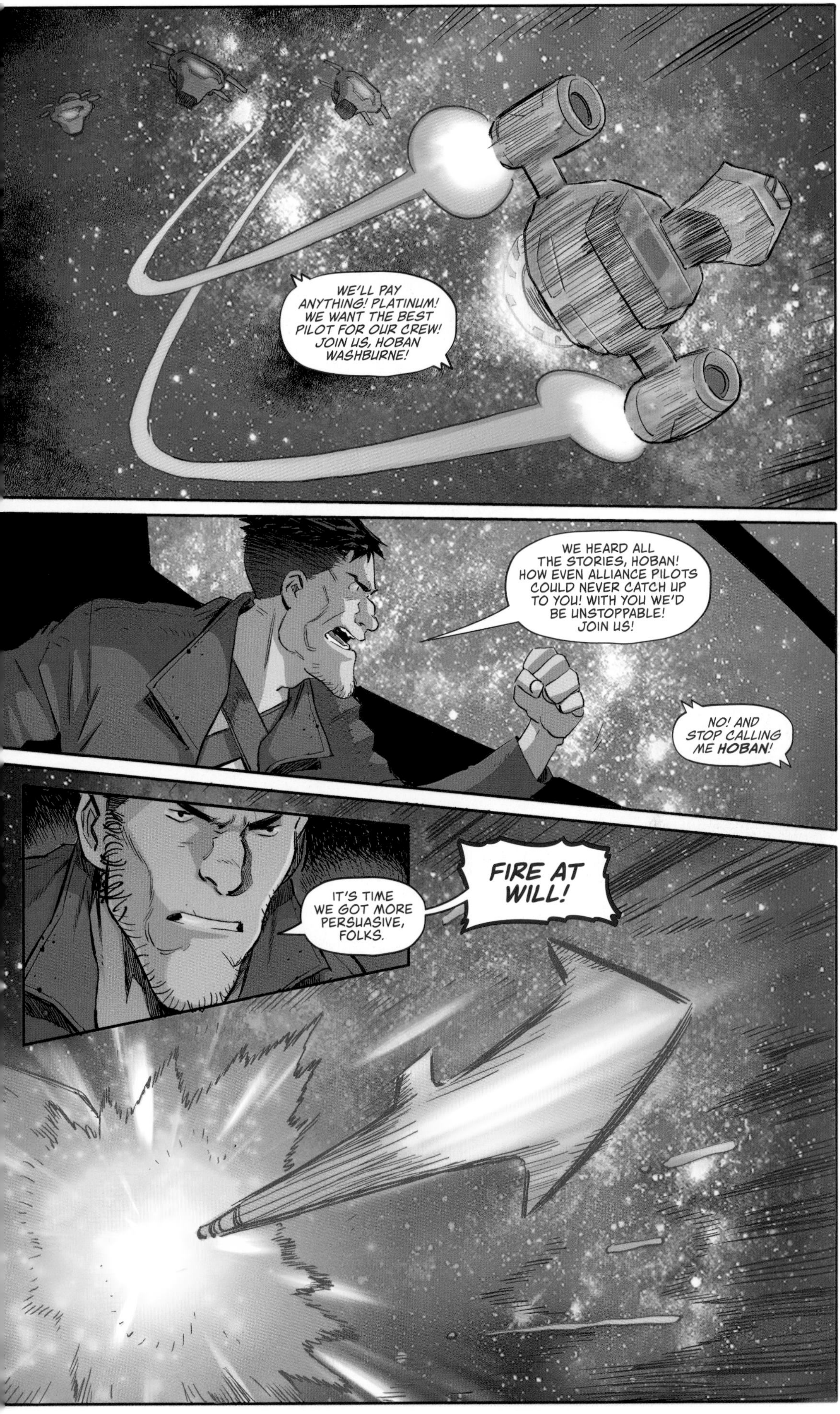
WE'LL PAY ANYTHING! PLATINUM! WE WANT THE BEST PILOT FOR OUR CREW! JOIN US, HOBAN WASHBURNE!
WE HEARD ALL THE STORIES, HOBAN! HOW EVEN ALLIANCE PILOTS COULD NEVER CATCH UP TO YOU! WITH YOU WE'D BE UNSTOPPABLE! JOIN US!
NO! AND STOP CALLING ME **HOBAN**!
IT'S TIME WE GOT MORE PERSUASIVE, FOLKS.
FIRE AT WILL!

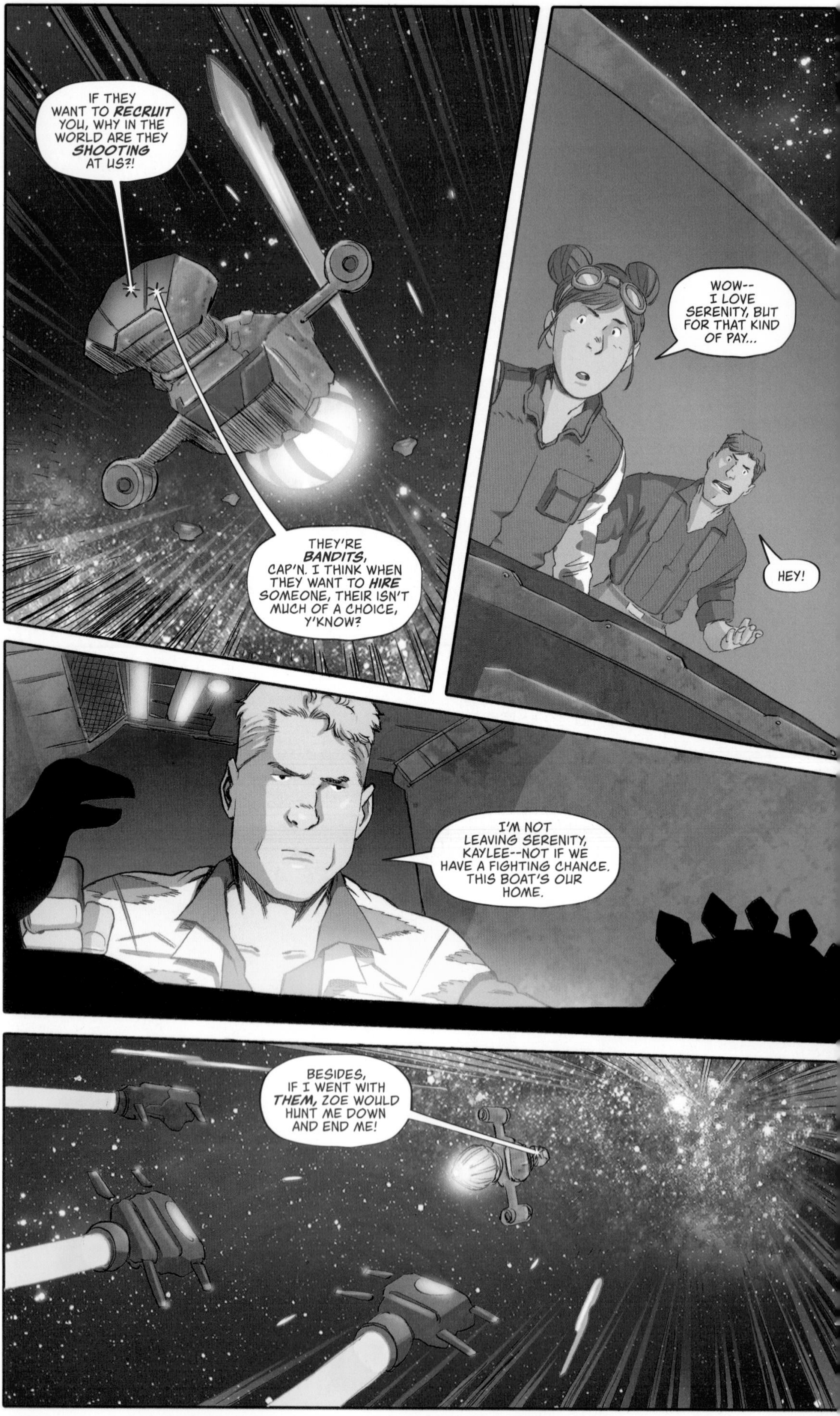
IF THEY WANT TO RECRUIT YOU, WHY IN THE WORLD ARE THEY SHOOTING AT US?!
THEY'RE BANDITS, CAP'N. I THINK WHEN THEY WANT TO HIRE SOMEONE, THEIR ISN'T MUCH OF A CHOICE, Y'KNOW?
WOW-- I LOVE SERENITY, BUT FOR THAT KIND OF PAY...
HEY!
I'M NOT LEAVING SERENITY, KAYLEE--NOT IF WE HAVE A FIGHTING CHANCE. THIS BOAT'S OUR HOME.
BESIDES, IF I WENT WITH THEM, ZOE WOULD HUNT ME DOWN AND END ME!

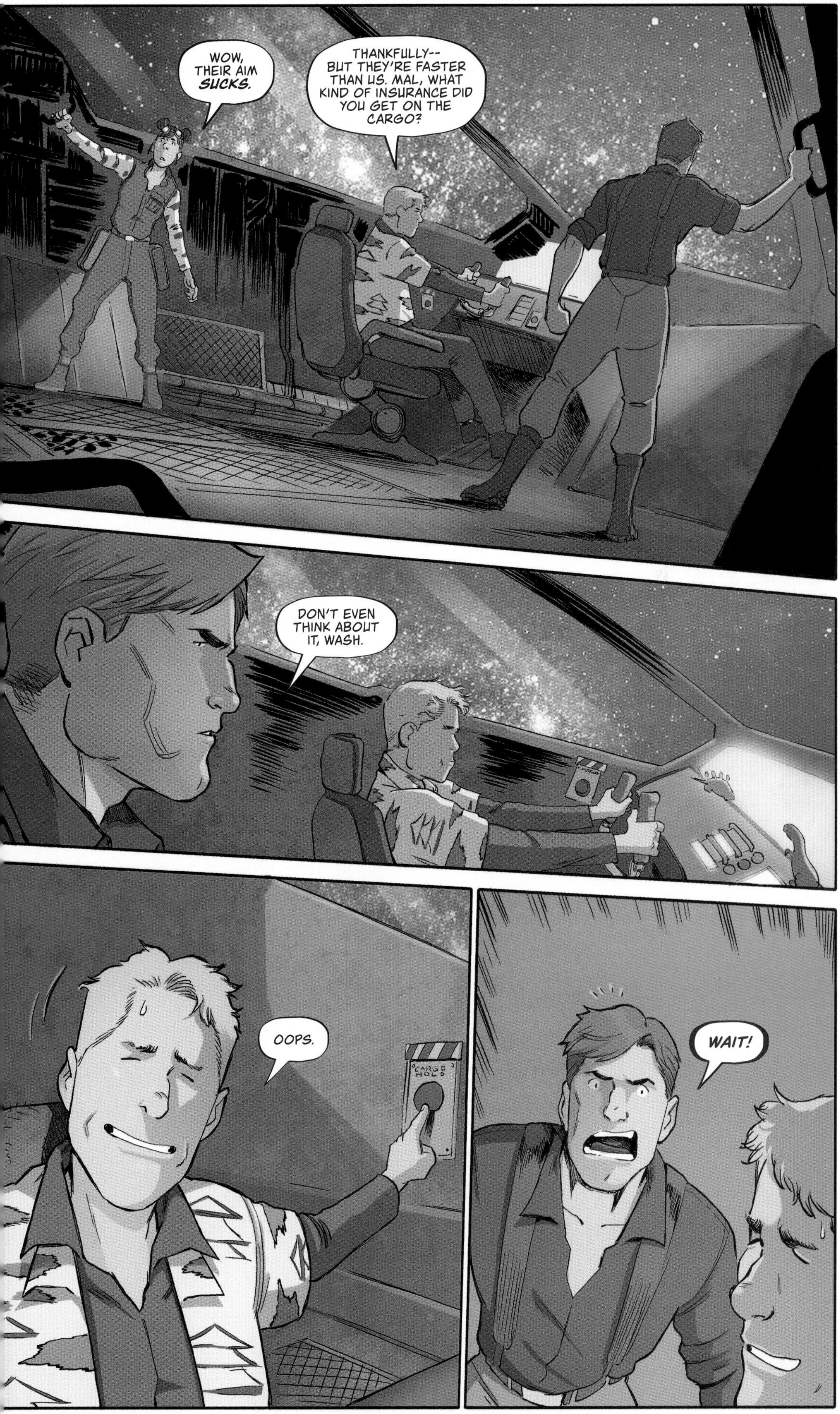
WOW, THEIR AIM SUCKS.
THANKFULLY-- BUT THEY'RE FASTER THAN US. MAL, WHAT KIND OF INSURANCE DID YOU GET ON THE CARGO?
DON'T EVEN THINK ABOUT IT, WASH.
OOPS.
WAIT!

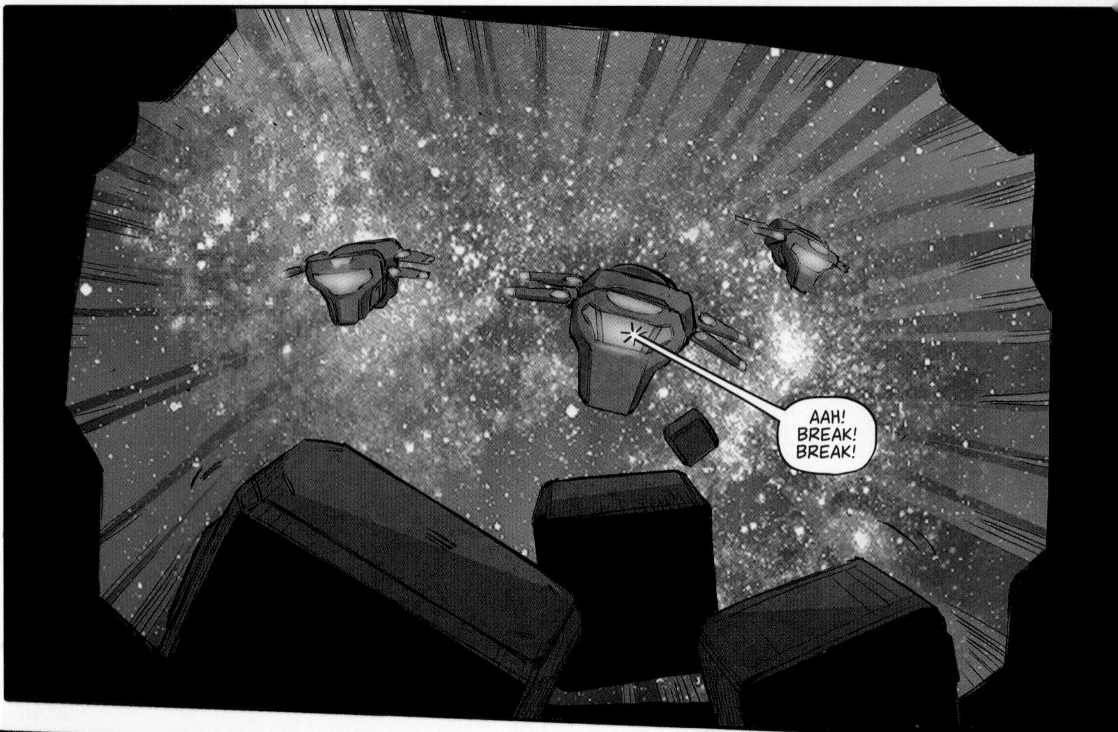
AAH! BREAK! BREAK!

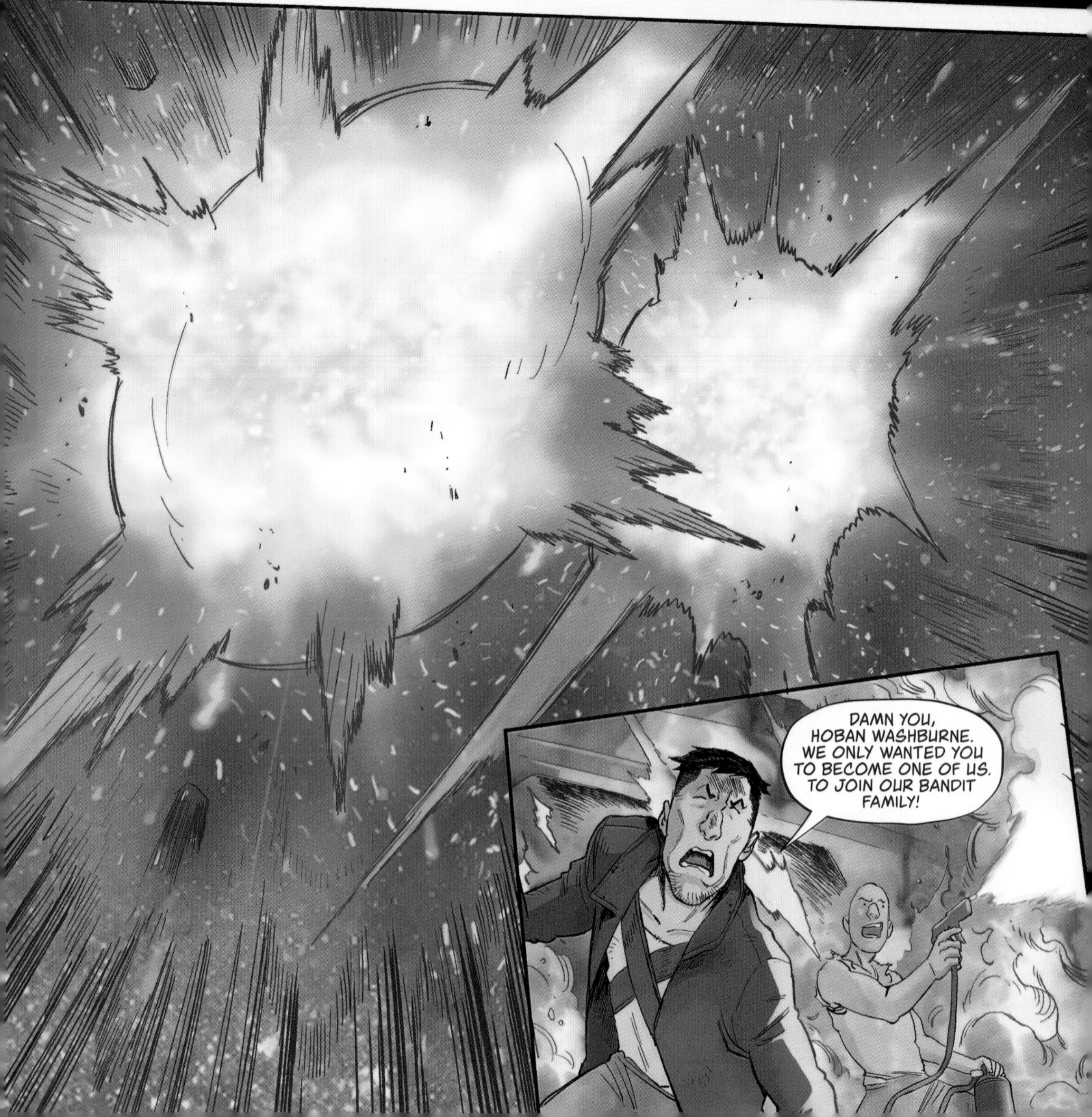
DAMN YOU, HOBAN WASHBURNE. WE ONLY WANTED YOU TO BECOME ONE OF US. TO JOIN OUR BANDIT FAMILY!

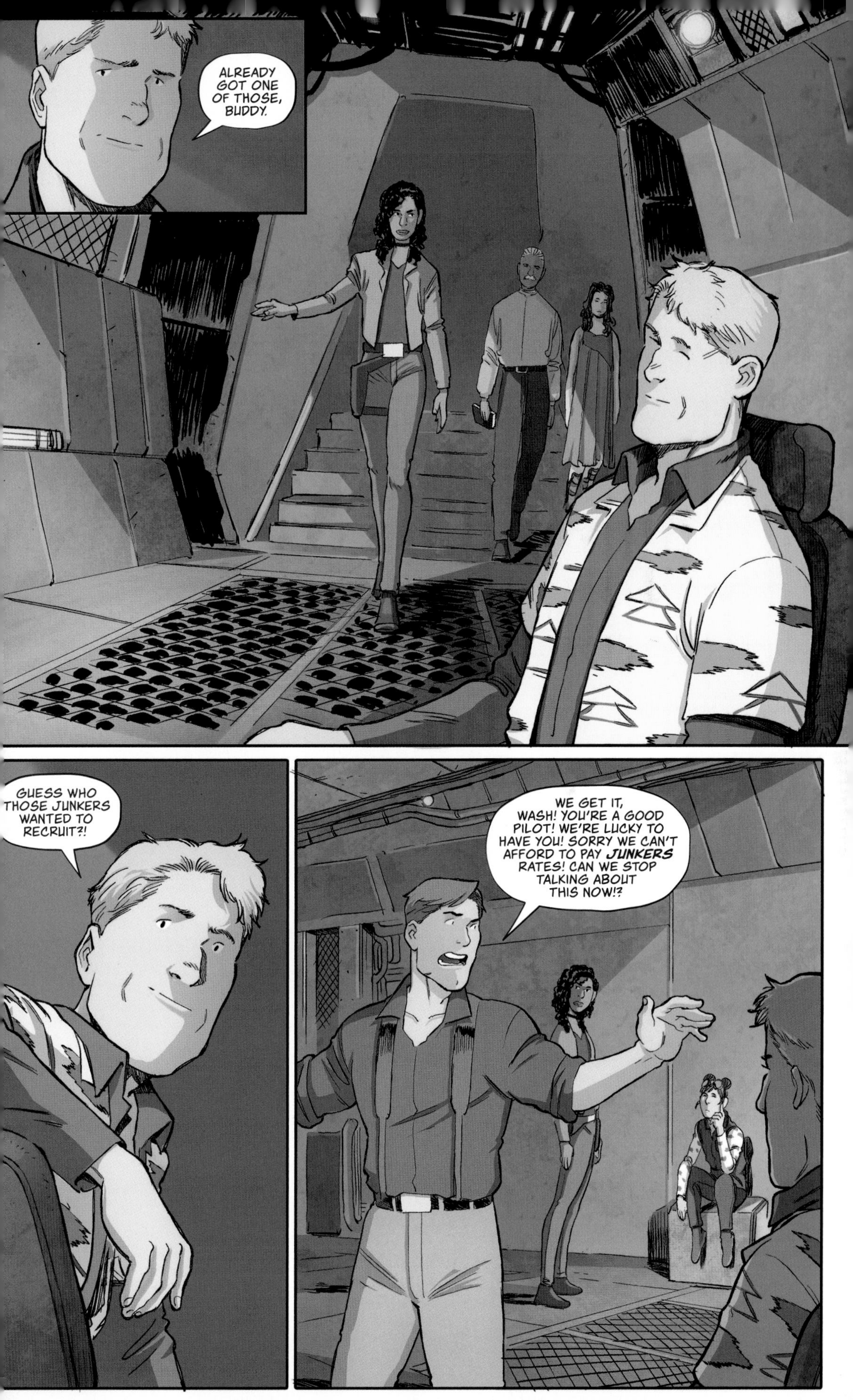
ALREADY GOT ONE OF THOSE, BUDDY.
GUESS WHO THOSE JUNKERS WANTED TO RECRUIT?!
WE GET IT, WASH! YOU'RE A GOOD PILOT! WE'RE LUCKY TO HAVE YOU! SORRY WE CAN'T AFFORD TO PAY JUNKERS RATES! CAN WE STOP TALKING ABOUT THIS NOW!?

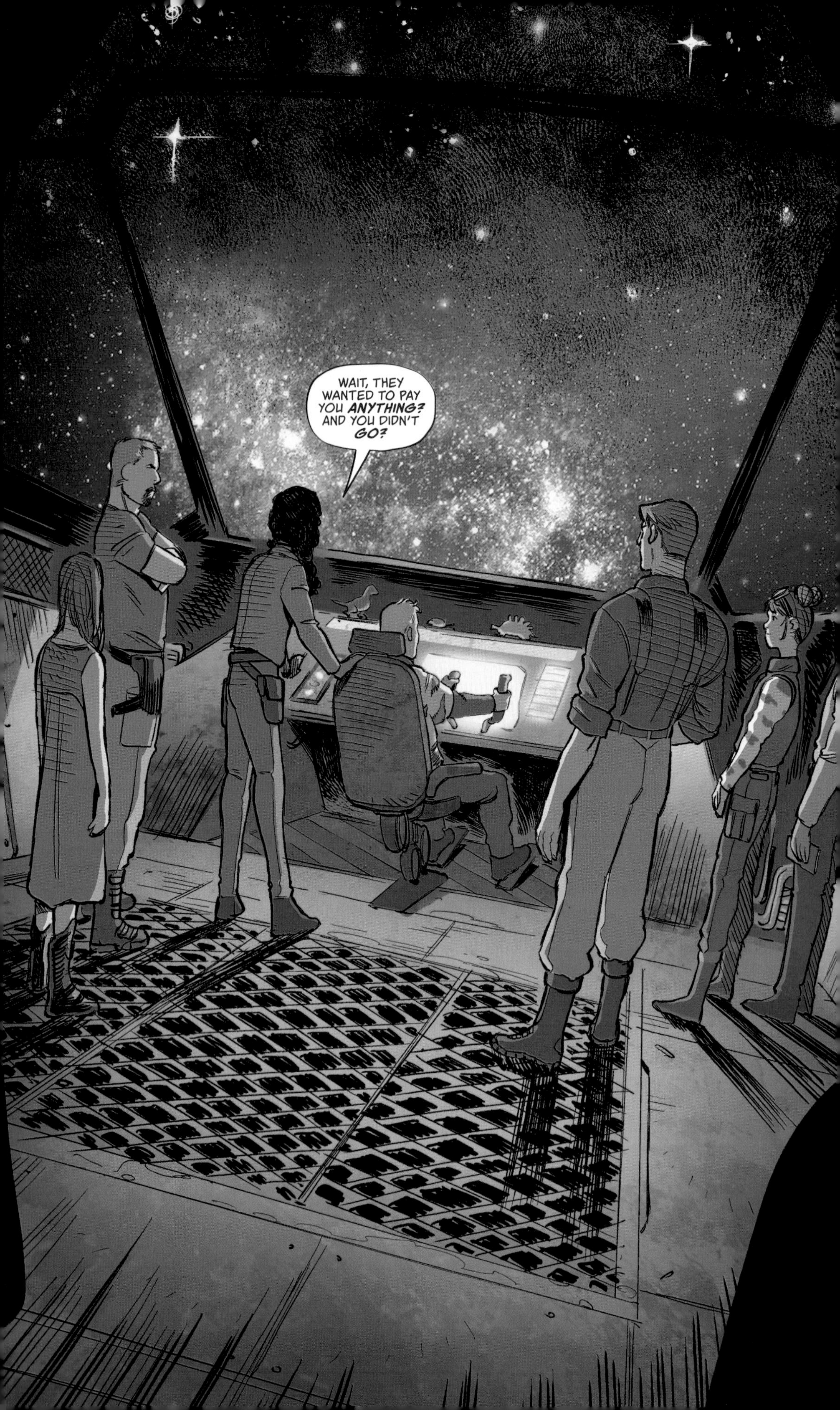
WAIT, THEY WANTED TO PAY YOU ANYTHING? AND YOU DIDN'T GO?

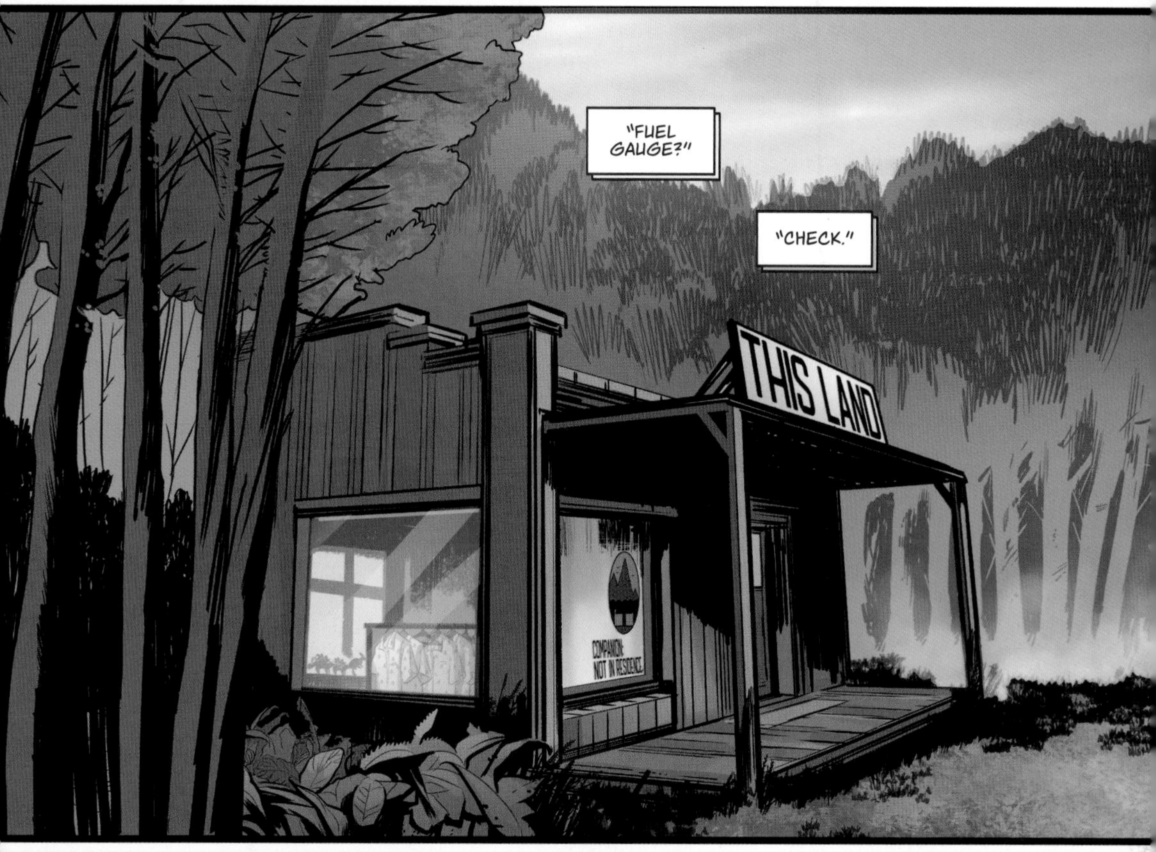
"FUEL GAUGE?"
"CHECK."
THIS LAND
COMPANION: NOT IN RESIDENCE

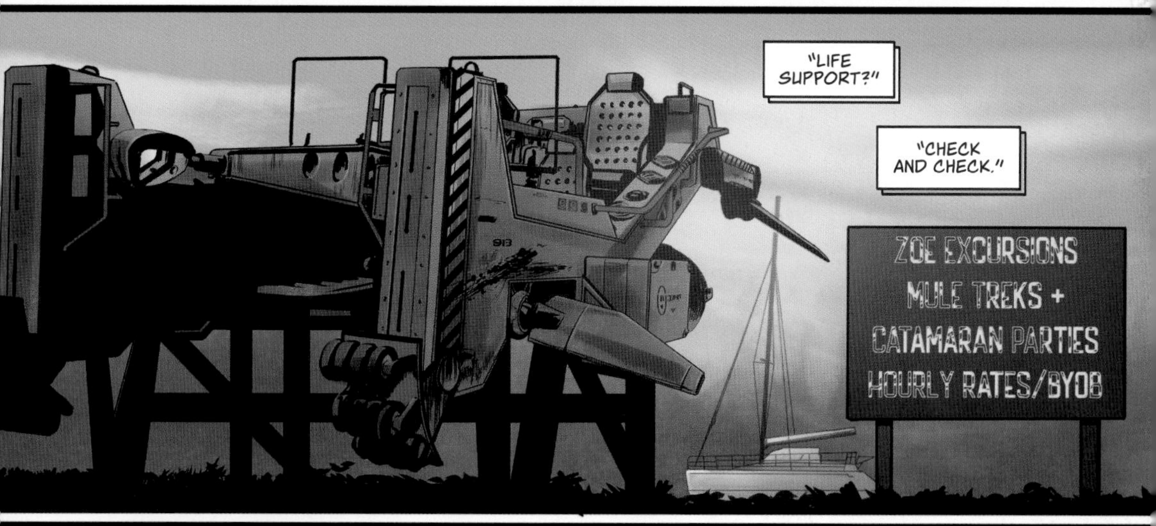
"LIFE SUPPORT?"
"CHECK AND CHECK."
ZOE EXCURSIONS
MULE TREKS +
CATAMARAN PARTIES
HOURLY RATES/BYOB

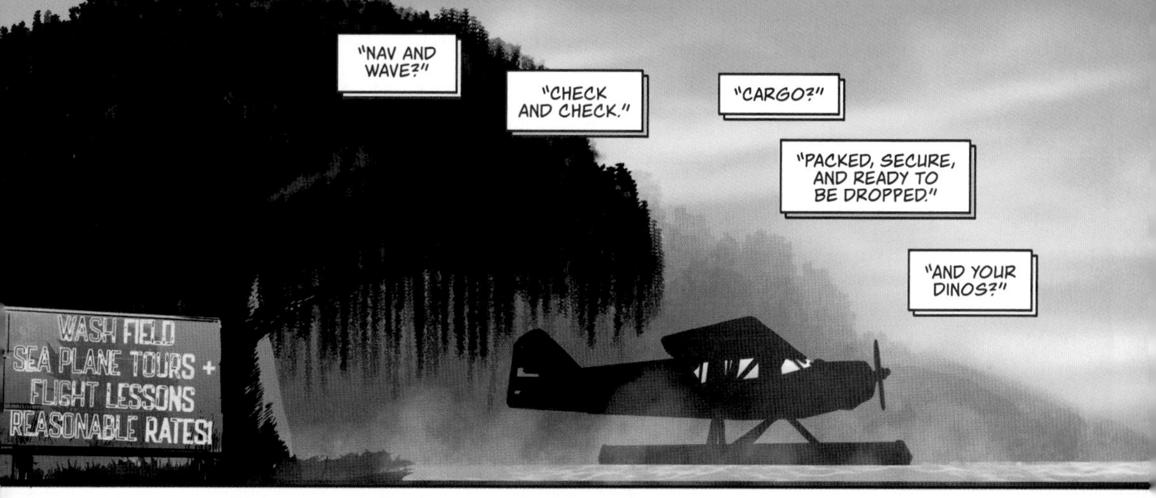
"NAV AND WAVE?"
"CHECK AND CHECK."
"CARGO?"
"PACKED, SECURE, AND READY TO BE DROPPED."
"AND YOUR DINOS?"
WASH FIELD
SEA PLANE TOURS +
FLIGHT LESSONS
REASONABLE RATES!

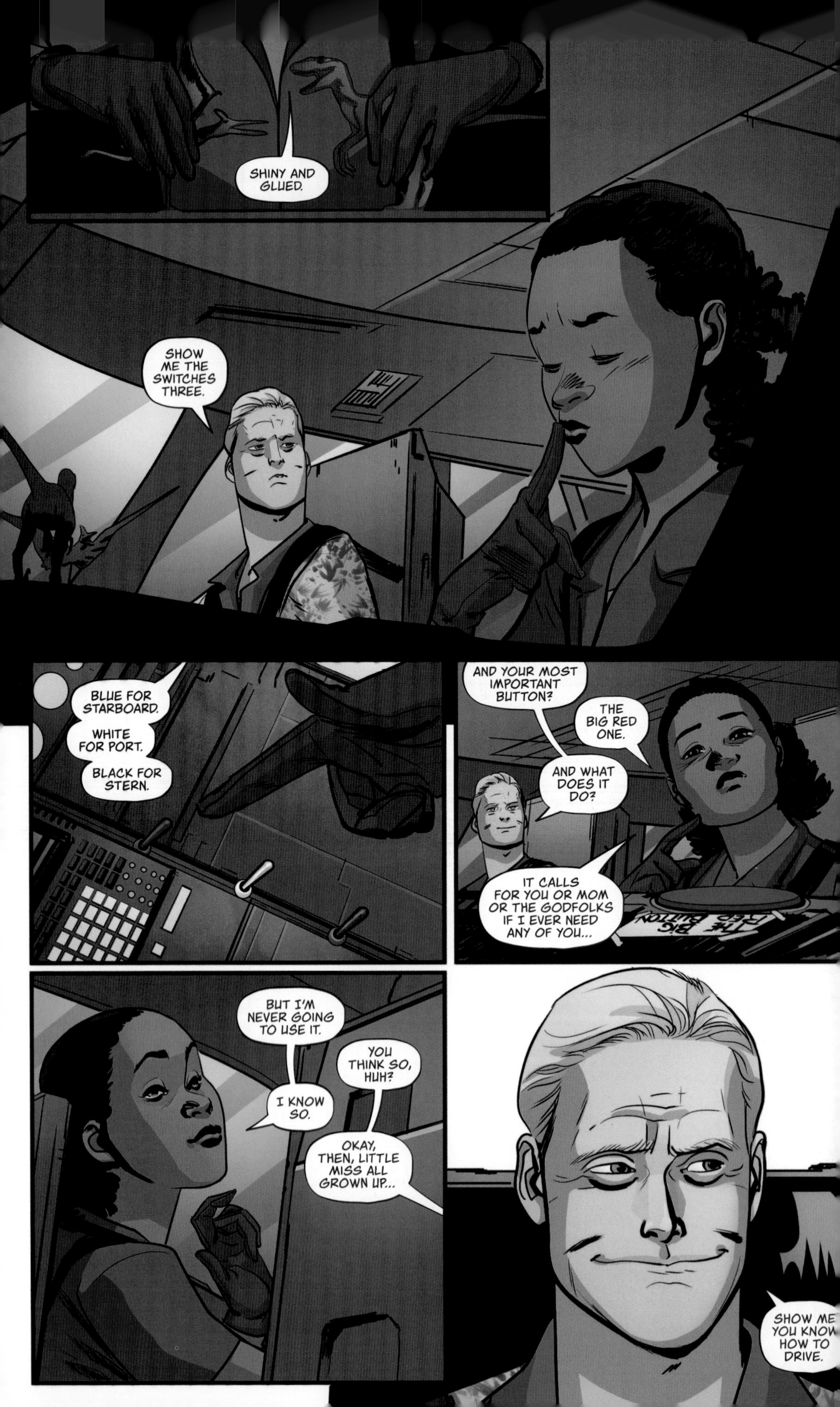
SHINY AND GLUED.
SHOW ME THE SWITCHES THREE.
BLUE FOR STARBOARD.
WHITE FOR PORT.
BLACK FOR STERN.
AND YOUR MOST IMPORTANT BUTTON?
THE BIG RED ONE.
AND WHAT DOES IT DO?
IT CALLS FOR YOU OR MOM OR THE GODFOLKS IF I EVER NEED ANY OF YOU...
THE BIG RED BUTTON
BUT I'M NEVER GOING TO USE IT.
YOU THINK SO, HUH?
I KNOW SO.
OKAY, THEN, LITTLE MISS ALL GROWN UP...
SHOW ME YOU KNOW HOW TO DRIVE.

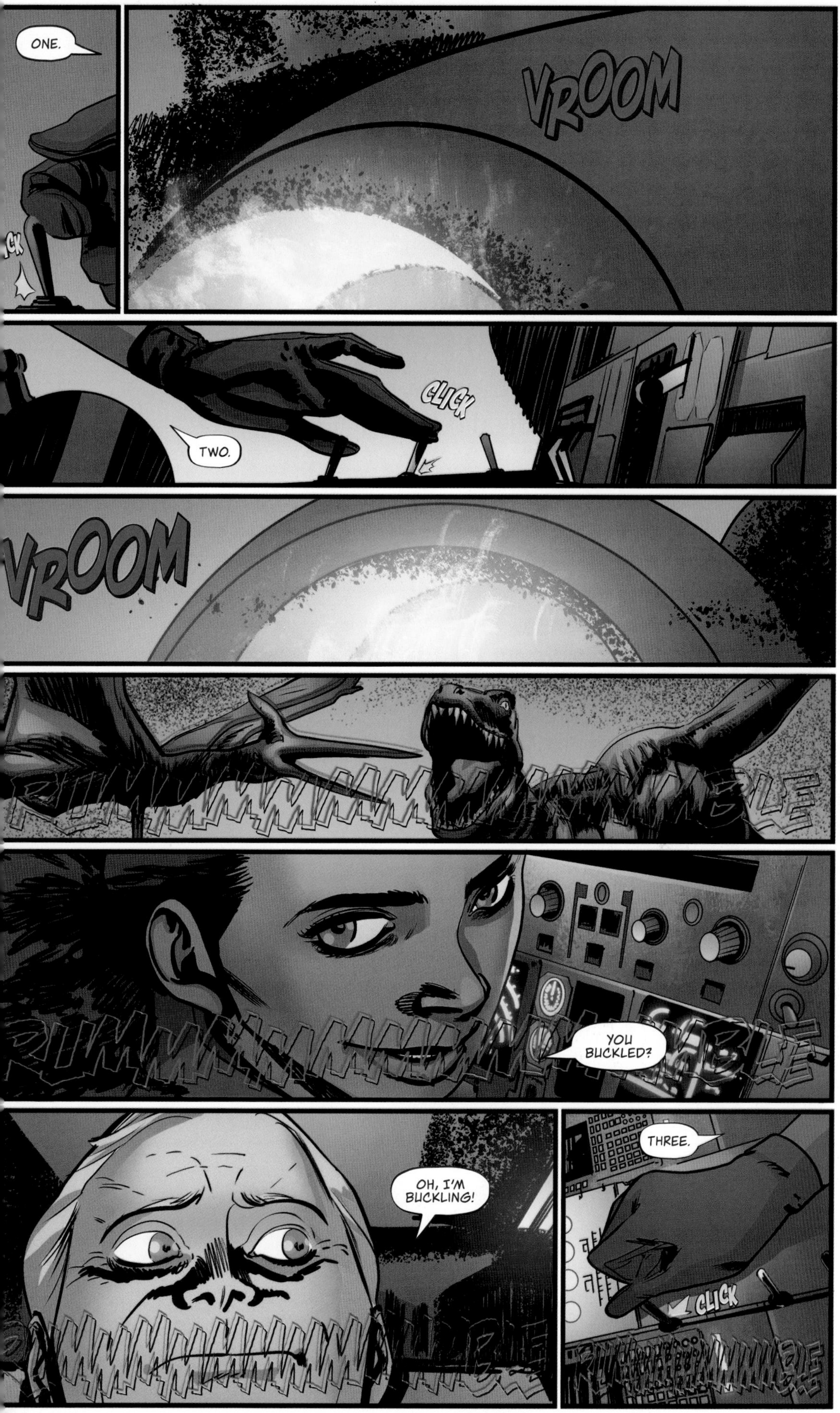
ONE.
VROOM
CLICK
TWO.
VROOM
YOU BUCKLED?
OH, I'M BUCKLING!
THREE.
CLICK

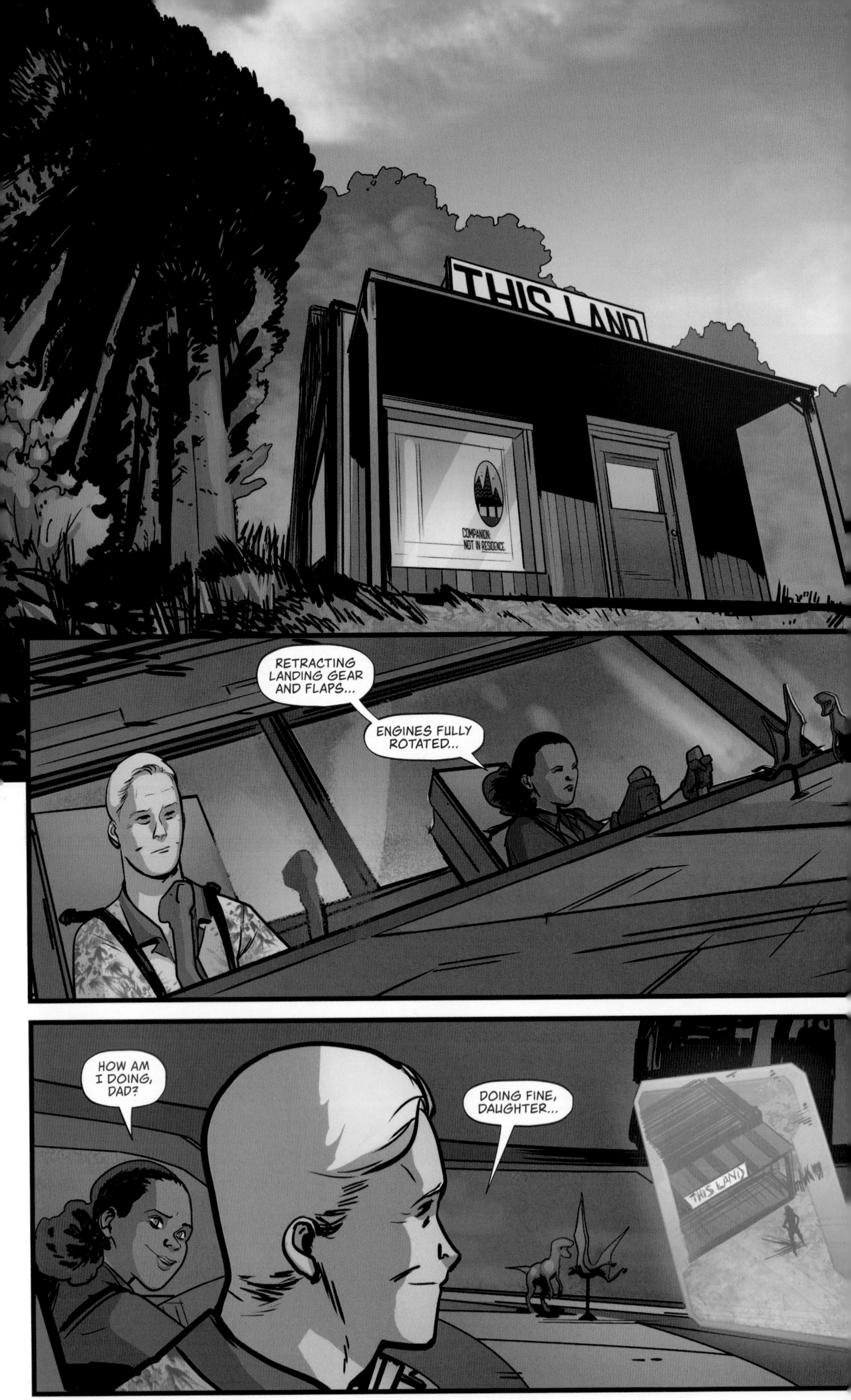
THIS LAND
COMPANION: NOT IN RESIDENCE
RETRACTING LANDING GEAR AND FLAPS...
ENGINES FULLY ROTATED...
HOW AM I DOING, DAD?
DOING FINE, DAUGHTER...
THIS LAND

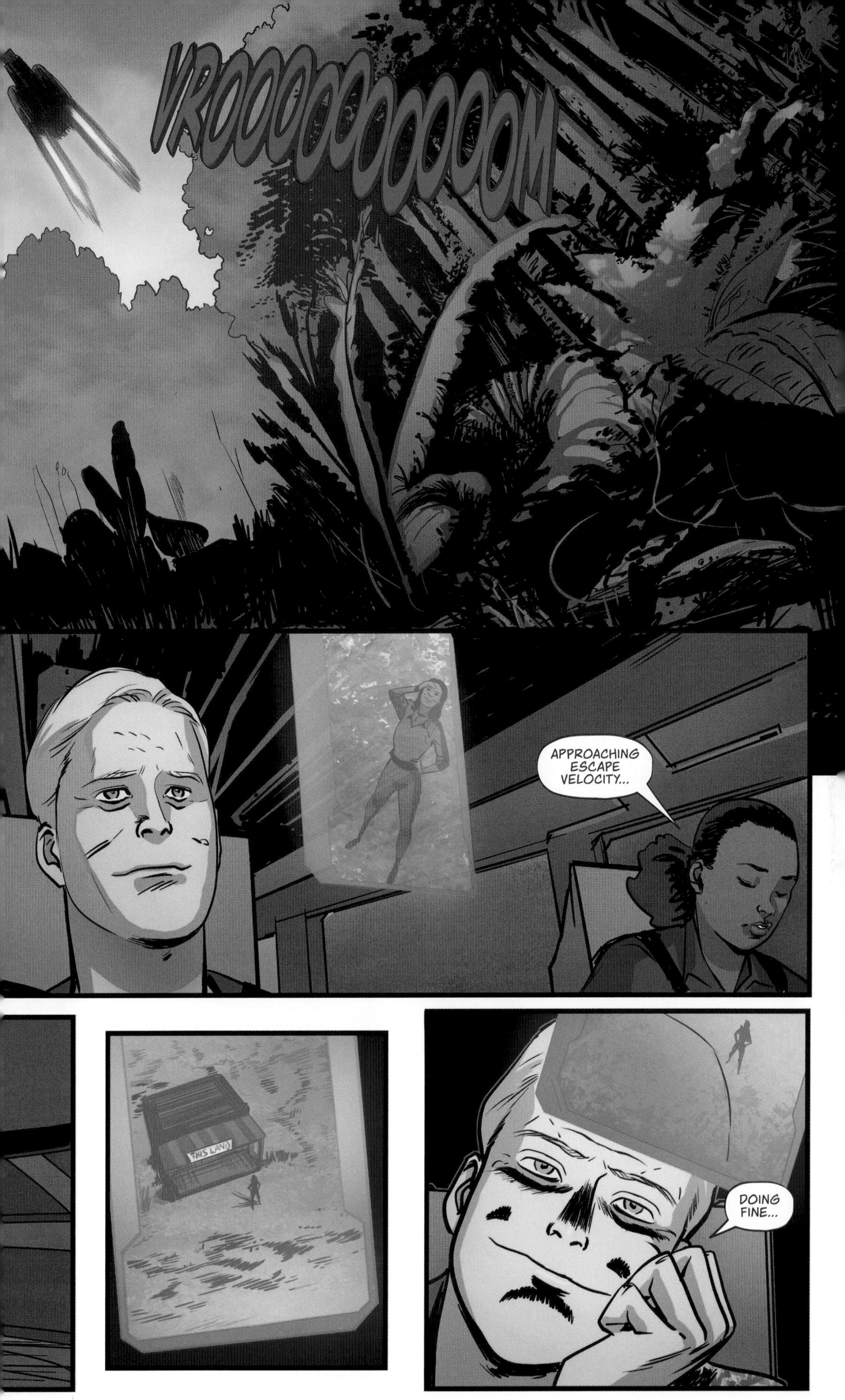
VROOOOOOOOOOM
APPROACHING ESCAPE VELOCITY...
THIS LAND
DOING FINE...

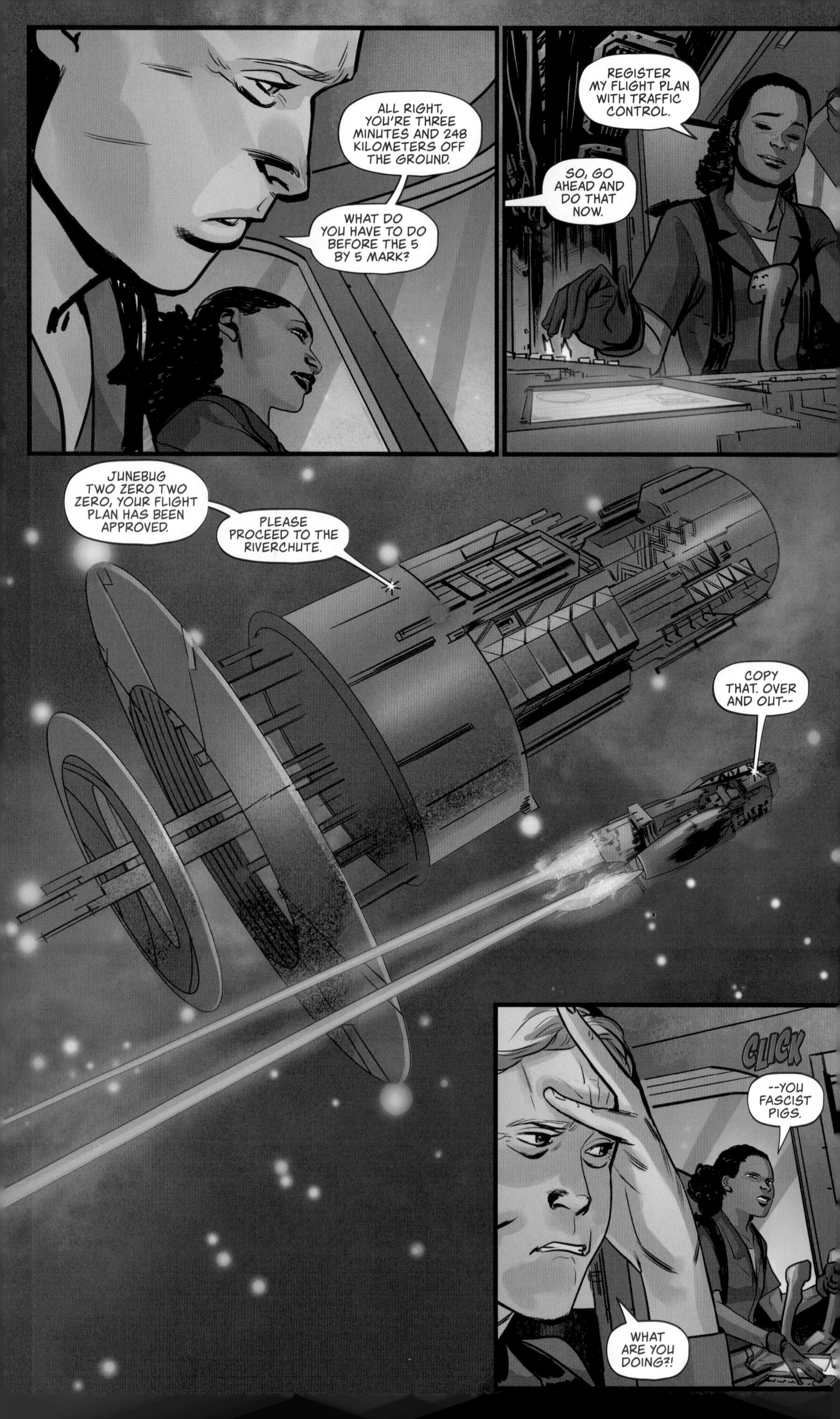
ALL RIGHT, YOU'RE THREE MINUTES AND 248 KILOMETERS OFF THE GROUND.
WHAT DO YOU HAVE TO DO BEFORE THE 5 BY 5 MARK?
REGISTER MY FLIGHT PLAN WITH TRAFFIC CONTROL.
SO, GO AHEAD AND DO THAT NOW.
JUNEBUG TWO ZERO TWO ZERO, YOUR FLIGHT PLAN HAS BEEN APPROVED.
PLEASE PROCEED TO THE RIVERCHUTE.
COPY THAT. OVER AND OUT--
CLICK
--YOU FASCIST PIGS.
WHAT ARE YOU DOING?!

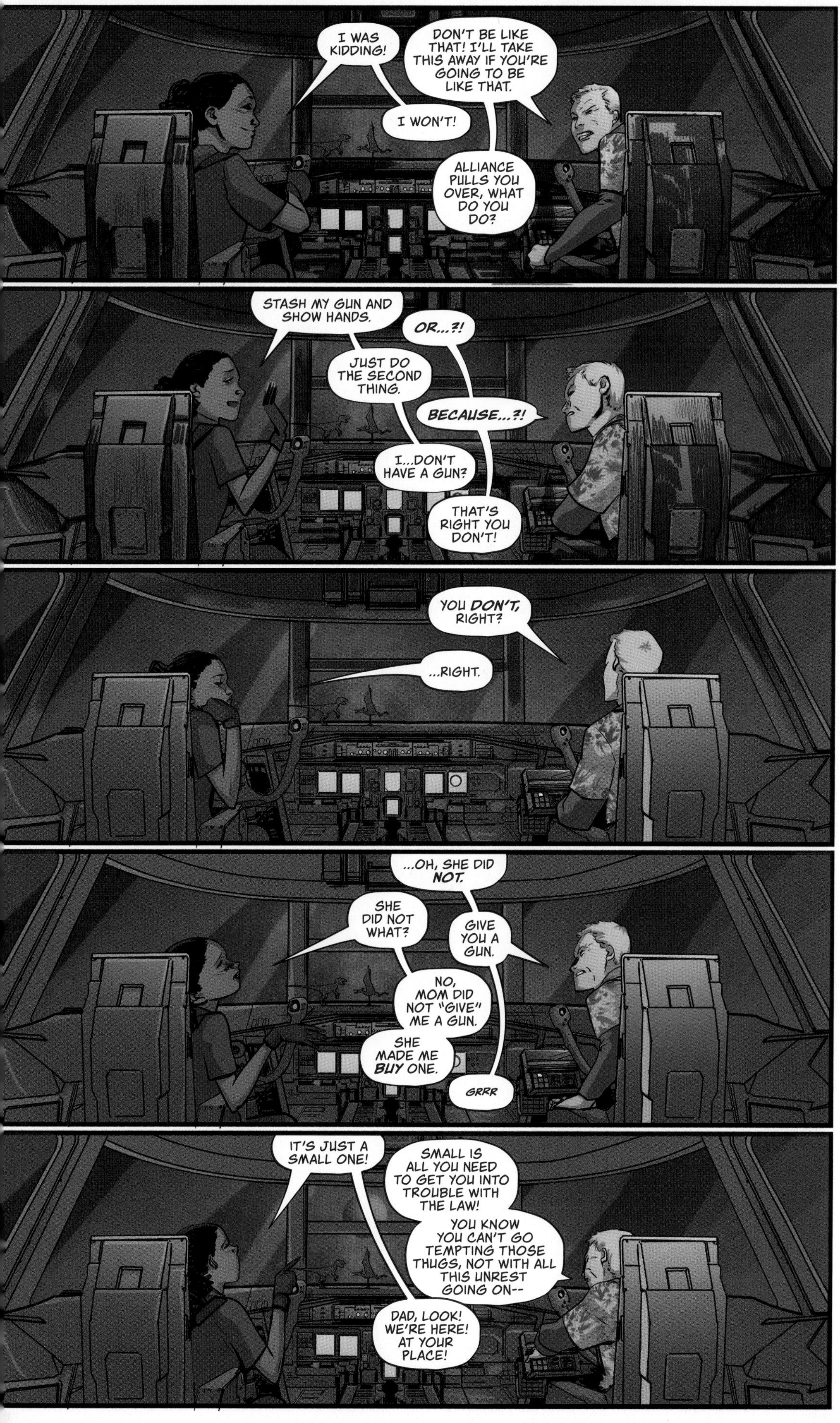

I WAS KIDDING!
DON'T BE LIKE THAT! I'LL TAKE THIS AWAY IF YOU'RE GOING TO BE LIKE THAT.
I WON'T!
ALLIANCE PULLS YOU OVER, WHAT DO YOU DO?
STASH MY GUN AND SHOW HANDS.
OR...?!
JUST DO THE SECOND THING.
BECAUSE...?!
I...DON'T HAVE A GUN?
THAT'S RIGHT YOU DON'T!
YOU DON'T, RIGHT?
...RIGHT.
...OH, SHE DID NOT.
SHE DID NOT WHAT?
GIVE YOU A GUN.
NO, MOM DID NOT "GIVE" ME A GUN.
SHE MADE ME BUY ONE.
GRRR
IT'S JUST A SMALL ONE!
SMALL IS ALL YOU NEED TO GET YOU INTO TROUBLE WITH THE LAW!
YOU KNOW YOU CAN'T GO TEMPTING THOSE THUGS, NOT WITH ALL THIS UNREST GOING ON--
DAD, LOOK! WE'RE HERE! AT YOUR PLACE!

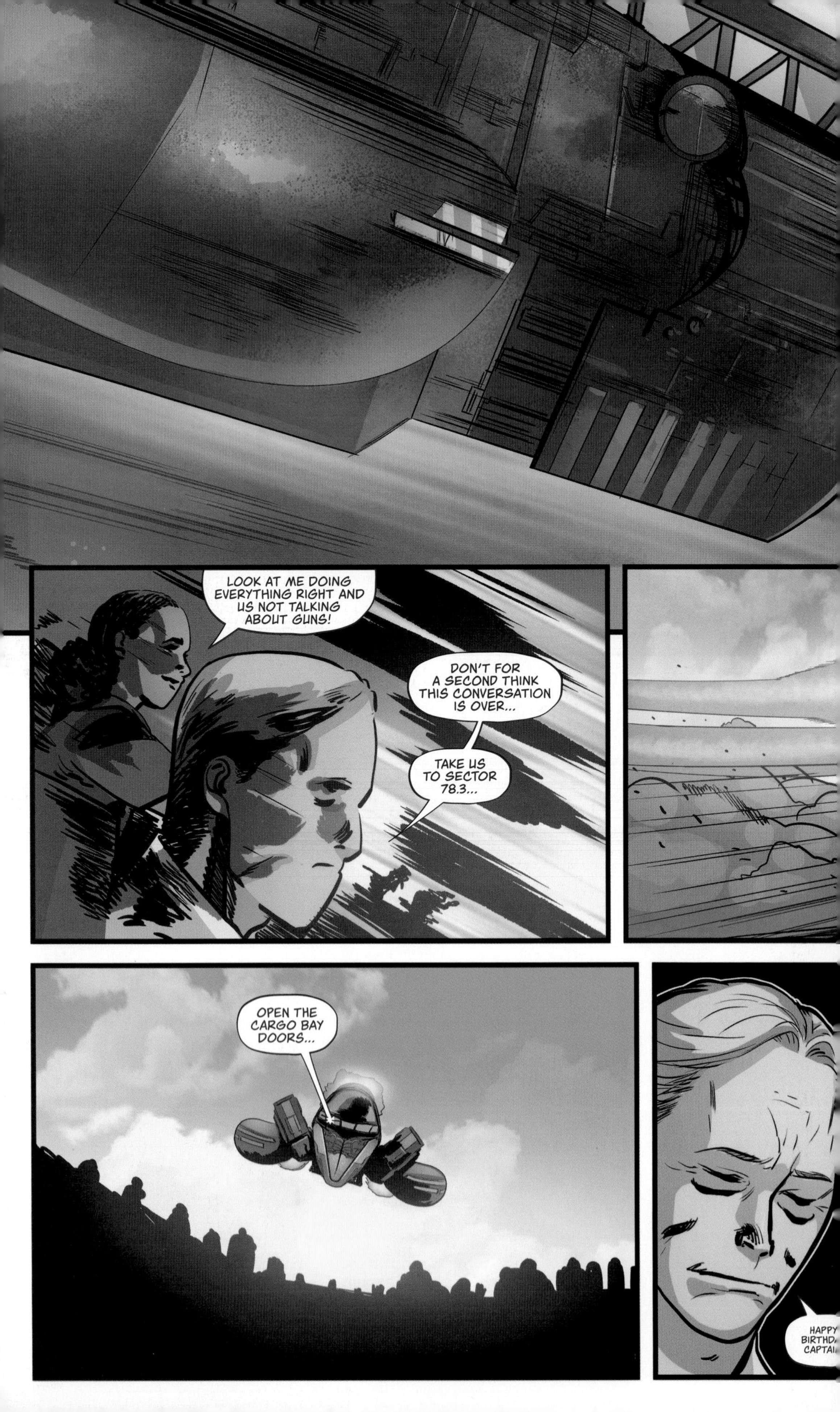
LOOK AT ME DOING EVERYTHING RIGHT AND US NOT TALKING ABOUT GUNS!
DON'T FOR A SECOND THINK THIS CONVERSATION IS OVER...
TAKE US TO SECTOR 78.3...
OPEN THE CARGO BAY DOORS...
HAPPY

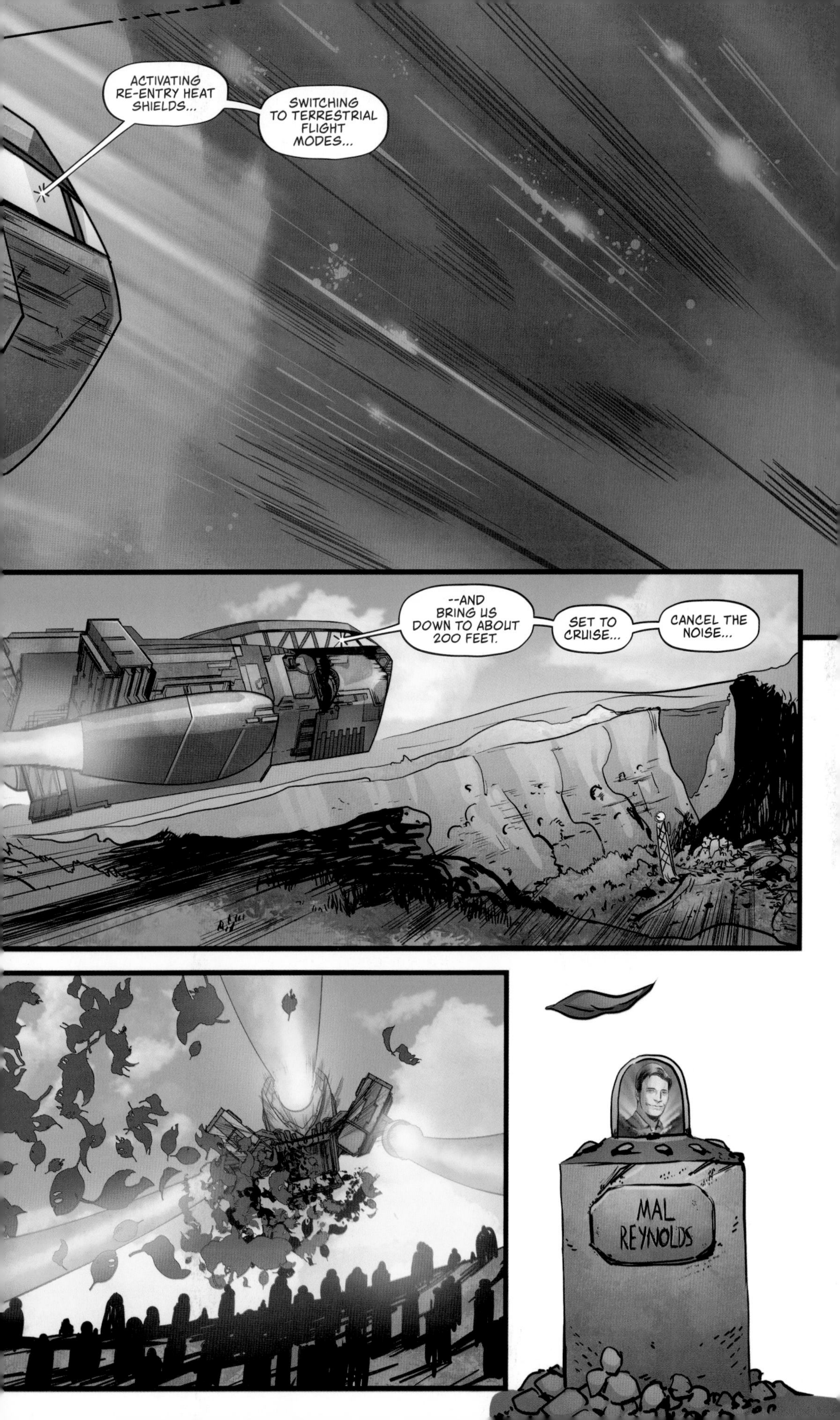
ACTIVATING RE-ENTRY HEAT SHIELDS...
SWITCHING TO TERRESTRIAL FLIGHT MODES...
--AND BRING US DOWN TO ABOUT 200 FEET.
SET TO CRUISE...
CANCEL THE NOISE...
MAL REYNOLDS

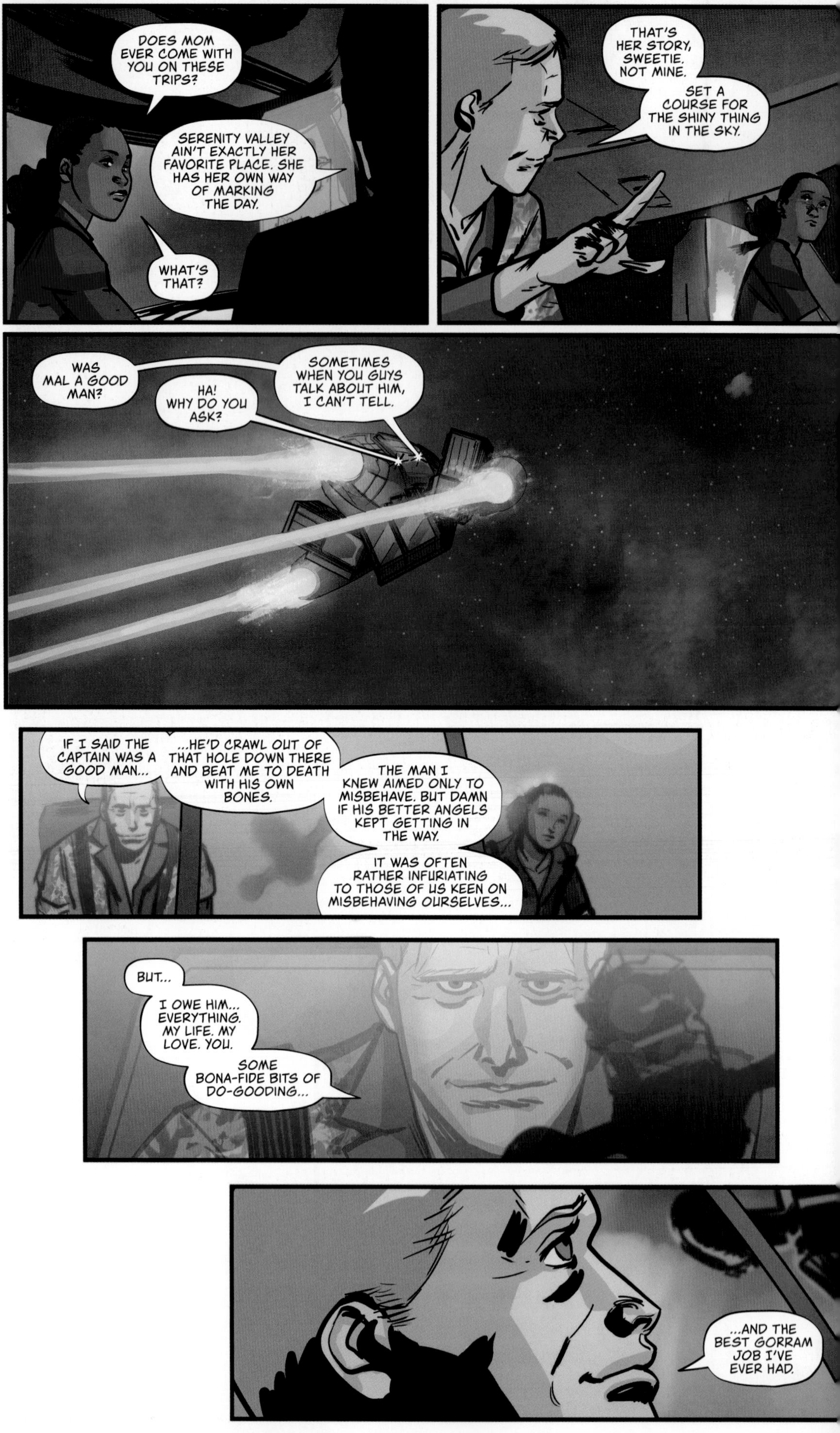
DOES MOM EVER COME WITH YOU ON THESE TRIPS?
SERENITY VALLEY AIN'T EXACTLY HER FAVORITE PLACE. SHE HAS HER OWN WAY OF MARKING THE DAY.
WHAT'S THAT?
THAT'S HER STORY, SWEETIE. NOT MINE.
SET A COURSE FOR THE SHINY THING IN THE SKY.
WAS MAL A GOOD MAN?
SOMETIMES WHEN YOU GUYS TALK ABOUT HIM, I CAN'T TELL.
HA! WHY DO YOU ASK?
IF I SAID THE CAPTAIN WAS A GOOD MAN...
...HE'D CRAWL OUT OF THAT HOLE DOWN THERE AND BEAT ME TO DEATH WITH HIS OWN BONES.
THE MAN I KNEW AIMED ONLY TO MISBEHAVE. BUT DAMN IF HIS BETTER ANGELS KEPT GETTING IN THE WAY.
IT WAS OFTEN RATHER INFURIATING TO THOSE OF US KEEN ON MISBEHAVING OURSELVES...
BUT...
I OWE HIM... EVERYTHING. MY LIFE. MY LOVE. YOU.
SOME BONA-FIDE BITS OF DO-GOODING...
...AND THE BEST GORRAM JOB I'VE EVER HAD.

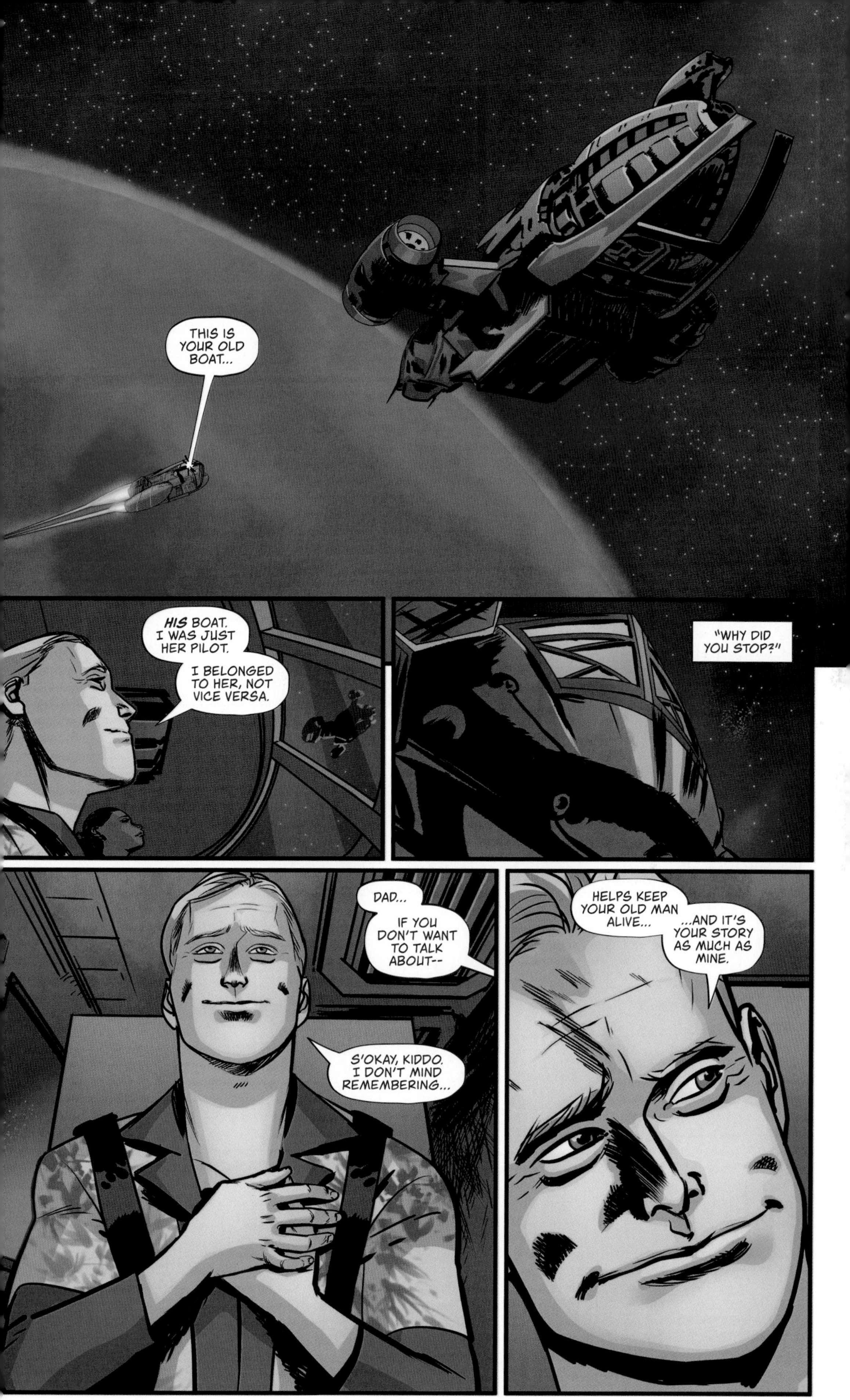
THIS IS YOUR OLD BOAT...
HIS BOAT. I WAS JUST HER PILOT.
I BELONGED TO HER, NOT VICE VERSA.
"WHY DID YOU STOP?"
DAD...
IF YOU DON'T WANT TO TALK ABOUT--
S'OKAY, KIDDO. I DON'T MIND REMEMBERING...
HELPS KEEP YOUR OLD MAN ALIVE...
...AND IT'S YOUR STORY AS MUCH AS MINE.

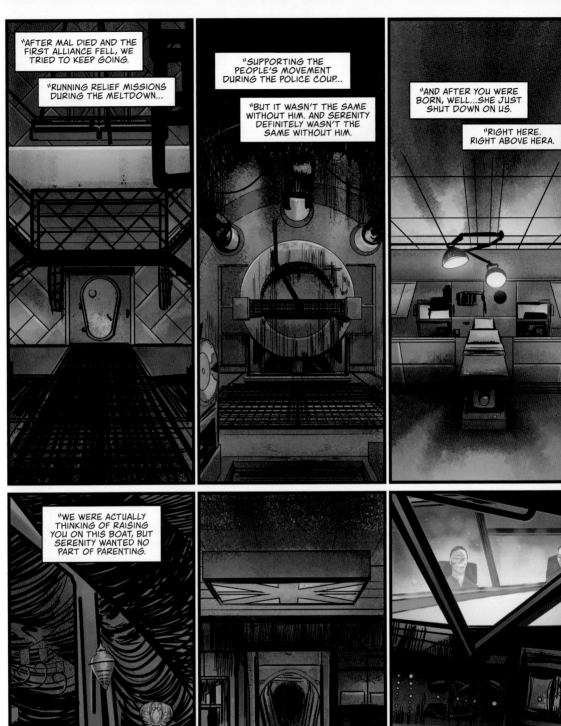

"AFTER MAL DIED AND THE FIRST ALLIANCE FELL, WE TRIED TO KEEP GOING.

"RUNNING RELIEF MISSIONS DURING THE MELTDOWN...

"SUPPORTING THE PEOPLE'S MOVEMENT DURING THE POLICE COUP...

"BUT IT WASN'T THE SAME WITHOUT HIM. AND SERENITY DEFINITELY WASN'T THE SAME WITHOUT HIM.

"AND AFTER YOU WERE BORN, WELL...SHE JUST SHUT DOWN ON US.

"RIGHT HERE. RIGHT ABOVE HERA.

"WE WERE ACTUALLY THINKING OF RAISING YOU ON THIS BOAT, BUT SERENITY WANTED NO PART OF PARENTING.

"SHE LOVED US. BUT SHE COULDN'T TAKE CARE OF US, NOT LIKE WE NEEDED TAKEN CARE OF...

"SERENITY'S WAY IS WILD, AND THE DOMESTIC LIFE AIN'T FOR HER."

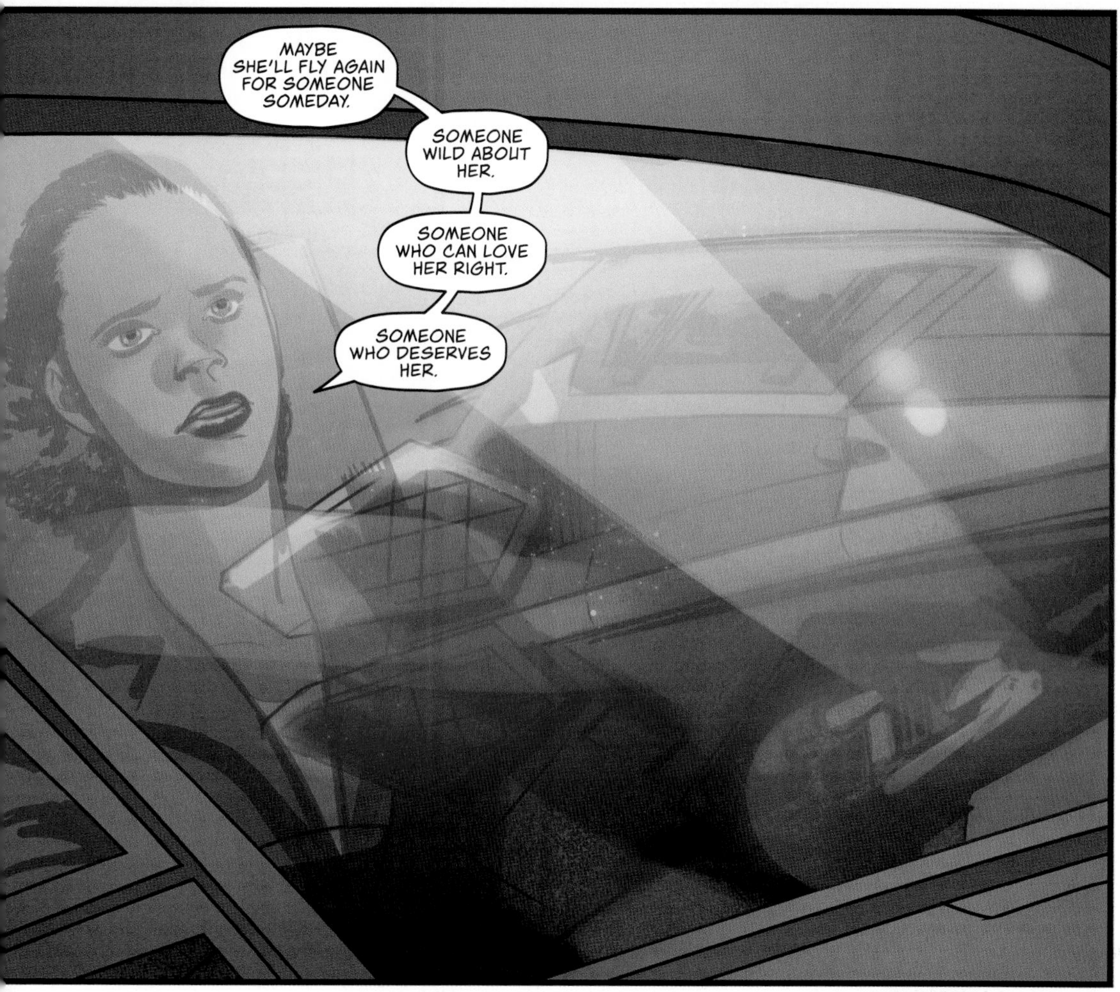
MAYBE SHE'LL FLY AGAIN FOR SOMEONE SOMEDAY.
SOMEONE WILD ABOUT HER.
SOMEONE WHO CAN LOVE HER RIGHT.
SOMEONE WHO DESERVES HER.

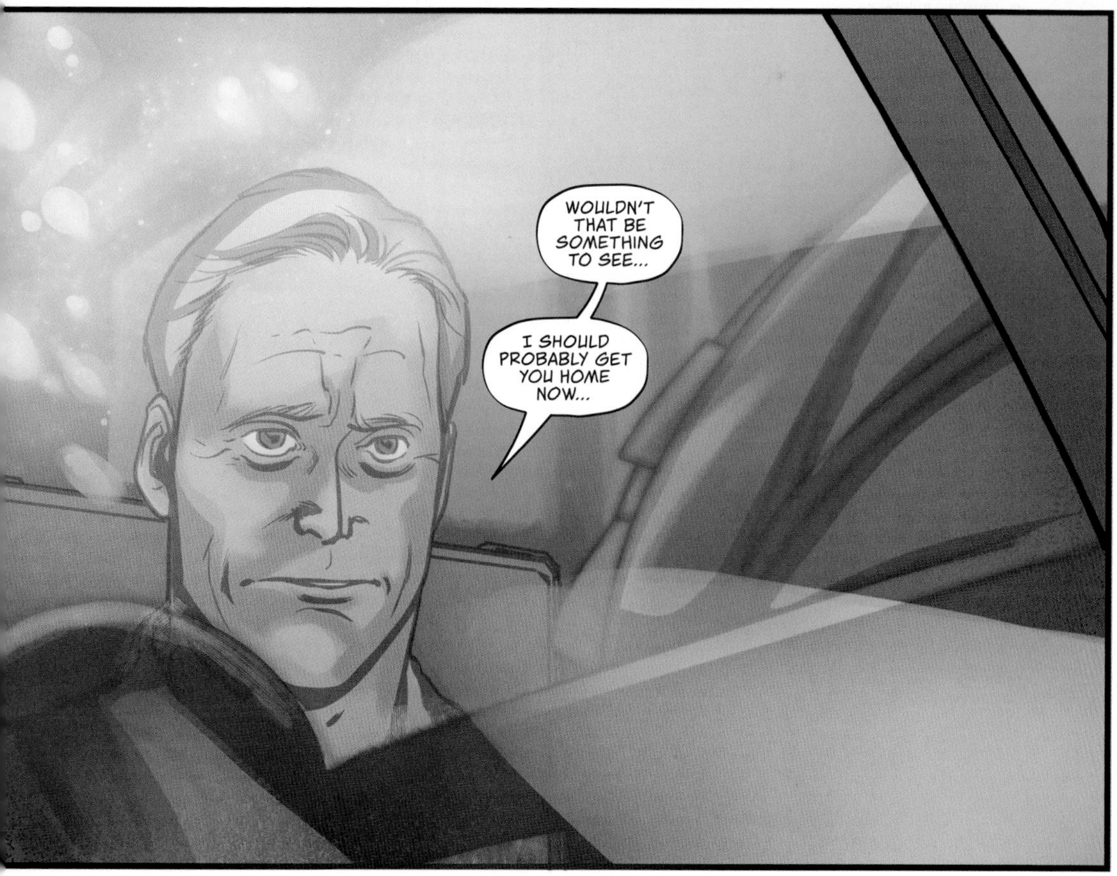
WOULDN'T THAT BE SOMETHING TO SEE...
I SHOULD PROBABLY GET YOU HOME NOW...

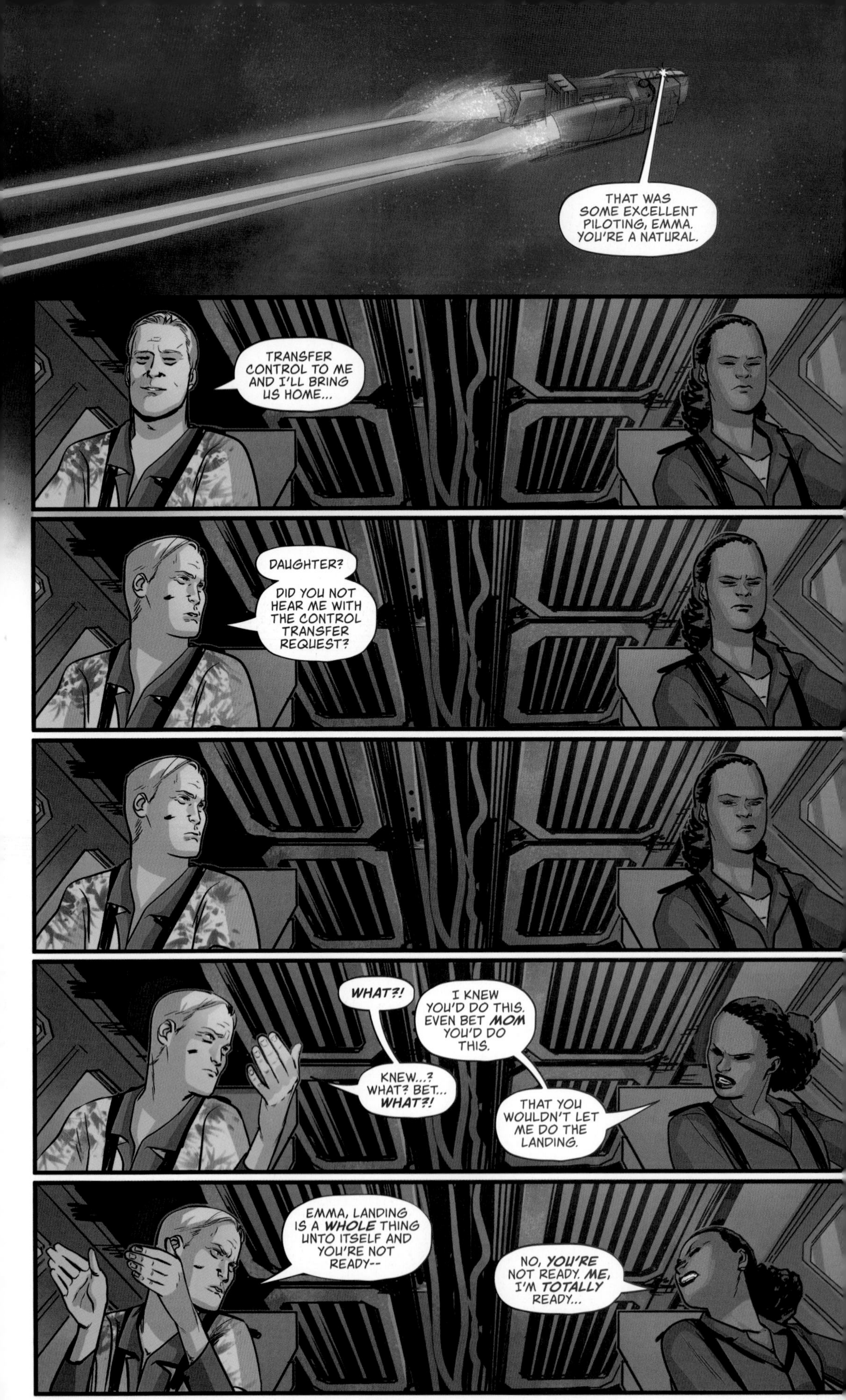
THAT WAS SOME EXCELLENT PILOTING, EMMA. YOU'RE A NATURAL.
TRANSFER CONTROL TO ME AND I'LL BRING US HOME...
DAUGHTER?
DID YOU NOT HEAR ME WITH THE CONTROL TRANSFER REQUEST?
WHAT?!
I KNEW YOU'D DO THIS. EVEN BET MOM YOU'D DO THIS.
KNEW...? WHAT? BET... WHAT?!
THAT YOU WOULDN'T LET ME DO THE LANDING.
EMMA, LANDING IS A WHOLE THING UNTO ITSELF AND YOU'RE NOT READY--
NO, YOU'RE NOT READY. ME, I'M TOTALLY READY...

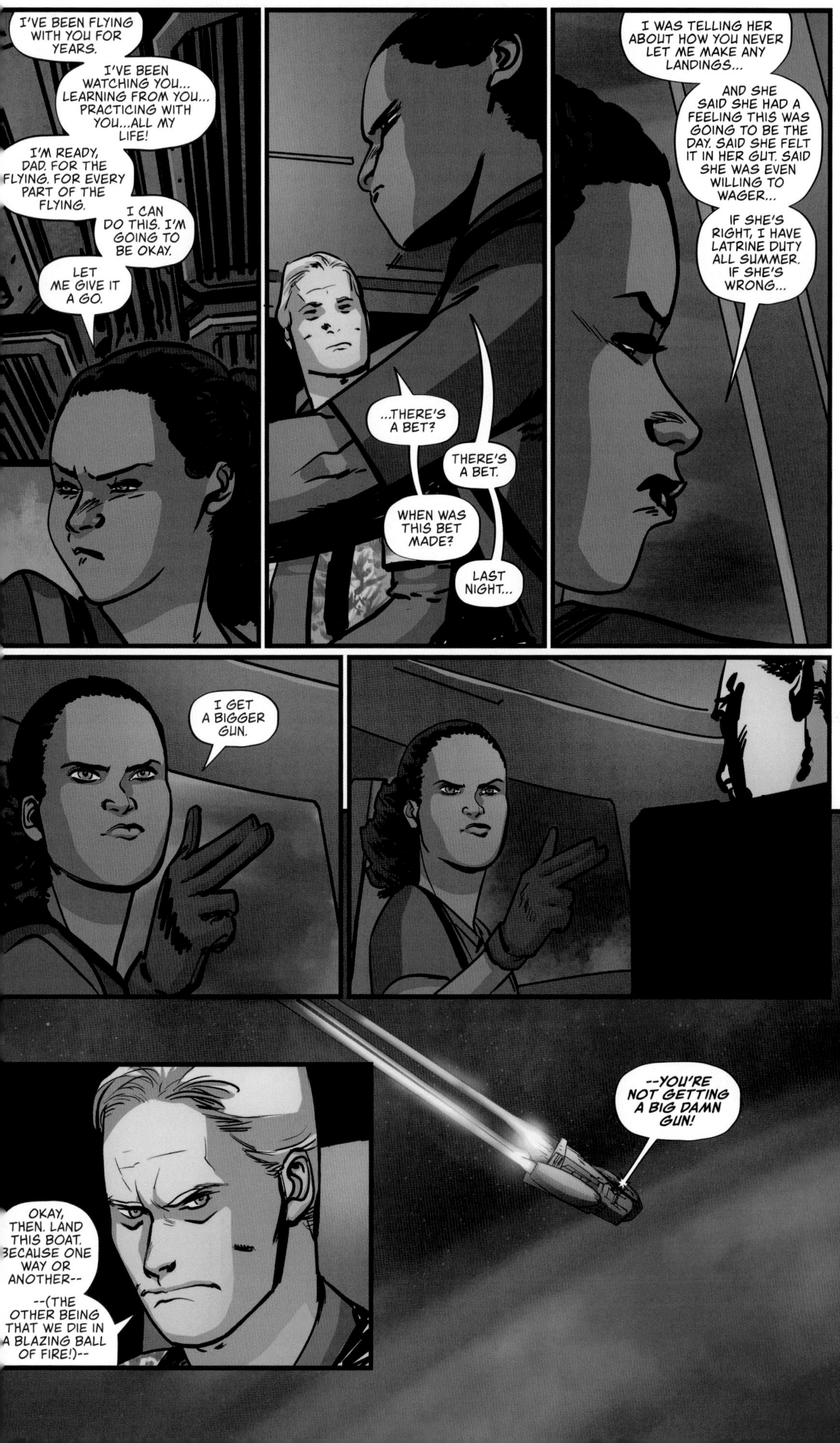
I'VE BEEN FLYING WITH YOU FOR YEARS.
I'VE BEEN WATCHING YOU... LEARNING FROM YOU... PRACTICING WITH YOU...ALL MY LIFE!
I'M READY, DAD. FOR THE FLYING. FOR EVERY PART OF THE FLYING.
I CAN DO THIS. I'M GOING TO BE OKAY.
LET ME GIVE IT A GO.
...THERE'S A BET?
THERE'S A BET.
WHEN WAS THIS BET MADE?
LAST NIGHT...
I WAS TELLING HER ABOUT HOW YOU NEVER LET ME MAKE ANY LANDINGS...
AND SHE SAID SHE HAD A FEELING THIS WAS GOING TO BE THE DAY. SAID SHE FELT IT IN HER GUT. SAID SHE WAS EVEN WILLING TO WAGER...
IF SHE'S RIGHT, I HAVE LATRINE DUTY ALL SUMMER. IF SHE'S WRONG...
I GET A BIGGER GUN.
OKAY, THEN. LAND THIS BOAT. BECAUSE ONE WAY OR ANOTHER--
--(THE OTHER BEING THAT WE DIE IN A BLAZING BALL OF FIRE!)--
--YOU'RE NOT GETTING A BIG DAMN GUN!

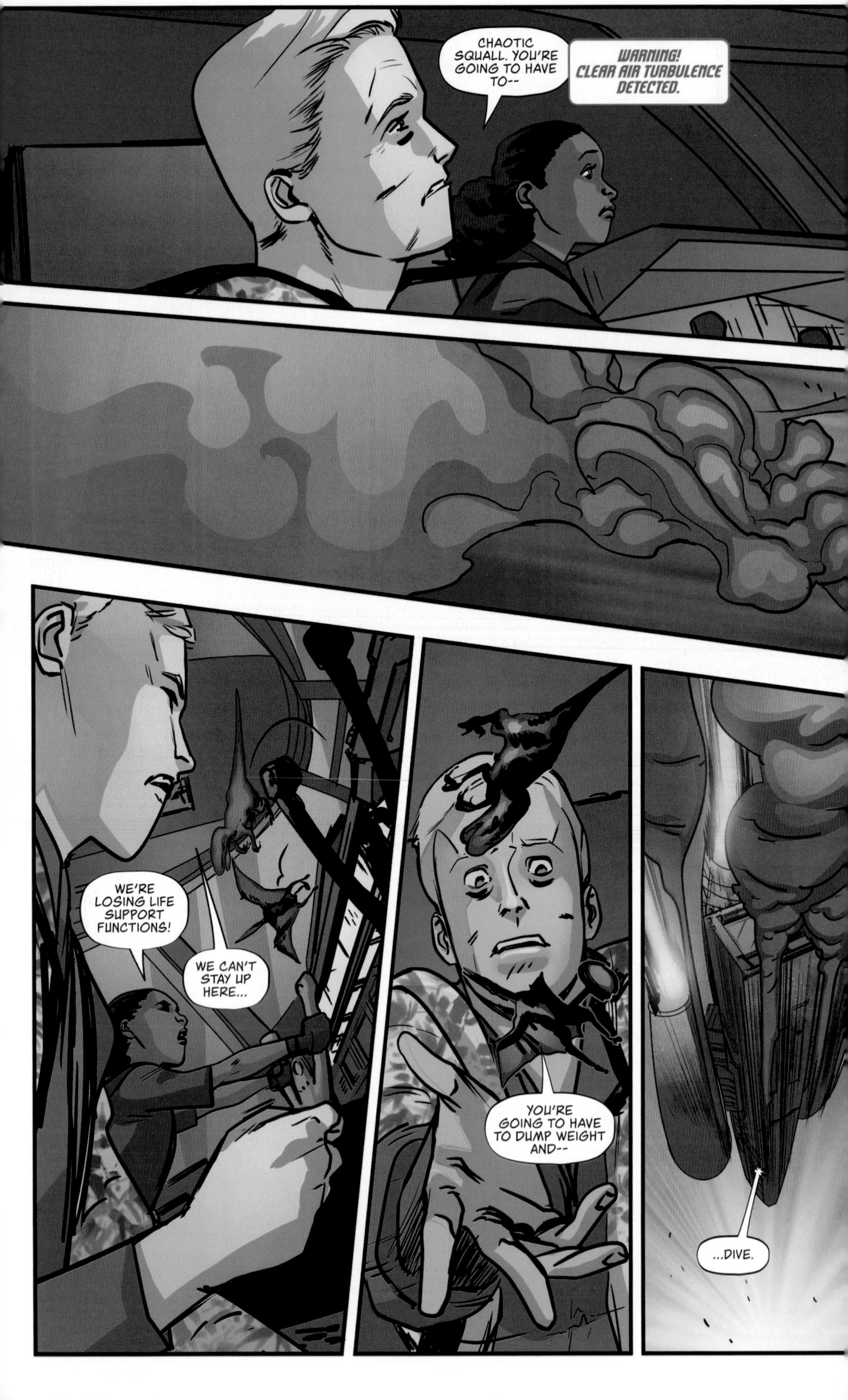
CHAOTIC SQUALL, YOU'RE GOING TO HAVE TO--
WARNING! CLEAR AIR TURBULENCE DETECTED.
WE'RE LOSING LIFE SUPPORT FUNCTIONS!
WE CAN'T STAY UP HERE...
YOU'RE GOING TO HAVE TO DUMP WEIGHT AND--
...DIVE.

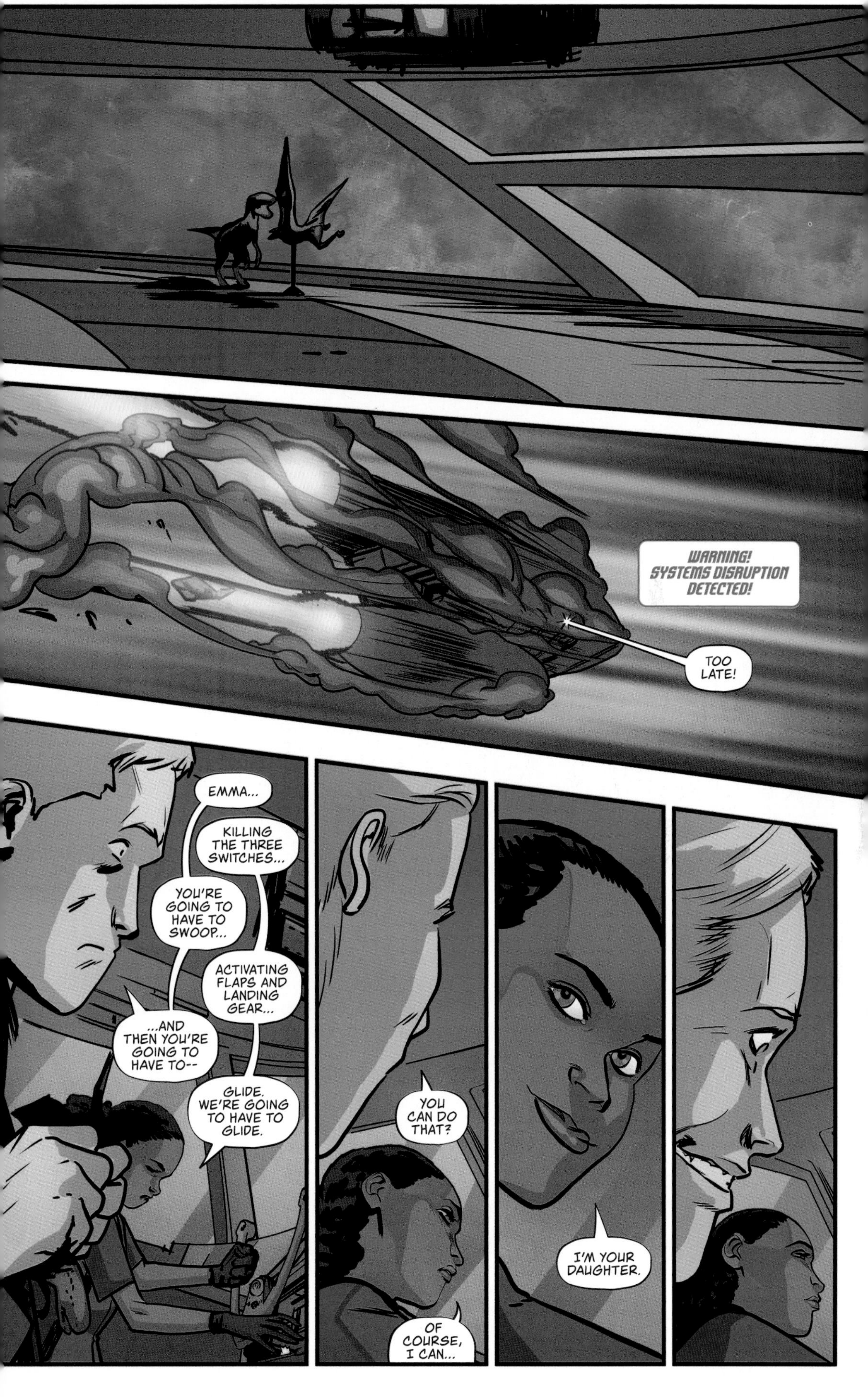
WARNING! SYSTEMS DISRUPTION DETECTED!
TOO LATE!
EMMA...
KILLING THE THREE SWITCHES...
YOU'RE GOING TO HAVE TO SWOOP...
ACTIVATING FLAPS AND LANDING GEAR...
...AND THEN YOU'RE GOING TO HAVE TO--
GLIDE. WE'RE GOING TO HAVE TO GLIDE.
YOU CAN DO THAT?
OF COURSE, I CAN...
I'M YOUR DAUGHTER.

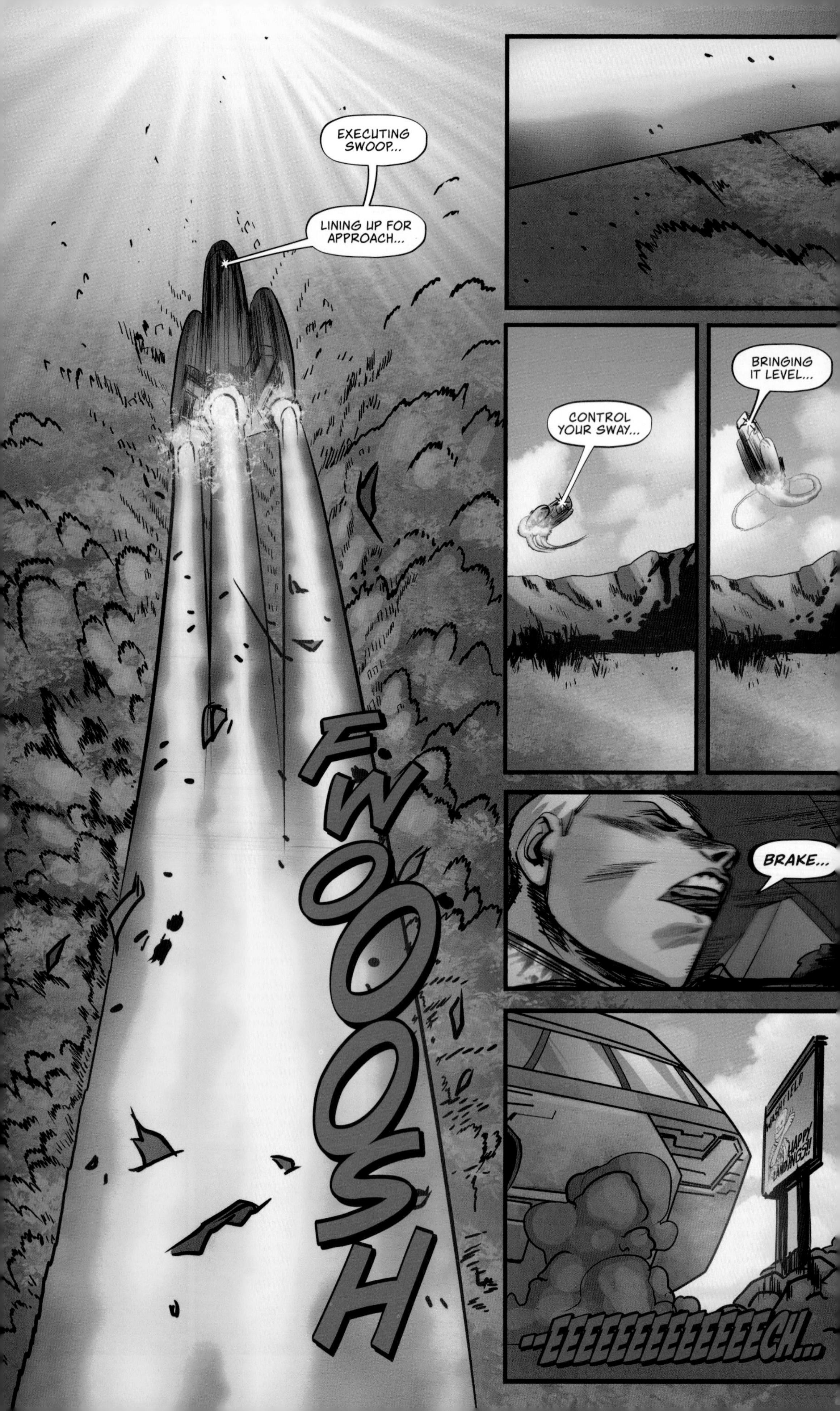
EXECUTING SWOOP...
LINING UP FOR APPROACH...
FWOOOOSH
CONTROL YOUR SWAY...
BRINGING IT LEVEL...
BRAKE...
--EEEEEEEEEEEEECH..

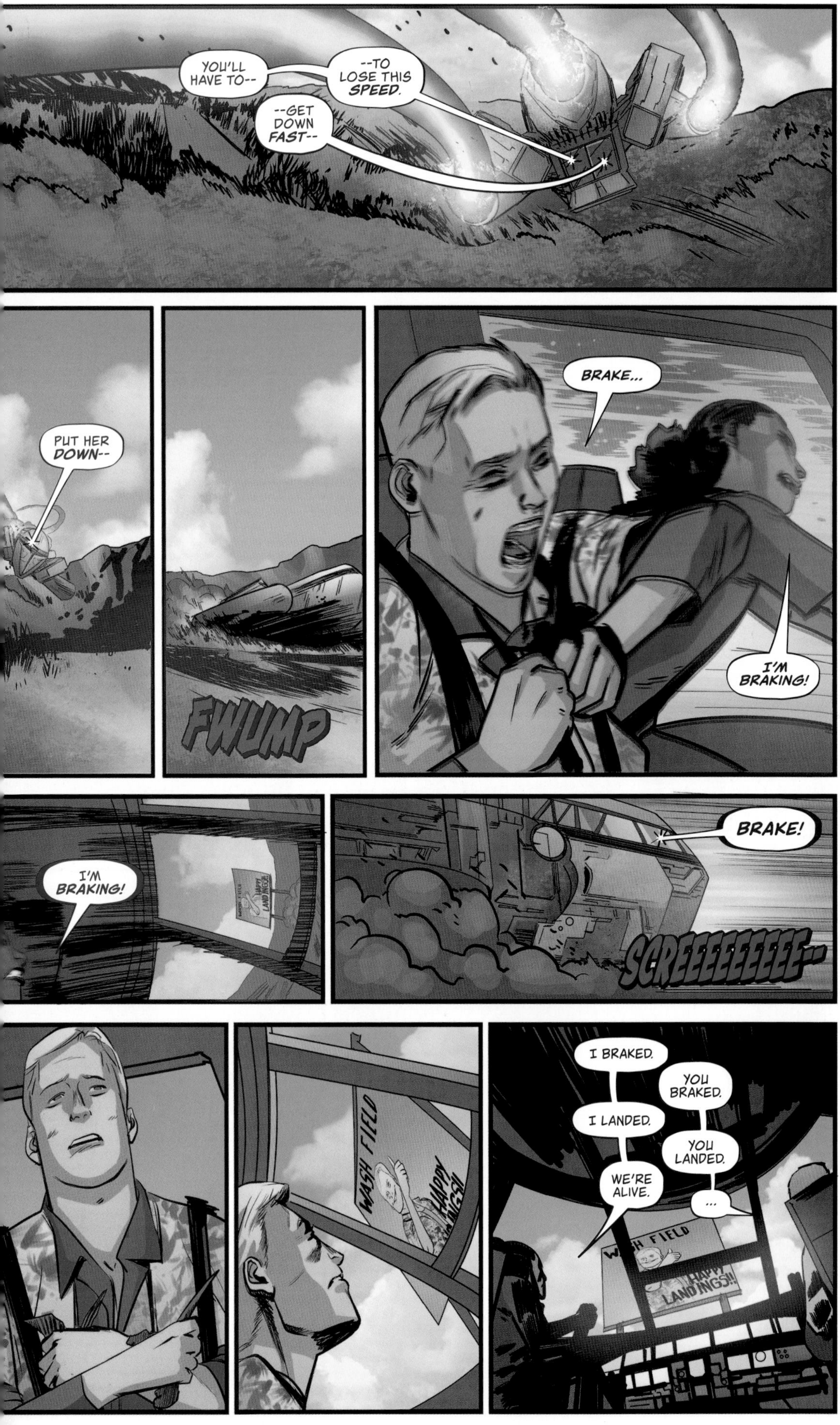
YOU'LL HAVE TO--
--TO LOSE THIS SPEED.
--GET DOWN FAST--
PUT HER DOWN--
FWUMP
BRAKE...
I'M BRAKING!
I'M BRAKING!
BRAKE!
SCREEEEEEEEEE--
WASH FIELD
HAPPY LANDINGS!!
I BRAKED.
YOU BRAKED.
I LANDED.
YOU LANDED.
WE'RE ALIVE.
...

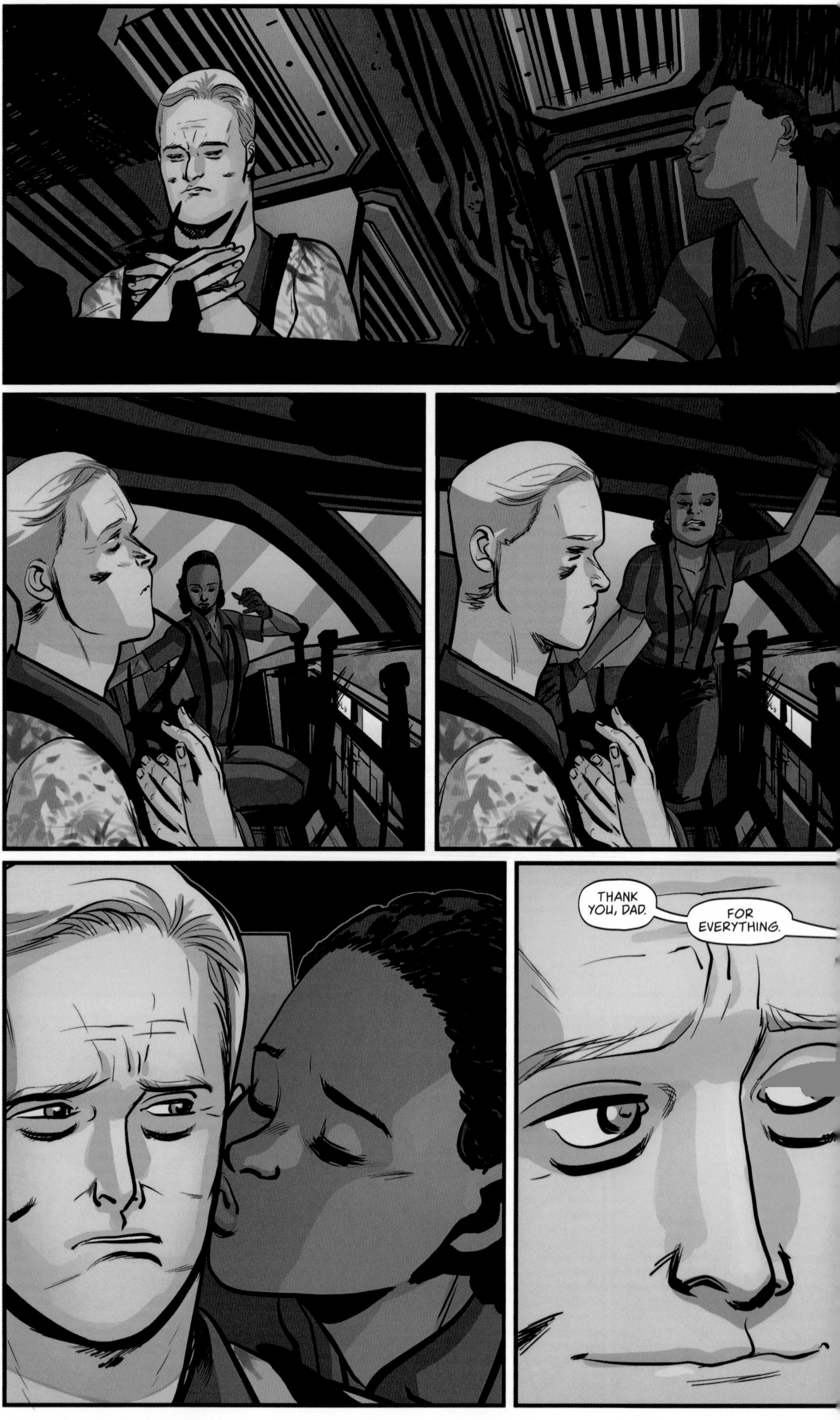
THANK YOU, DAD.
FOR EVERYTHING.

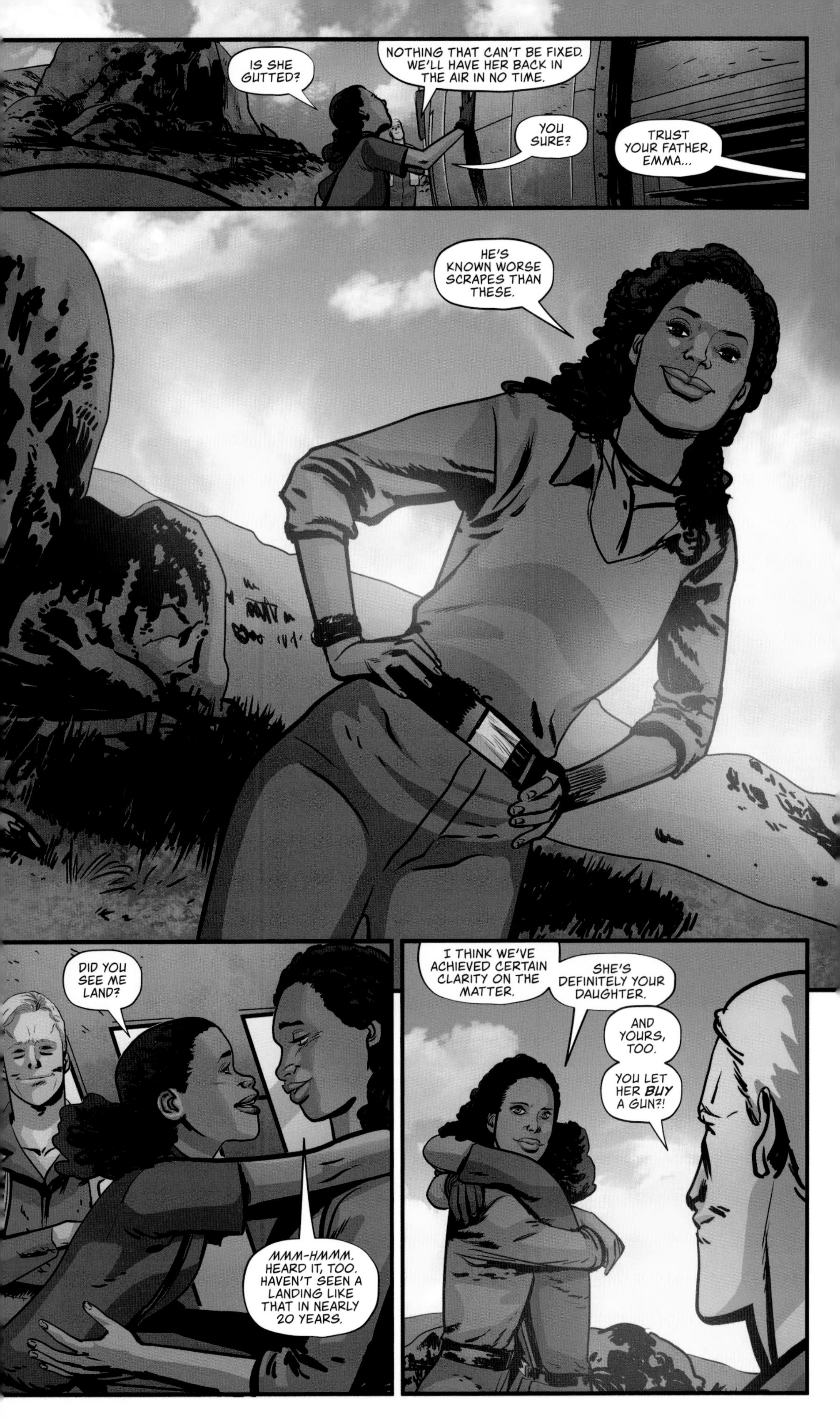
IS SHE GUTTED?
NOTHING THAT CAN'T BE FIXED. WE'LL HAVE HER BACK IN THE AIR IN NO TIME.
YOU SURE?
TRUST YOUR FATHER, EMMA...
HE'S KNOWN WORSE SCRAPES THAN THESE.
DID YOU SEE ME LAND?
MMM-HMMM. HEARD IT, TOO. HAVEN'T SEEN A LANDING LIKE THAT IN NEARLY 20 YEARS.
I THINK WE'VE ACHIEVED CERTAIN CLARITY ON THE MATTER.
SHE'S DEFINITELY YOUR DAUGHTER.
AND YOURS, TOO.
YOU LET HER BUY A GUN?!

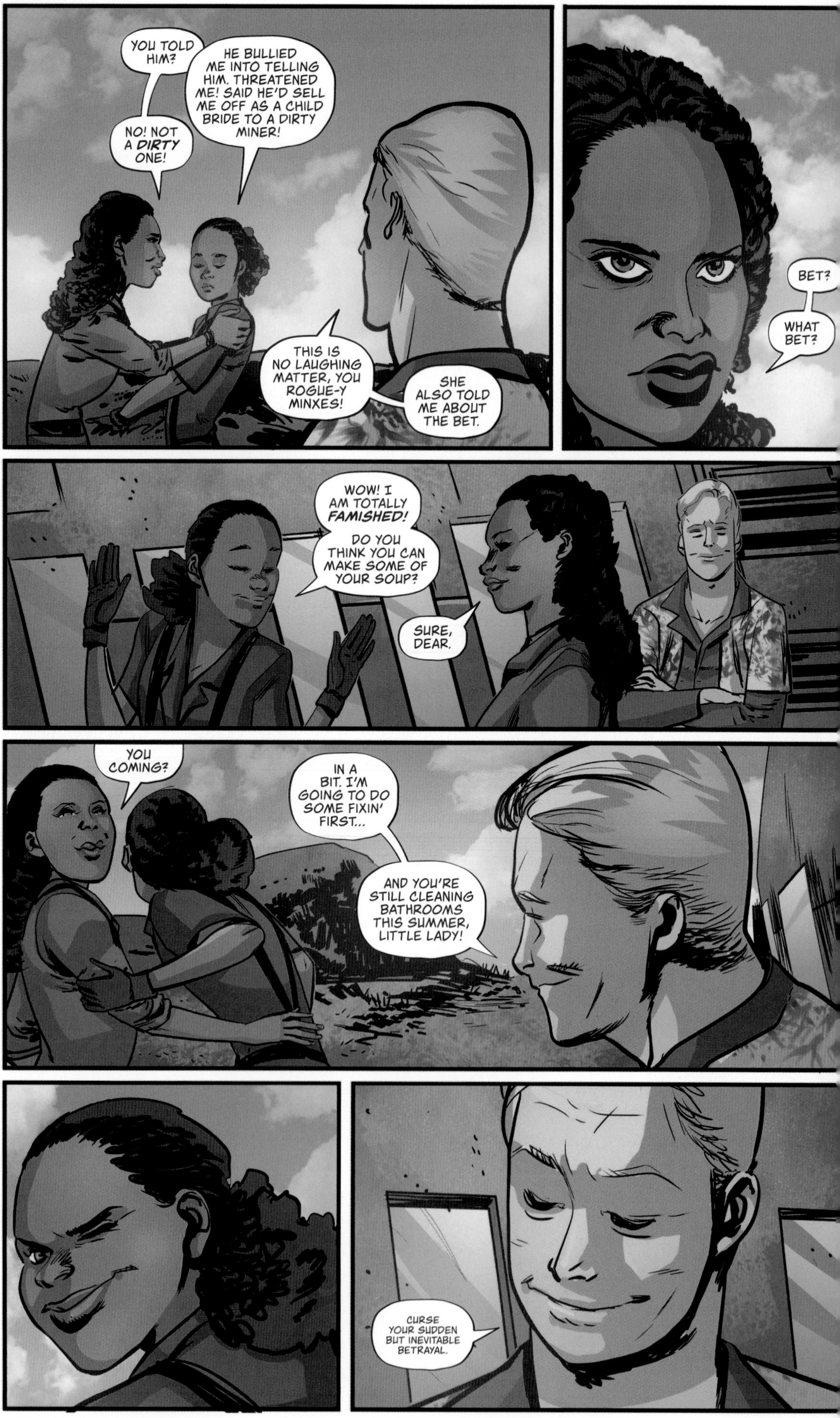
YOU TOLD HIM?
HE BULLIED ME INTO TELLING HIM. THREATENED ME! SAID HE'D SELL ME OFF AS A CHILD BRIDE TO A DIRTY MINER!
NO! NOT A *DIRTY* ONE!
THIS IS NO LAUGHING MATTER, YOU ROGUE-Y MINXES!
SHE ALSO TOLD ME ABOUT THE BET.
BET?
WHAT BET?
WOW! I AM TOTALLY ***FAMISHED!***
DO YOU THINK YOU CAN MAKE SOME OF YOUR SOUP?
SURE, DEAR.
YOU COMING?
IN A BIT. I'M GOING TO DO SOME FIXIN' FIRST...
AND YOU'RE STILL CLEANING BATHROOMS THIS SUMMER, LITTLE LADY!
CURSE YOUR SUDDEN BUT INEVITABLE BETRAYAL.

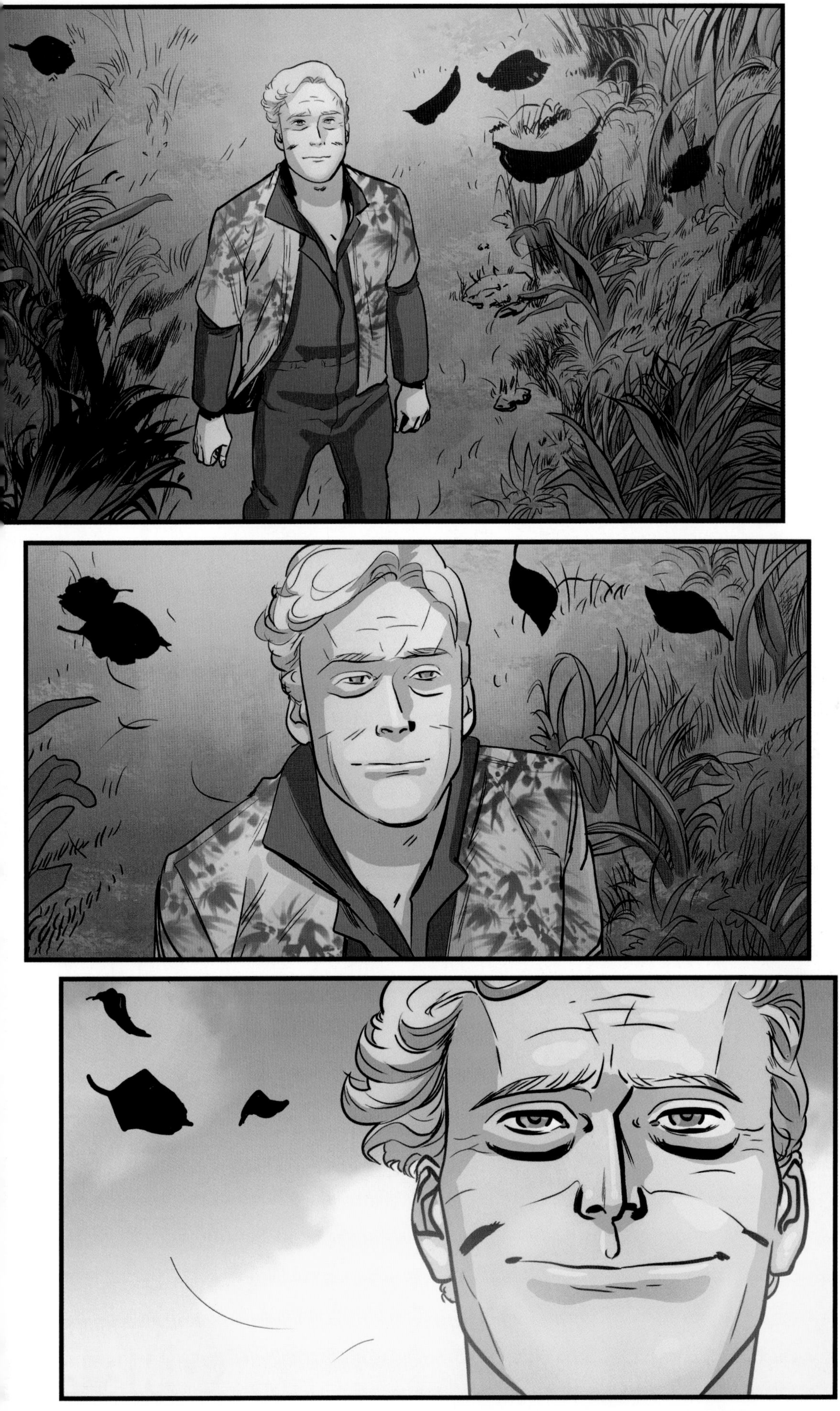

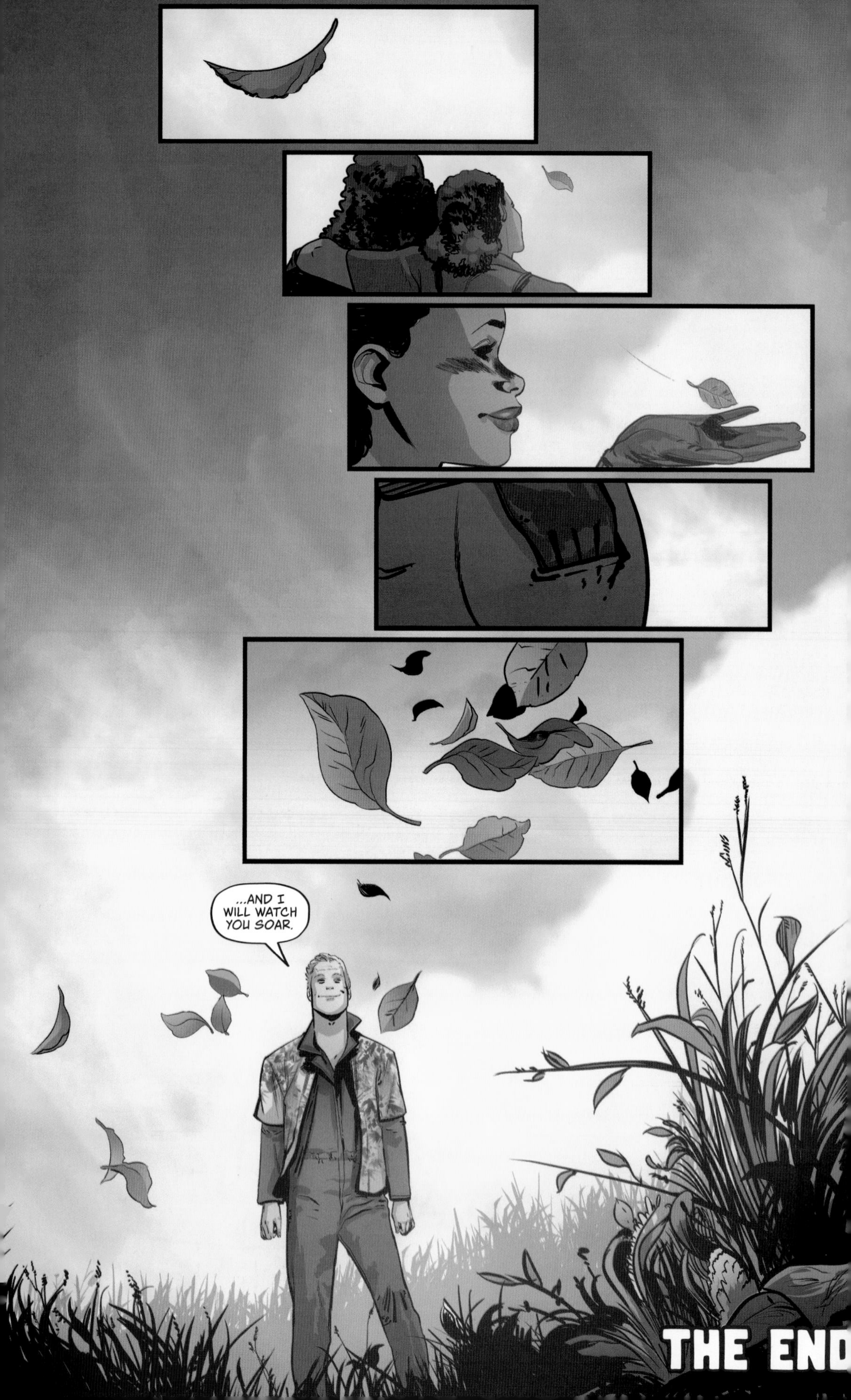
...AND I WILL WATCH YOU SOAR.
THE END

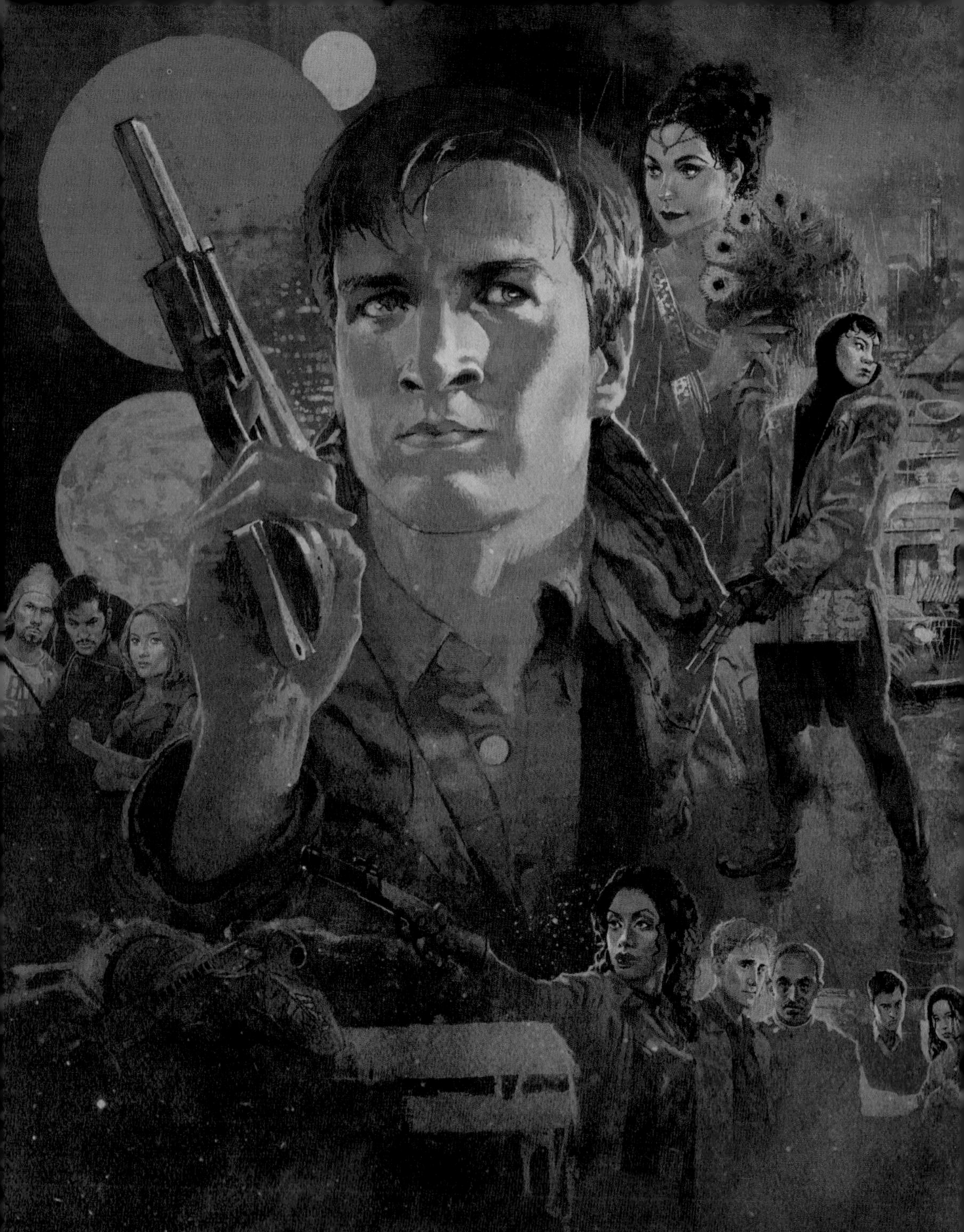

PREVIEW OF "OUTLAW MA REYNOLDS" FROM

FIREFLY: NEW SHERIFF IN THE 'VERSE VOL. 1

Written by
Greg Pak

Illustrated by
Davide Gianfelice
& **George Kambadais**

Colored by
Joana Lafuente

Lettered by
Jim Campbell

IN STORES NOW!

Chapter One
Her Damnable Son

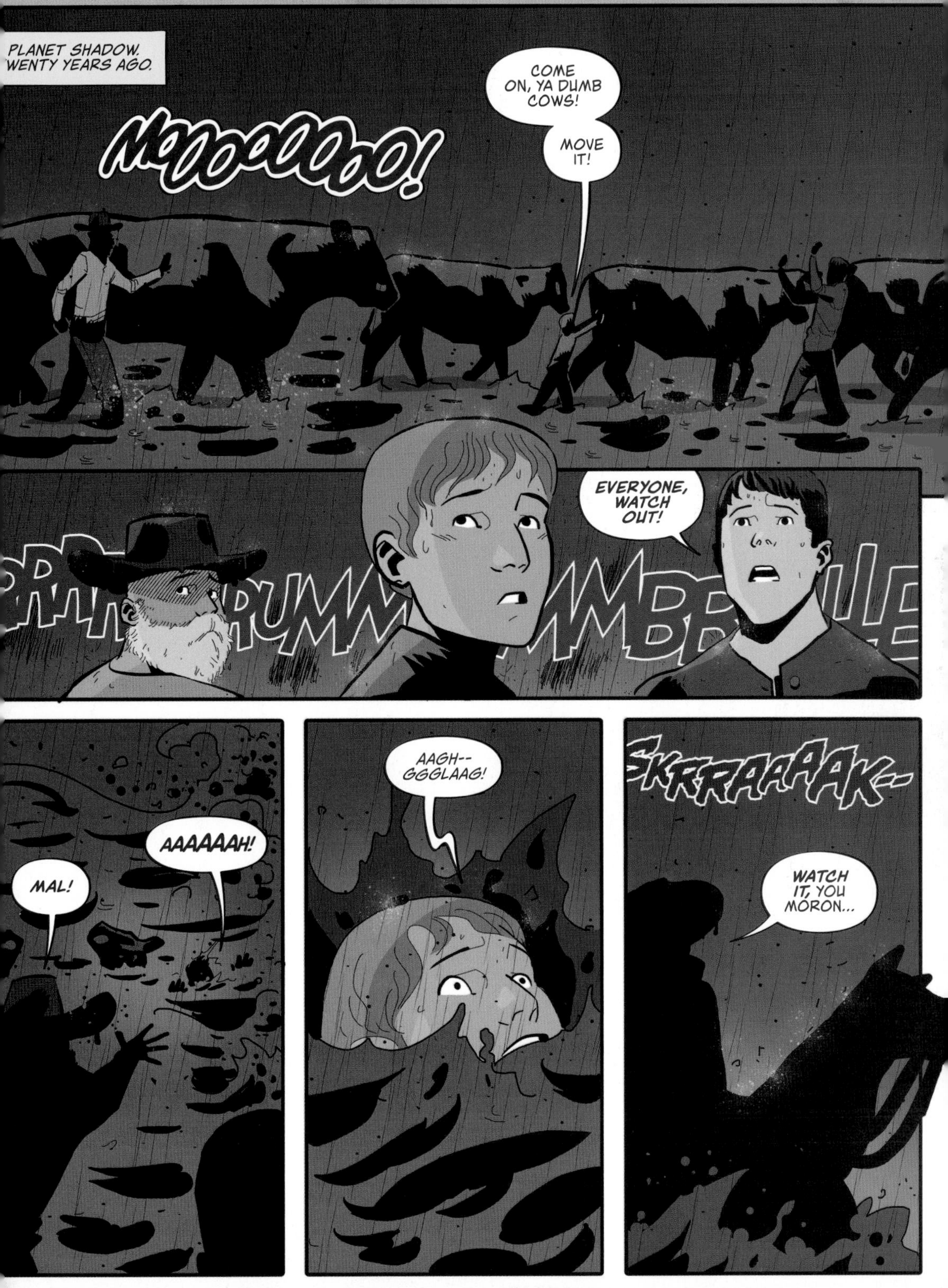
PLANET SHADOW.
WENTY YEARS AGO.
MOOOOOOOOOO!
COME ON, YA DUMB COWS!
MOVE IT!
RRRRUMMMMMBRRULE
EVERYONE, WATCH OUT!
MAL!
AAAAAAH!
AAGH-- GGGLAAG!
KRRAAAAK--
WATCH IT, YOU MORON...

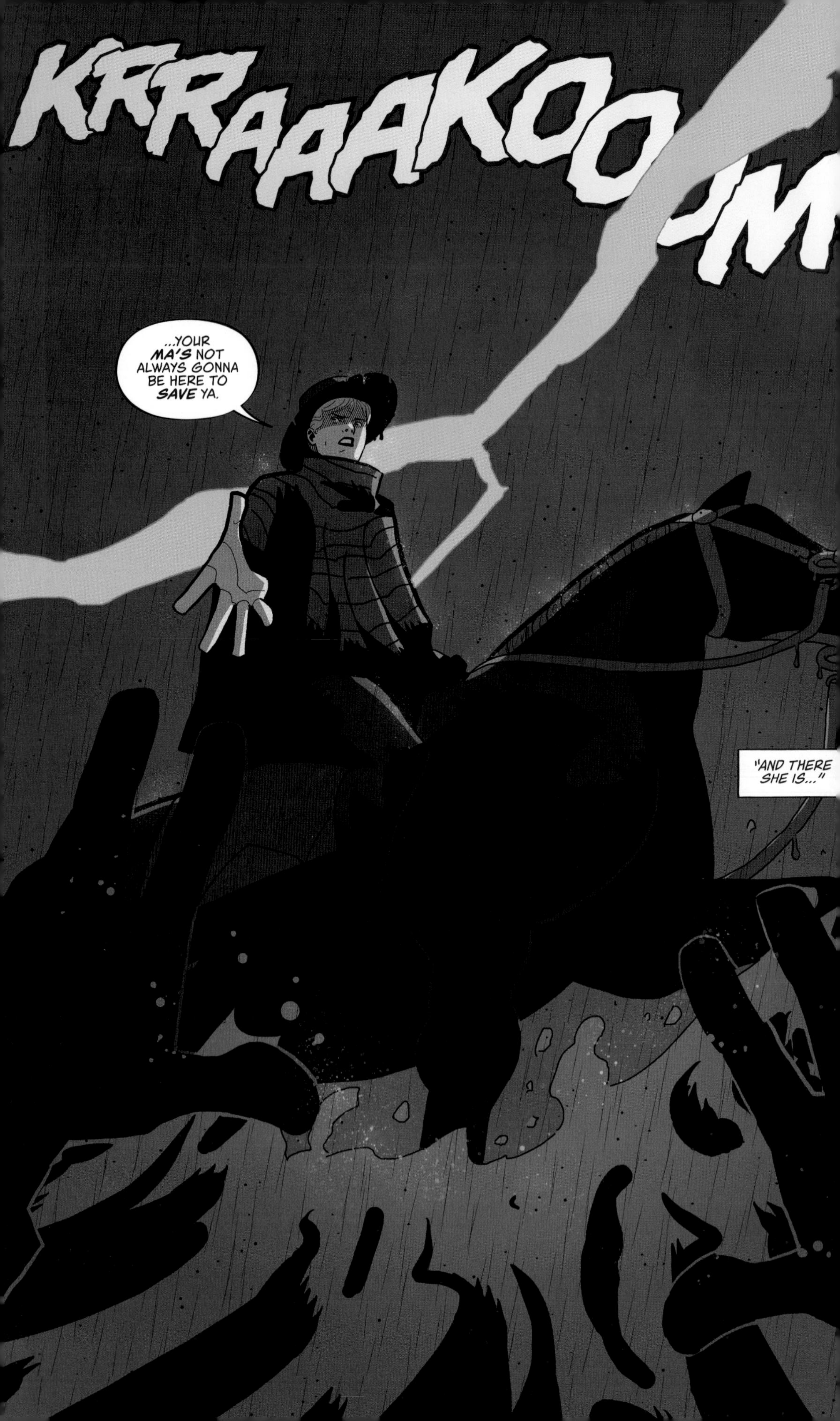
KRRAAAKOOOM
...YOUR MA'S NOT ALWAYS GONNA BE HERE TO SAVE YA.
"AND THERE SHE IS..."

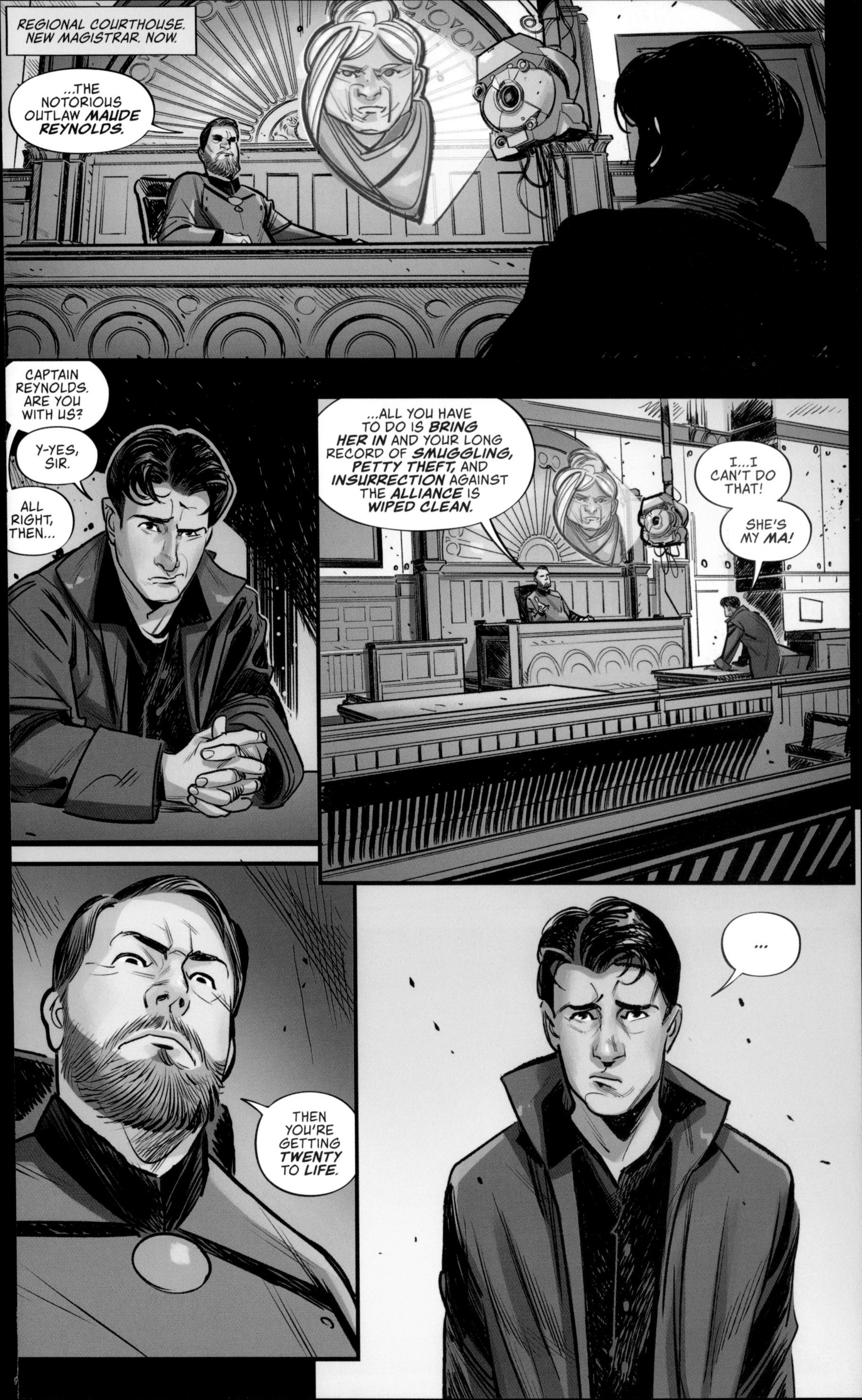
REGIONAL COURTHOUSE. NEW MAGISTRAR. NOW.
...THE NOTORIOUS OUTLAW MAUDE REYNOLDS.
CAPTAIN REYNOLDS. ARE YOU WITH US?
Y-YES, SIR.
ALL RIGHT, THEN...
...ALL YOU HAVE TO DO IS BRING HER IN AND YOUR LONG RECORD OF SMUGGLING, PETTY THEFT, AND INSURRECTION AGAINST THE ALLIANCE IS WIPED CLEAN.
I...I CAN'T DO THAT!
SHE'S MY MA!
THEN YOU'RE GETTING TWENTY TO LIFE.
...

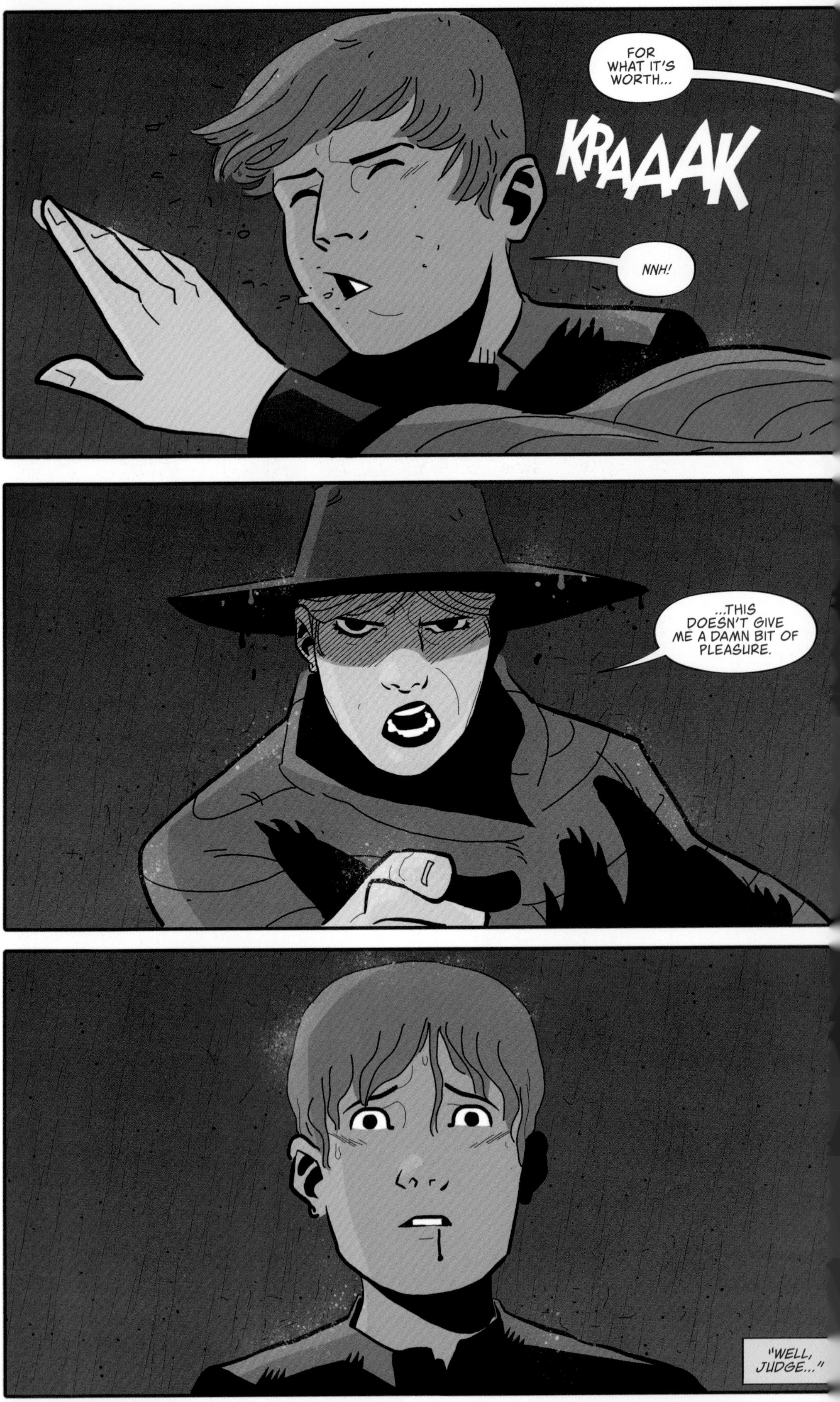
FOR WHAT IT'S WORTH...
KRAAAK
NNH!
...THIS DOESN'T GIVE ME A DAMN BIT OF PLEASURE.
"WELL, JUDGE..."

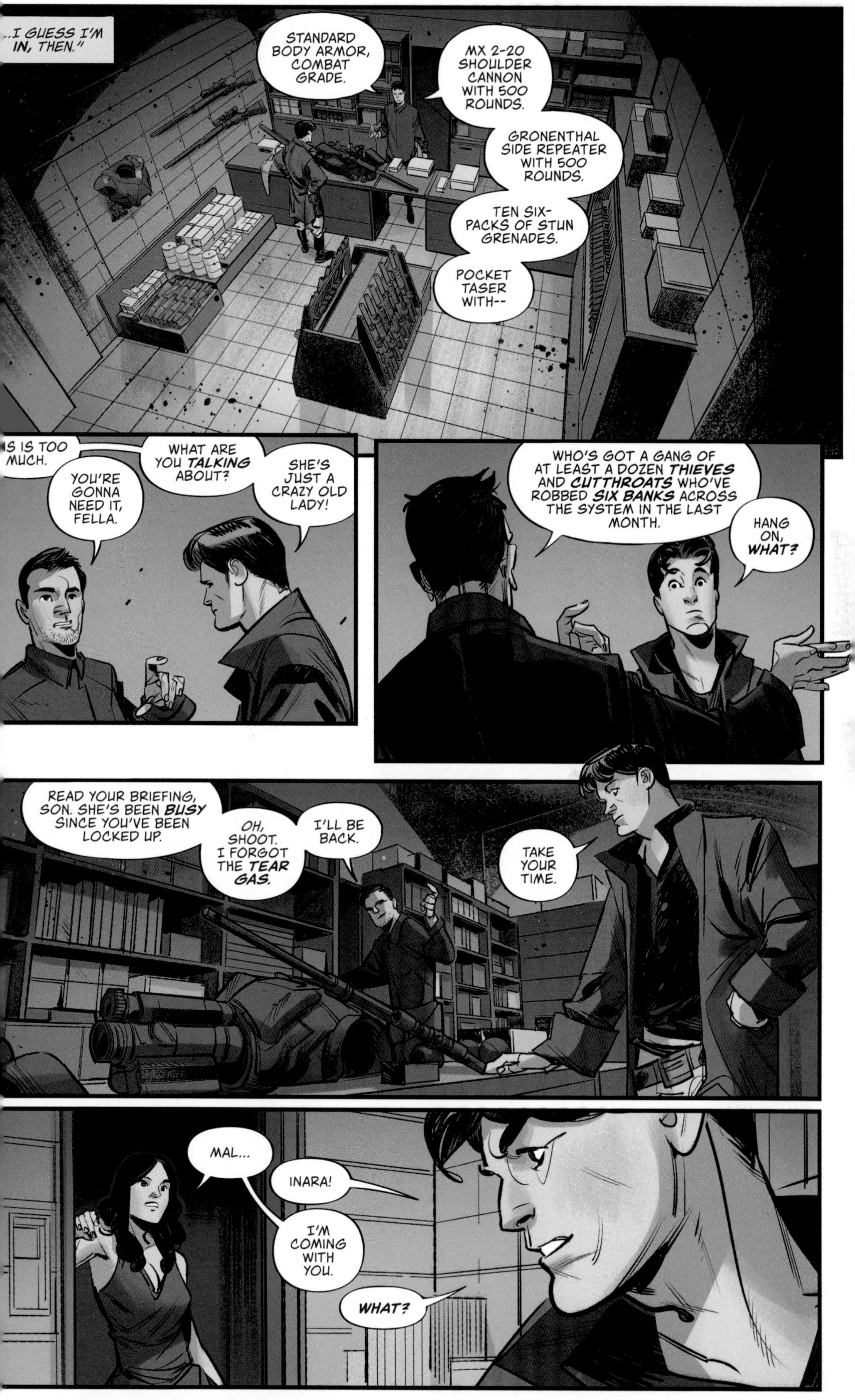

..I GUESS I'M IN, THEN."
STANDARD BODY ARMOR, COMBAT GRADE.
MX 2-20 SHOULDER CANNON WITH 500 ROUNDS.
GRONENTHAL SIDE REPEATER WITH 500 ROUNDS.
TEN SIX-PACKS OF STUN GRENADES.
POCKET TASER WITH--
S IS TOO MUCH.
YOU'RE GONNA NEED IT, FELLA.
WHAT ARE YOU TALKING ABOUT?
SHE'S JUST A CRAZY OLD LADY!
WHO'S GOT A GANG OF AT LEAST A DOZEN THIEVES AND CUTTHROATS WHO'VE ROBBED SIX BANKS ACROSS THE SYSTEM IN THE LAST MONTH.
HANG ON, WHAT?
READ YOUR BRIEFING, SON. SHE'S BEEN BUSY SINCE YOU'VE BEEN LOCKED UP.
OH, SHOOT. I FORGOT THE TEAR GAS.
I'LL BE BACK.
TAKE YOUR TIME.
MAL...
INARA!
I'M COMING WITH YOU.
WHAT?

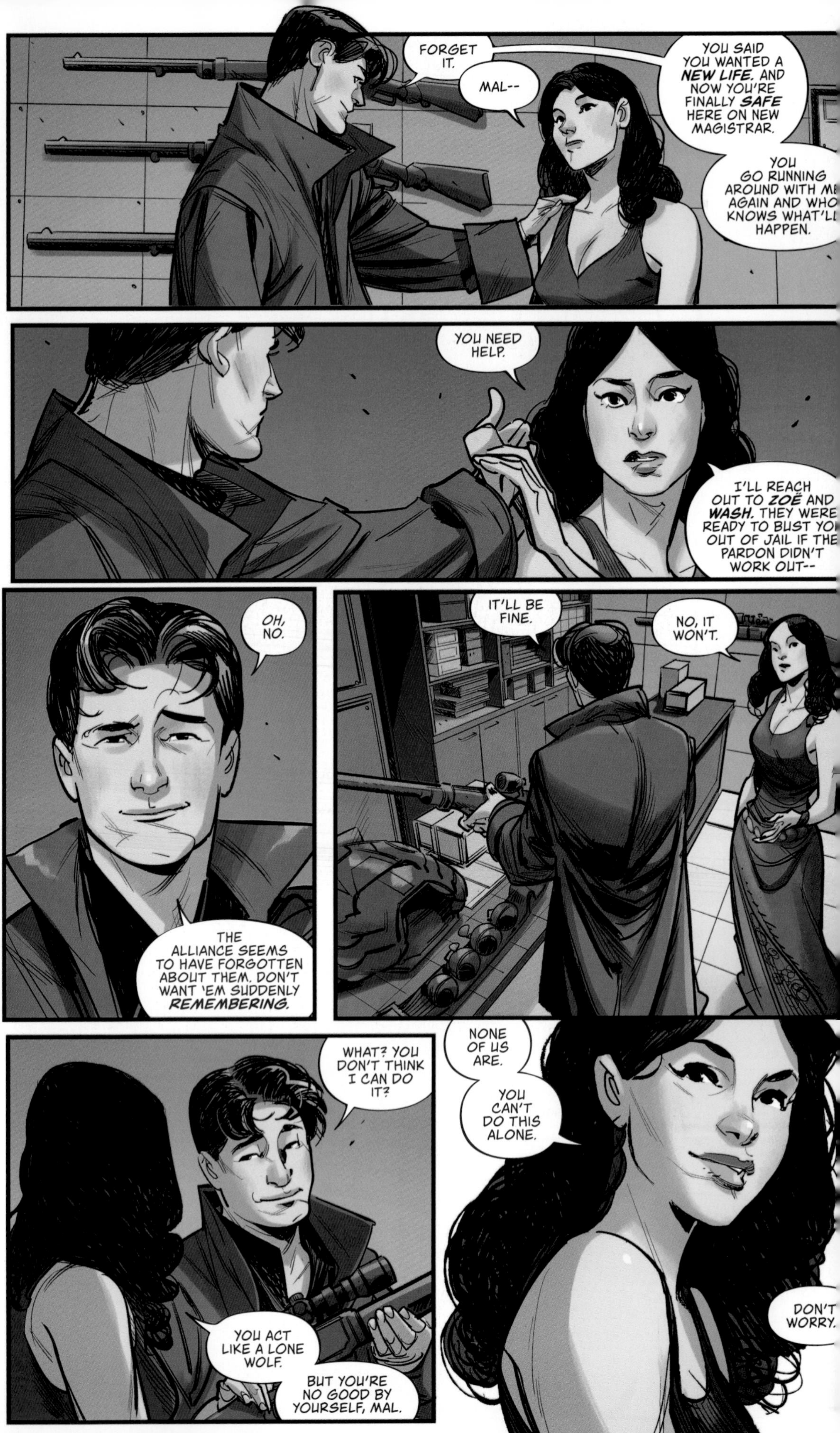
FORGET IT.
MAL--
YOU SAID YOU WANTED A NEW LIFE. AND NOW YOU'RE FINALLY SAFE HERE ON NEW MAGISTRAR.
YOU GO RUNNING AROUND WITH ME AGAIN AND WHO KNOWS WHAT'LL HAPPEN.
YOU NEED HELP.
I'LL REACH OUT TO ZOË AND WASH. THEY WERE READY TO BUST YOU OUT OF JAIL IF THE PARDON DIDN'T WORK OUT--
OH, NO.
THE ALLIANCE SEEMS TO HAVE FORGOTTEN ABOUT THEM. DON'T WANT 'EM SUDDENLY REMEMBERING.
IT'LL BE FINE.
NO, IT WON'T.
WHAT? YOU DON'T THINK I CAN DO IT?
YOU ACT LIKE A LONE WOLF.
BUT YOU'RE NO GOOD BY YOURSELF, MAL.
NONE OF US ARE.
YOU CAN'T DO THIS ALONE.
DON'T WORRY.

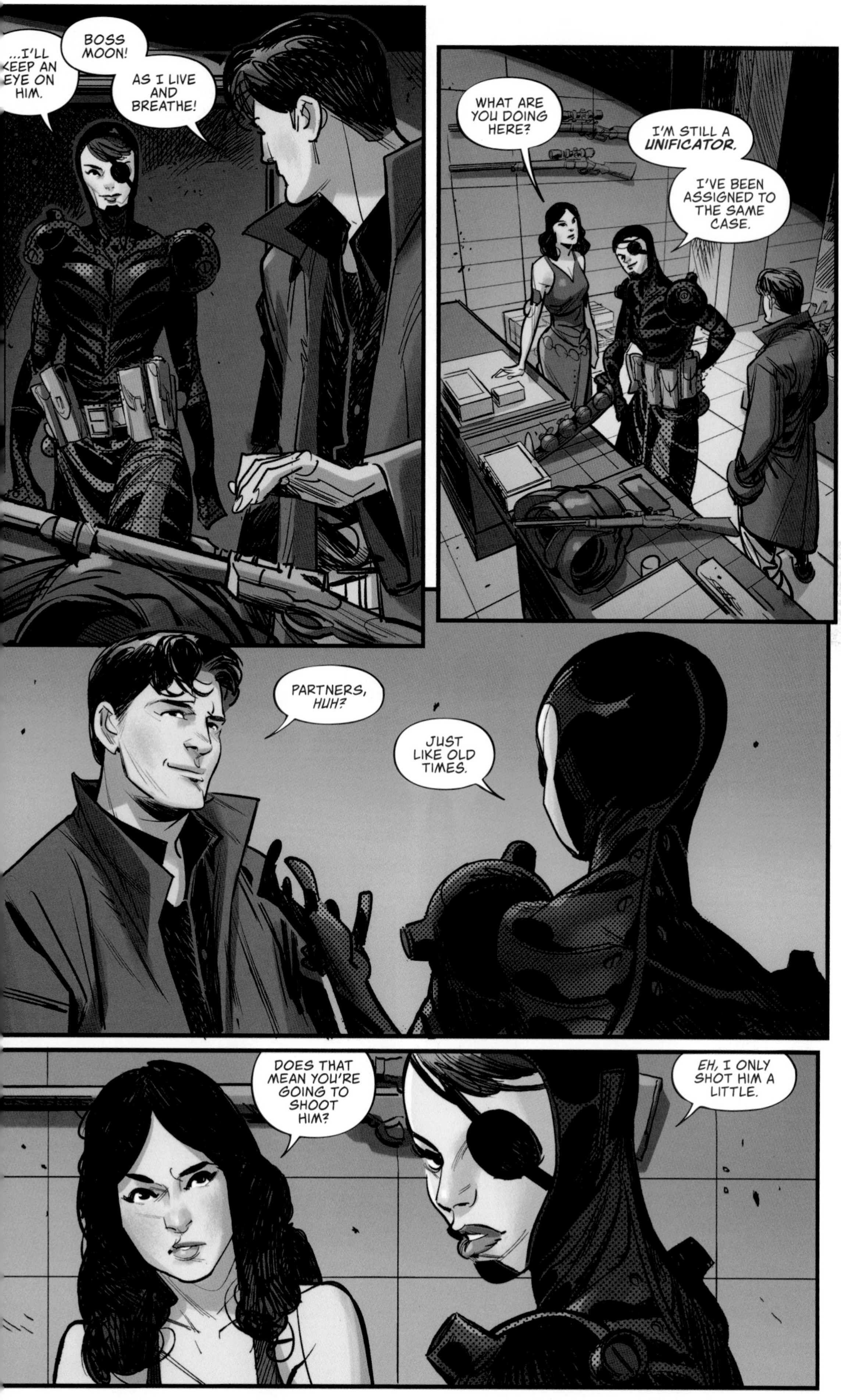
BOSS MOON!
...I'LL KEEP AN EYE ON HIM.
AS I LIVE AND BREATHE!
WHAT ARE YOU DOING HERE?
I'M STILL A *UNIFICATOR.*
I'VE BEEN ASSIGNED TO THE SAME CASE.
PARTNERS, *HUH?*
JUST LIKE OLD TIMES.
DOES THAT MEAN YOU'RE GOING TO SHOOT HIM?
EH, I ONLY SHOT HIM A LITTLE.

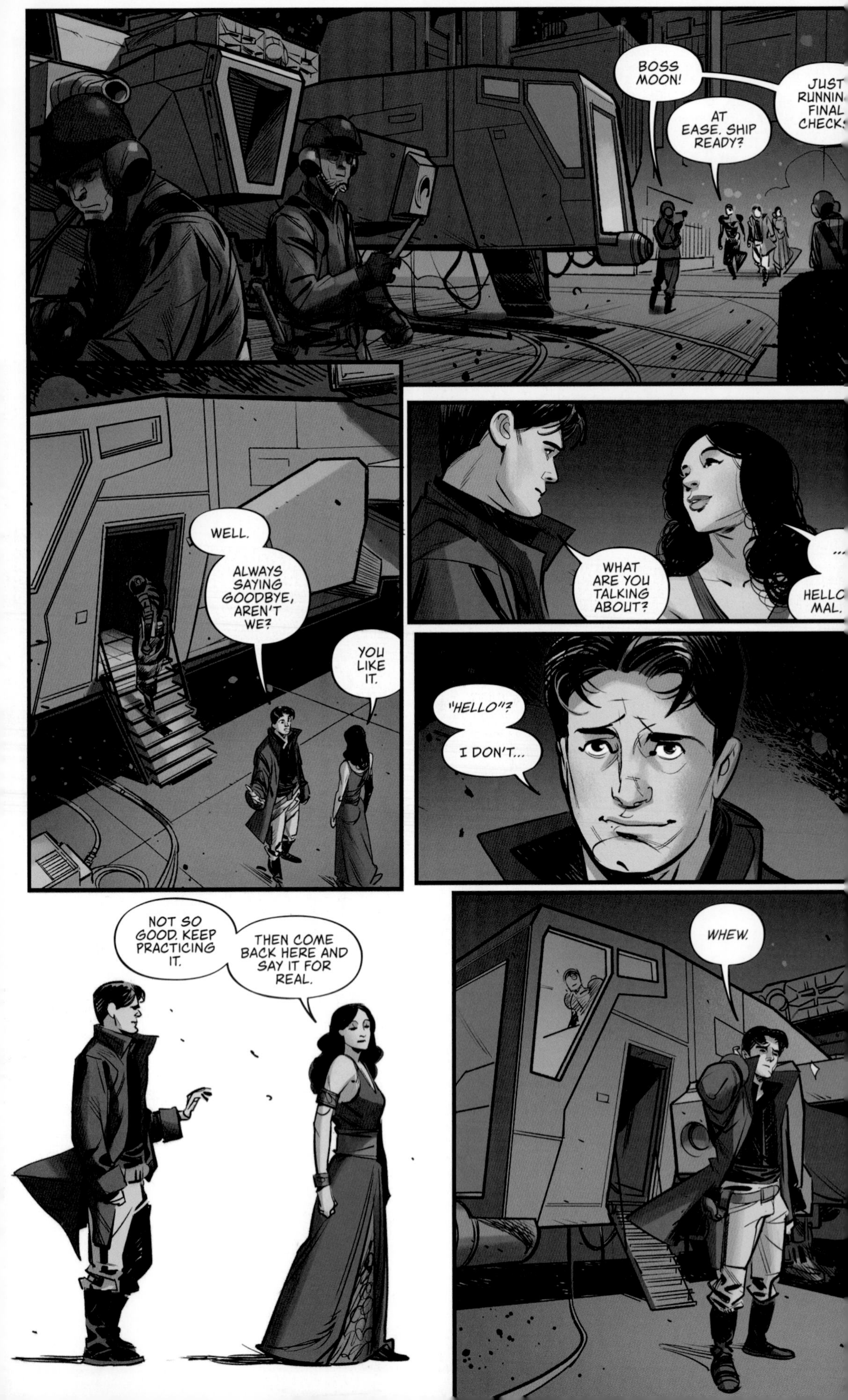

BOSS MOON!
AT EASE. SHIP READY?
JUST RUNNIN FINAL CHECK
WELL.
ALWAYS SAYING GOODBYE, AREN'T WE?
YOU LIKE IT.
WHAT ARE YOU TALKING ABOUT?
...
HELLO MAL.
"HELLO"?
I DON'T...
NOT SO GOOD. KEEP PRACTICING IT.
THEN COME BACK HERE AND SAY IT FOR REAL.
WHEW.

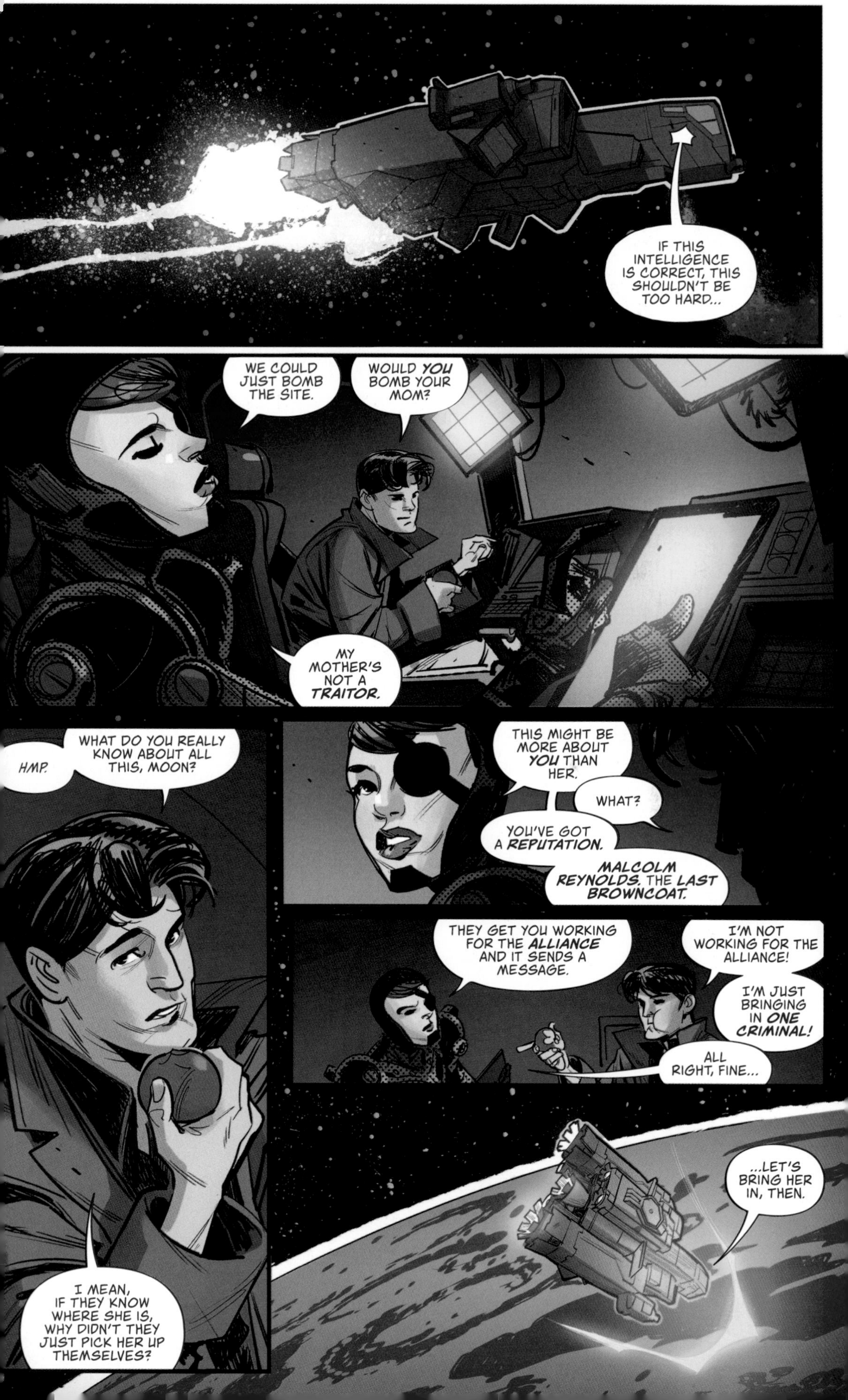
IF THIS INTELLIGENCE IS CORRECT, THIS SHOULDN'T BE TOO HARD...
WE COULD JUST BOMB THE SITE.
WOULD YOU BOMB YOUR MOM?
MY MOTHER'S NOT A TRAITOR.
HMP.
WHAT DO YOU REALLY KNOW ABOUT ALL THIS, MOON?
THIS MIGHT BE MORE ABOUT YOU THAN HER.
WHAT?
YOU'VE GOT A REPUTATION.
MALCOLM REYNOLDS. THE LAST BROWNCOAT.
THEY GET YOU WORKING FOR THE ALLIANCE AND IT SENDS A MESSAGE.
I'M NOT WORKING FOR THE ALLIANCE!
I'M JUST BRINGING IN ONE CRIMINAL!
ALL RIGHT, FINE...
I MEAN, IF THEY KNOW WHERE SHE IS, WHY DIDN'T THEY JUST PICK HER UP THEMSELVES?
...LET'S BRING HER IN, THEN.

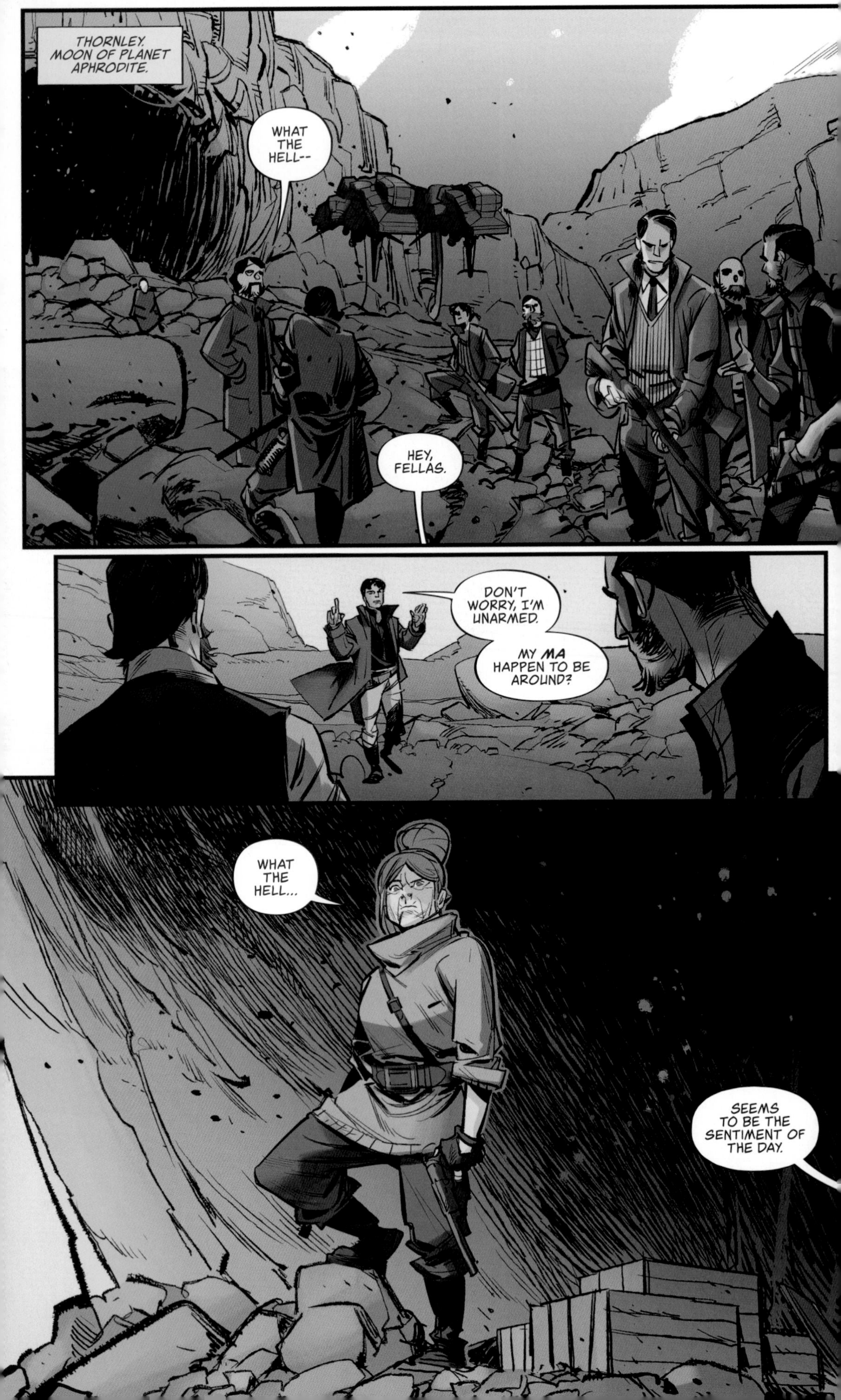
THORNLEY. MOON OF PLANET APHRODITE.
WHAT THE HELL--
HEY, FELLAS.
DON'T WORRY, I'M UNARMED.
MY MA HAPPEN TO BE AROUND?
WHAT THE HELL...
SEEMS TO BE THE SENTIMENT OF THE DAY.

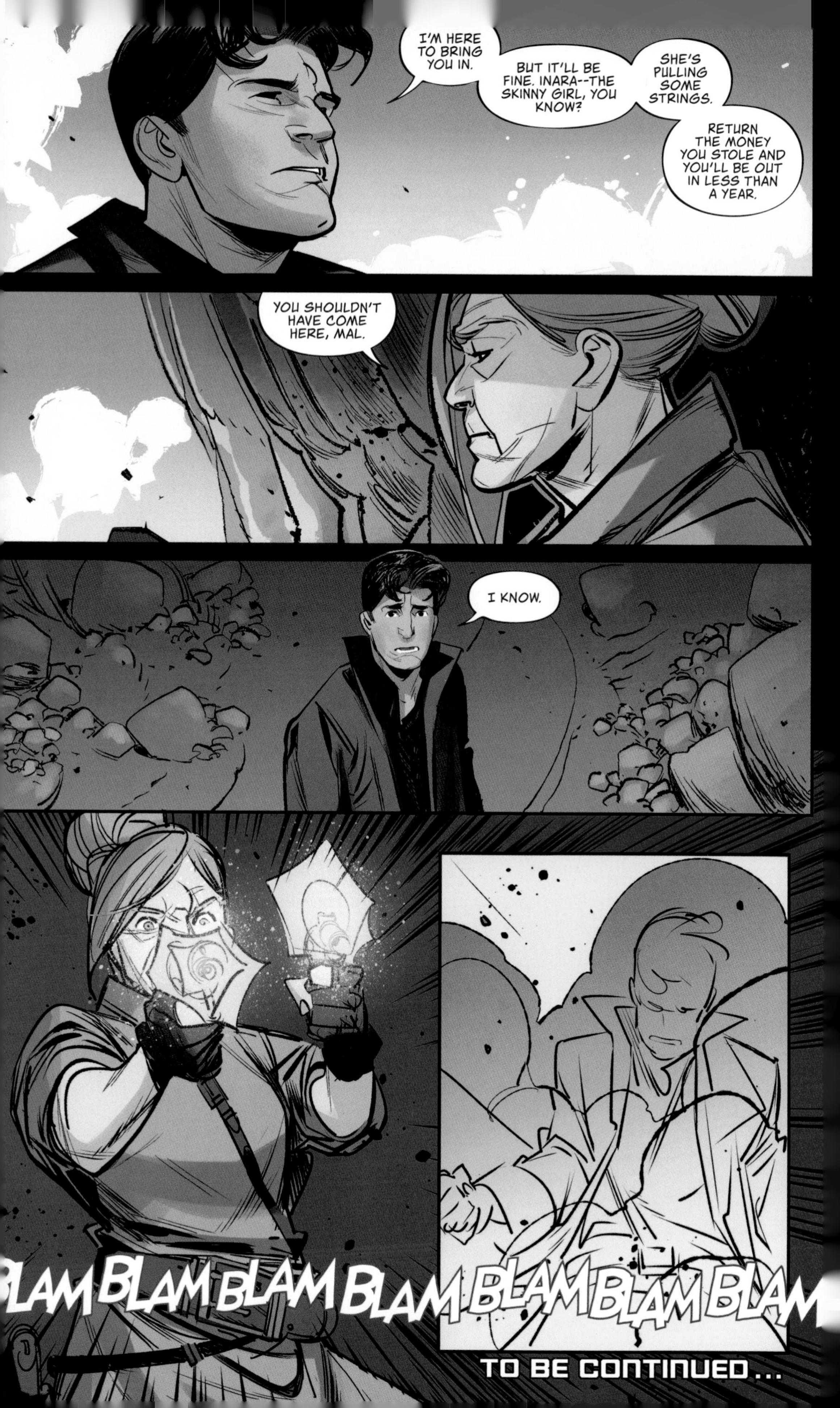
I'M HERE TO BRING YOU IN.
BUT IT'LL BE FINE. INARA--THE SKINNY GIRL, YOU KNOW?
SHE'S PULLING SOME STRINGS.
RETURN THE MONEY YOU STOLE AND YOU'LL BE OUT IN LESS THAN A YEAR.
YOU SHOULDN'T HAVE COME HERE, MAL.
I KNOW.
BLAM BLAM BLAM BLAM BLAM BLAM BLAM
TO BE CONTINUED...

BIOGRAPHIES

Fabio Amelia is an Italian comic book letterer born in Naples. He serves as Editorial Production Manager and Letterer at Arancia Studio. Fabio has lettered for publishing houses like The Walt Disney Company, Image Comics, BOOM! Studios, Glénat, Panini Comics, Edizioni Star Comics, Zenescope, and many others.

He is the letterer of the Mirka Andolfo's best-selling books: *Unnatural*, *Mercy*, and *Un/Sacred*. He also works on localization for the Italian editions of Marvel, DC, and Valiant comics and several mangas. Parallel to this, after graduating in BA (Hons) Information and Interface Design with a First-Class Honours at the University of the Arts London, he started working as a UX and UI Designer.

Maxflan Araujo is a Brazilian colorist who lives in the city of Maceio-AL. He has colored comic books since 2009 and has worked for many publishers on various titles, including *Vampirella*, *Evil Ernie*, *Red Sonja*, *John Carter*, *The Green Hornet*, and *Van Helsing*.

Jorge Corona is a Venezuelan sequential artist and winner of the 2015 Russ Manning Award. Writer and illustrator, his work includes *We are...Robin*, *Nightwing*, and *The Flash* for DC Comics; *Big Trouble in Little China*, *Adventure Time*, *Jim Henson's The Storyteller*, among others for BOOM! Entertainment; as well as co-creator of *Goners* and *Number One With a Bullet* (nominated for the 2018 Eisner Awards for Best Cover Artist) alongside Jacob Semahn for Image Comics, and creator of *Feathers*, his all ages dark fantasy, for Archaia.

Recently he finished Image comic's *Middlewest* with writer Skottie Young. Jorge now lives in Denver, CO with his wife and fellow artist Morgan Beem.

Jared Cullum is a cartoonist, writer, and painter with a deep passion for connecting with people through visual storytelling. Between developing stories, he teaches traditional plein-air painting and anatomy. He has also written and painted story-art for BOOM!/Archaia and Jim Henson Productions, working on such titles as *Planet of the Apes*, *Labyrinth*, *Fraggle Rock*, and *The Storyteller*. Jared currently has a middle-grade graphic novel out, *Kodi* which he wrote and illustrated. He resides in Pittsburgh, PA.

Jeff Jensen is a screenwriter, comic book writer, basically a writer of many things, who makes his home somewhere near Long Beach, California. He was a story editor on HBO's *Watchmen*, earning Hugo and Nebula nominations for his writing, and he served as an executive producer on Disney's *Tomorrowland*. His Eisner award-winning graphic novel with artist Jonathan Case, *Green River Killer: A True Detective*, dramatized the life and investigative work of his father, Tom Jensen. During his nineteen years as a reporter and critic for *Entertainment Weekly*, Jeff covered the short life—and enduring legacy—of Joss Whedon's Firefly. He's been inside Serenity. He's even sat in Wash's chair. But he knows nothing of leaves. Jeff has three children, including a teenage daughter whose driving scares the Gorram hell out of him. This story is for her.

Fabiana Mascolo is a freelance comic-book artist based in Rome, Italy. Upon graduating top of her class in 2015, she started working in the comics industry both as a penciler and a colorist. Her pencil works include the horror series *Caput Mundi*, her original graphic novel *Ruggine*, and a six-issue run for Scout Comics called *Yasmeen*. She also illustrated an animated episode of the series *Move it or Lose it* for SkyArte, the poster art of the 35th Venice Critics Week Film Festival, and several children's books.

As a colorist, she's been working with BOOM! Studios on the series *The Dark Crystal* and *An Unkindness of Ravens* as well as with Italian publishers Feltrinelli and Editoriale Aurea.

Giada Marchisio is an Italian colorist. She was a ballet dancer in Scala theatre in Milan before moving into comics professionally. After the end of her studies at the International School of Comics and the iMasterArt, she began working as an illustrator for Rizzoli. In 2017 she became a colorist for the Sergio Bonelli Editore with *Dragonero*, before coloring covers for *The Platoon* from Marvel comics. Her other books include *The Origins of the Punisher*, *Astonishing X-Men*, *Cloak and Dagger*, *Avengers #700*, "The Spectacular Spider-Man", Marvel Comics #1000 "BloodBath", *Star Wars: Target Vader*, and *Hit Girl* with Honk Kong/Image Comics/Mark Millar. Currently she is collaborating with Arancia Studios.

Giannis Milonogiannis was born in 1988 and has been writing and drawing comics since 2010. Works include *Ronin Island*, *Old City Blues*, *Prophet*, *Ghost in the Shell: Global Neural Network*, and others.

Jorge Monlongo is a Spanish comic book artist and character designer. His most recent works include *Over The Garden Wall: Hollow Town* (BOOM! Studios) and *Napoleon Dynamite: Impeach Pedro* (IDW). He also made Hello Kitty travel through alternate dimensions and fight post-apocalyptic warriors (VIZ).

Jordi Pérez Estevez was born in 1978 in Malgrat de Mar (Barcelona). He has most recently worked for Dynamite Comics on Issue #3 of *Xena* (2019) and a special issue of *James Bond* (2020). His other works include *Queen of Bad Dreams* for Vault Comics and *RET:CON* for 133art.

Ethan Young was born and raised in New York City. He is best known for *Nanjing: The Burning City*, winner of the 2016 Reuben Award for Best Graphic Novel and featured on multiple Top 10 lists. He also received Eisner and Harvey nominations that same year.

His other graphic novels include *The Battles of Bridget Lee*, *Life Between Panels*, and *The Dragon Path* (arriving in 2021 from Graphix/Scholastic)

DISCOVER
VISIONARY CREATORS

THE
WOODS
JAMES TYNION IV • MICHAEL DIALYNAS
VOL 1
THE ARROW

"The Spire is fantastic! My kind of genre free-for-all."
—BRIAN K. VAUGHAN
(Saga)
THE
SPIRE
SIMON SPURRIER
JEFF STOKELY
ANDRÉ MAY

MARK WAID • PETER KRAUSE
IRREDEEMABLE
AFTERWORD BY
GRANT MORRISON

MARK WAID • JEAN DIAZ
INCORRUPTIBLE

MICHAEL ALAN NELSON
DAN MORA
GABRIEL CASSATA
HEXED
THE HARLOT & THE THIEF VOLUME ONE

ABNETT & CULBARD
WILD'S
END
FIRST LIGHT
"IT'S REALLY GREAT!"
JEFF LEMIRE

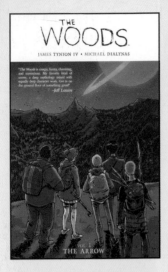

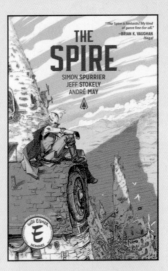

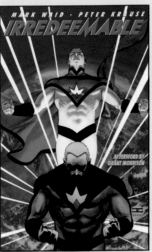

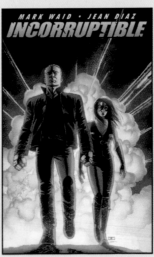

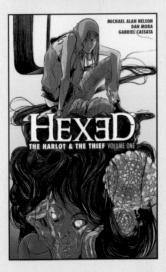

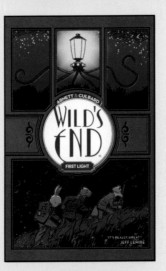

James Tynion IV

The Woods

Volume 1
ISBN: 978-1-60886-454-6 | $9.99 US
Volume 2
ISBN: 978-1-60886-495-9 | $14.99 US
Volume 3
ISBN: 978-1-60886-773-8 | $14.99 US

The Backstagers

Volume 1
ISBN: 978-1-60886-993-0 | $14.99 US

Simon Spurrier

Six-Gun Gorilla

ISBN: 978-1-60886-390-7 | $19.99 US

The Spire

ISBN: 978-1-60886-913-8 | $29.99 US

Weavers

ISBN: 978-1-60886-963-3 | $19.99 US

Mark Waid

Irredeemable

Volume 1
ISBN: 978-1-93450-690-5 | $16.99 US
Volume 2
ISBN: 978-1-60886-000-5 | $16.99 US

Incorruptible

Volume 1
ISBN: 978-1-60886-015-9 | $16.99 US
Volume 2
ISBN: 978-1-60886-028-9 | $16.99 US

Michael Alan Nelson

Hexed The Harlot & The Thief

Volume 1
ISBN: 978-1-60886-718-9 | $14.99 US
Volume 2
ISBN: 978-1-60886-816-2 | $14.99 US

Day Men

Volume 1
ISBN: 978-1-60886-393-8 | $9.99 US
Volume 2
ISBN: 978-1-60886-852-0 | $9.99 US

Dan Abnett

Wild's End

Volume 1: First Light
ISBN: 978-1-60886-735-6 | $19.99 US
Volume 2: The Enemy Within
ISBN: 978-1-60886-877-3 | $19.99 US

Hypernaturals

Volume 1
ISBN: 978-1-60886-298-6 | $16.99 US
Volume 2
ISBN: 978-1-60886-319-8 | $19.99 US

BOOM! STUDIOS

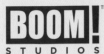

AVAILABLE AT YOUR LOCAL COMICS SHOP AND BOOKSTORE

To find a comics shop in your area, visit www.comicshoplocator.com

WWW.**BOOM-STUDIOS**.COM

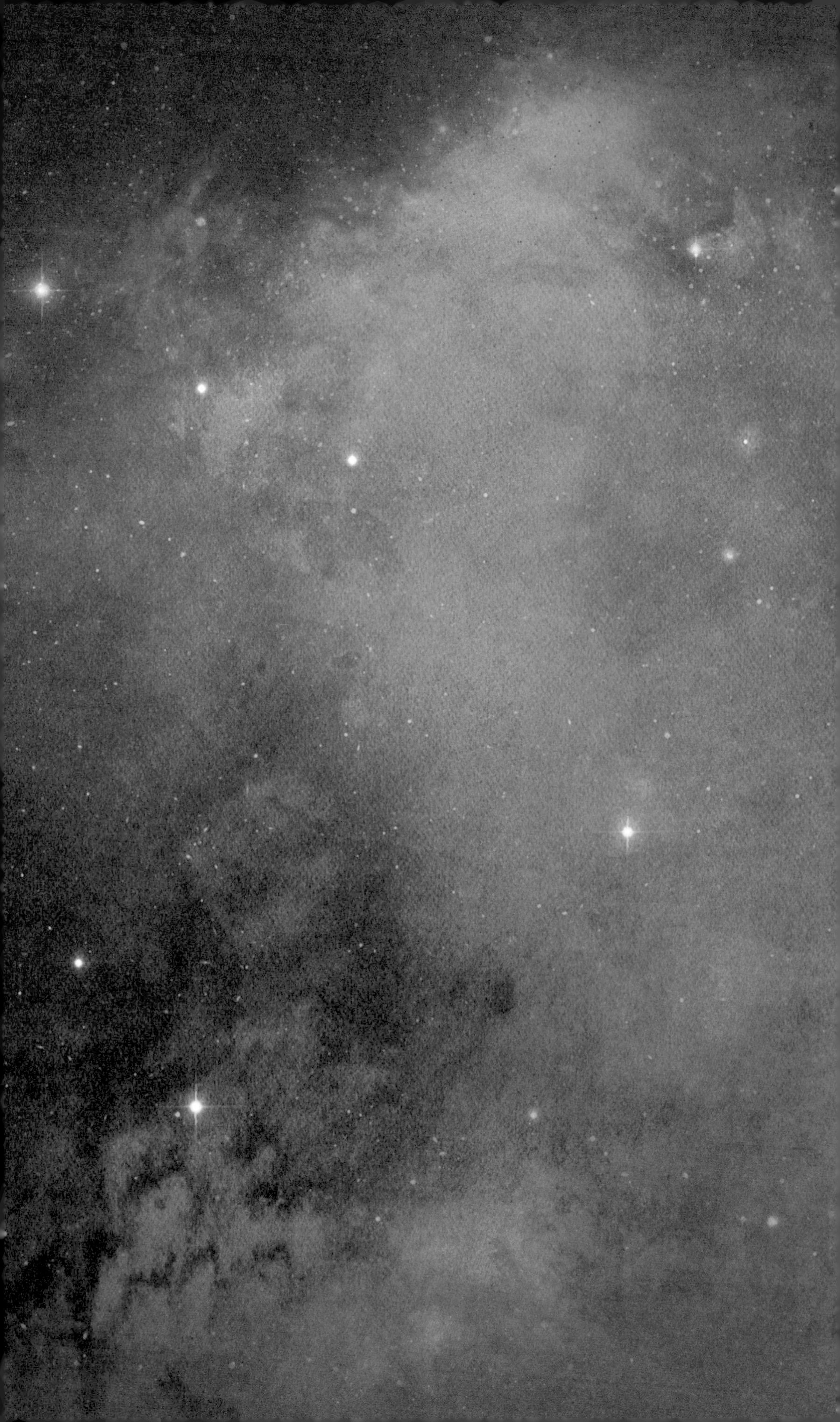